# Theory and measurement

*Historical Perspectives on Modern Economics*

*General Editor: Craufurd D. Goodwin, Duke University*

This series contains original works that challenge and enlighten historians of economics. For the profession as a whole, it promotes better understanding of the origin and content of modern economics.

Other books in the series:

# Theory and measurement

## Causality issues in Milton Friedman's monetary economics

**J. Daniel Hammond**
Wake Forest University

CAMBRIDGE
UNIVERSITY PRESS

CAMBRIDGE UNIVERSITY PRESS
Cambridge, New York, Melbourne, Madrid, Cape Town, Singapore, São Paulo

Cambridge University Press
The Edinburgh Building, Cambridge CB2 2RU, UK

Published in the United States of America by Cambridge University Press, New York

www.cambridge.org
Information on this title: www.cambridge.org/9780521552059

First published 1996
This digitally printed first paperback version 2005

*A catalogue record for this publication is available from the British Library*

*Library of Congress Cataloguing in Publication data*
Hammond, J. Daniel.
Theory and measurement : causality issues in Milton Friedman's
monetary economics / J. Daniel Hammond.
    p.   cm. – (Historical perspectives on modern economics)
Includes bibliographical references.
ISBN 0-521-55205-2 (hc)
1. Friedman, Milton, 1912–  .  2. Money.  3. Business cycles.
4. Neoclassical school of economics.  I. Title.  II. Series.
HB119.F84H36   1996
330.15′7–dc20                                        95-19324
                                                          CIP

ISBN-13 978-0-521-55205-9 hardback
ISBN-10 0-521-55205-2 hardback

ISBN-13 978-0-521-02264-4 paperback
ISBN-10 0-521-02264-9 paperback

*To Claire, Joe, Pat, and Jane*

# Contents

# Contents

# Acknowledgments

Over the course of the research project that led to this book I have accumulated debts of gratitude to many people. Warren Samuels supported my initial work on causality issues in the debate between Milton Friedman and his critics over money's macroeconomic role. Warren, Neil de Marchi, Abraham Hirsch, and Kevin Hoover were immensely helpful in the early stages as I tried to discover exactly what the project was to consist of. Through conversation, their writings on Friedman and the Chicago School, and their criticism of my papers, they helped me transform broad questions and somewhat vague hunches into clearer and more meaningful questions and answers.

The project, and ultimately this book, began to take a biographical turn in the fall of 1987 when Milton Friedman agreed to my request for an interview. In May of the following year Mr. Friedman spent a half day with me at Stanford University's Hoover Institution responding to a very long list of questions about his debates with critics over money's role as cause and effect and about his education and training in economics and statistics. During that visit something happened that illustrates both the role of serendipity in research and Milton Friedman's generosity and liberality. Just a week or so before, he had dug out from his files his graduate school class notes for someone who was writing a paper on Jacob Viner's University of Chicago price theory course. When we completed my interview he offered to me, for the next day, the use of all the class notes, his office, and a photocopy machine. I eagerly accepted this most generous offer, and from that point on I knew that my work on Milton Friedman's economics would be heavily biographical.

The following year I had the good fortune to interview Mr. Friedman once again, along with Rose D. Friedman. The Friedmans shared recollections of their lives and work in the half century since they met as University of Chicago graduate students in 1932. I have returned each summer since 1988 to work in the Milton Friedman Papers at the Hoover Institution Archives. On each of these visits Mr. Friedman's assistant, Gloria Valentine, has helped make my time at Hoover pleasant and productive. Both she and Mr. Friedman have generously provided me with materials from his active files. For my use of the papers deposited in the Hoover Institution Archives I am also grateful to the efficient and friendly archives staff.

ix

I had an R. J. Reynolds Company Research Leave from Wake Forest for the fall semester of 1987, which allowed me to write several papers that contained material that later found its way into this book. Wake Forest has continued to provide generous support for my research through, in various years, the William C. Archie Fund, the Research and Creative Activities Fund, and the Research and Publications Fund. Research grants from the Earhart Foundation in 1988 and 1989 and from the John William Pope Foundation in 1989 and 1990 provided financial support for my writing, the interviews with the Friedmans, and archival research at Stanford, the University of Chicago, and Columbia University.

I completed much of this book's first draft while I was an Honorary Visiting Fellow in the Department of Economics of University College London from January through May 1992. I am grateful for the hospitality of then department head, Richard Blundell, Victoria Chick, and Pat Fairbrother, department administrator, during my visit.

Claire Hammond, Abraham Hirsch, Kevin Hoover, Thomas Mayer, the late Don Patinkin, Anna Schwartz, John H. Wood, and Leland Yeager read and commented on the complete manuscript. Only the author can know how much better a book becomes because of the critical efforts of those who read it as it is being written. This book is much better because of the suggestions of these critics. I thank them.

Along the way, numerous other people provided valuable criticism of papers that led up to the book. Still others provided me with information or documents that made my work easier and more effective. These individuals include Paul Auerbach, Roger Backhouse, Jeff Biddle, Sir Samuel Brittan, Victoria Chick, David Colander, John Culbertson, Neil Ericsson, John Lodewijks, Don Moggridge, Edward Nelson, Eugene Rotwein, and Rutledge Vining. I have also benefited from discussions with participants in the Wake Forest Economics Workshop, the Duke Economic Thought Workshop, the Post Keynesian Economics Study Group (London), and the University of Birmingham Economics Club Seminar.

I thank my mother-in-law, Evelyn Rausch, for convivial accommodations during my trips to the Bay Area to do research at the Hoover Institution. And I am grateful to Faye Kisel, our department administrative assistant, for help with putting the manuscript together and especially for skillful transcription of the interviews.

Winston-Salem, North Carolina
*August 24, 1995*

# Introduction

In 1948 Milton Friedman and Anna J. Schwartz embarked on a National Bureau of Economic Research study of monetary factors in business cycles. According to a brief prospectus written by Friedman at the start of the project, their objectives included investigation of "the *causal role* of monetary and banking phenomena in producing cyclical fluctuations, intensifying or mitigating their severity, or determining their character ("Brief Statement," undated, p. 1, emphasis added). Their plan was to complete the project in three years, however, it continued for over three decades. It produced, among other publications, "Money and Business Cycles" (1963a), *A Monetary History of the United States, 1867–1960* (1963b), *Monetary Statistics of the United States: Estimates, Sources, and Methods* (1970), and *Monetary Trends in the United States and the United Kingdom: Their Relation to Income, Prices, and Interest Rates, 1867–1975* (1982).

The concept of causality carried no particular significance for Friedman and Schwartz in 1948. The pursuit of understanding money's role in business cycles, though a formidable challenge, seemed naturally and unobjectionably to call for analysis of causes and effects. As David Hume, himself a prominent eighteenth-century monetary economist as well as philosopher, noted, causality is the "cement of the universe." Our attempts to understand the material and social world around us through science are almost always attempts to sort out causes and effects and often then to gauge their magnitudes. Furthermore, the record of science reveals substantial success in attempts to do this sorting and measuring.

For Friedman and Schwartz, causality was to become a snare, or rather an issue that their critics would use to ensnare them. Throughout the project, their work in monetary economics was controversial, with a great part of the contention centered on their identification of causes and effects. Their quantity-theory conclusions, which assigned an important causal role for money and for the Federal Reserve, contrasted starkly with the prevailing Keynesian view that monetary policy lacked power. This difference between Friedman and Schwartz and their critics in *conclusions* about money's causal role is readily

1

apparent from even a cursory look at their books and articles and their critics' reactions to them.

Two other dimensions of Friedman and Schwartz's monetary economics also made their work distinctive and controversial. Their National Bureau business-cycle analysis techniques, or *methods*, were unorthodox and came under attack as the econometrics revolution swept through the profession. Friedman and Schwartz began their project just after Tjalling Koopmans's influential and scathing review (1947) had tagged Arthur Burns and Wesley Mitchell's National Bureau book *Measuring Business Cycles* (1946) as "measurement without theory." The third factor contributing to the controversy surrounding their work was the unorthodoxy of Friedman's Marshallian *methodology* in a macro- and monetary economics landscape dominated by the neo-Walrasian IS–LM analysis of John Hicks.[1]

Their distance from the economics mainstream on each of these three dimensions, their conclusions, their methods, and their methodology, made Friedman and Schwartz particularly susceptible to causality challenges. The chapters that follow will show that the clash between National Bureau and econometric methods and between Marshallian and Walrasian methodology were more fundamental factors in the disputatious reception of Friedman and Schwartz's substantive conclusions about money's role in business cycles than the conclusions themselves. Moreover, the unorthodox character of Friedman's methods and methodology help explain a wariness about causality that Friedman developed over the course of the monetary research project.

Friedman's original openness to the conception of their work as sorting causes and effects did not last. By 1964, when he prepared a summary of the National Bureau monetary studies for the National Bureau's annual report, Friedman was using carefully chosen language to give an account of the findings. He summarized the conclusions he and his colleagues had come to without using the word "cause."

. . . money does matter and matters very much. Changes in the quantity of money have important, and broadly predictable, economic effects. Long-period changes in the quantity of money relative to output determine the secular behavior of prices. Substantial expansions in the quantity of money over short periods have been a major proximate source of the accompanying

[1] The distinction between matters of method and of methodology is that method is *how* one pursues an investigation and methodology is the *justification* of one's method. Of course, the distinction should not be made too sharply because disagreements over method lead to arguments on methodology.

inflation in prices. Substantial contractions in the quantity of money over short periods have been a major factor in producing severe economic contractions. And cyclical variations in the quantity of money may well be an important element in the ordinary mild business cycle (1964a, p. 277).

Though it may astonish economists familiar with Friedman's monetary economics, who have come to think of monetarism in terms of catch phrases such as "inflation is always and everywhere a monetary phenomenon," Friedman deliberately avoided the word "cause." Its omission from the cited passage was not by chance. In a letter to me commenting on an analysis of the causality in his monetary economics (Hammond, 1986), Friedman wrote:

I have always regarded "cause" as a very tricky concept. In my technical scientific writings I have to the best of my ability tried to avoid using the word. In the quotation with which you start the paper I do not say at all that money stock is a cause. I believe that you will not be able to find a statement in the *Monetary History* or in other scientific writings of mine in which I make such an assertion (MF to JDH, June 13, 1985).

Clearly there existed something deeper than mere choice of words. Members of the economics community have interpreted Friedman's work as an attempt to sort out the cause–effect roles of money in business cycles, and that was exactly how he portrayed it when he and Schwartz commenced the research. How did Milton Friedman develop this sensitivity to causality? This is the question from which this book evolved. Friedman's methods and methodology in the context of post–World War II economics provide the key to this biographical puzzle.

This book is a history of Friedman's debates with his critics over money's causal role in business cycles. It is ordered chronologically, from the beginning of his collaboration with Anna Schwartz in 1948 through 1991. Most of the chapters are constructed around exchanges between Friedman or Friedman and Schwartz and their critics. The predominant issue in these exchanges was one or another dimension of causality. The chapters that do not cover criticisms of Friedman and Schwartz's monetary economics (Chapters 1, 2, and 3) provide background for understanding the disputes over money as cause and effect. Chapter 1 covers the "measurement without theory" issue concerning the National Bureau of Economic Research prior to Friedman and Schwartz's project. National Bureau methods, particularly those developed by Wesley C. Mitchell and Arthur F. Burns, which Friedman and Schwartz adopted for their studies, were highly controversial well before Friedman and Schwartz made public their conclusions about money's role in business cycles. Chapter 2 provides an exposition of Friedman's equally controversial Marshallian methodology. Of particular interest is the formation of Friedman's methodological position prior to the 1953 publication of "The Methodology of Positive Economics." Chapter 3 draws heavily on unpublished material for a history of the initial stage of Friedman and Schwartz's collaboration. Chapter 4 also uses unpublished documents to portray the initial critical reaction to their work, from colleagues at the National Bureau. Chapters 5 through 10 cover episodes of critical reaction to Friedman and Schwartz's publications at various stages of their extended project. Though much of the source material for these chapters is published, they too make use of correspondence and other unpublished documents.

Critics and allies of Friedman and Schwartz have regarded their views on money (monetarism versus Keynesianism) as the primary source of contention in the debate over Friedman and Schwartz's revival of monetary economics. But given the standards of the day, their use of National Bureau business-cycle methods and Friedman's Marshallian methodology played even larger roles in making Friedman and Schwartz's monetary economics unacceptable. Even though they were widely credited with revitalizing monetary economics and by and large dominated professional and popular discussions of macroeconomics, monetary theory, and monetary policy for a quarter century, Friedman and Schwartz labored from the beginning to the end of their collaboration under a cloud of professional doubt. The doubt was concerning the scientific credibility of their techniques, and thus of their results. The techniques in question were means of uncovering cause and effect roles, and the results were attributions of these roles. Even at the conclusion of the project, when the slow tide of professional and public opinion had turned their way, reviewers of *Monetary Trends* claimed *both* that Friedman and Schwartz had long since won the battle with their Keynesian foes over the power of money supply changes *and* that their book gave insufficient attention to issues of forward and reverse causation between money and income. To paraphrase Hume, causality was the cement of Friedman and Schwartz's monetary economics. It was also the Achilles' heel.

# CHAPTER 1

# Theory and measurement at the National Bureau

## Introduction

"Measurement Without Theory" was the title that Tjalling Koopmans gave his famous review of Arthur Burns and Wesley Mitchell's *Measuring Business Cycles*. That phrase seemed to sum up the differences between the ascendant Cowles Commission approach and the National Bureau of Economic Research (NBER) approach to macroeconomic, or business-cycle, analysis in 1947. Whereas both organizations shared a concern for understanding business-cycle phenomena in order to provide a basis for control, their means to this end differed markedly. The Cowles Commission objective was to wed neoclassical economic theory and modern probabilistically based econometrics. They were actually *creating* what came to be recognized as modern econometrics, their emphasis was on theory. The National Bureau objective, as Koopmans indicated, had much more to do with measurement. A large portion of the effort at the National Bureau went toward developing measurement concepts such as national income accounts and the "reference cycle," along with their related data series. National Bureau analysis of business cycles consisted of separating trends and cycles in time series, and relating patterns in cycles across different series. Burns and Mitchell's book epitomized for Koopmans the National Bureau's atheoretic approach and its fruitlessness for understanding business-cycle phenomena.

Koopmans was neither the first nor the last critic to bring the charge of "measurement without theory" against the National Bureau. The question of the relationship between the work done there under Mitchell's leadership and neoclassical economic theory was an old one. It was a common theme in reviews of Mitchell's work going all the way back to his 1913 *Business Cycles*, published seven years before the National Bureau was founded. Paul Homan (1928, pp. 410–11) speculated that the general lack of attention readers gave to the theoretical implications of Mitchell's analysis may have been due to the book's size. Mitchell himself later wrote that the National Bureau produced books that only readers with "keen interest in a problem and uncommon power to assimilate facts" can appreciate (1945, p. 12). The sheer quantity of facts could get in the way of seeing the theory. Later, Friedman and Schwartz's books sustained the "weighty tome" reputation of National Bureau publications.[1] In a number of guises, the "measurement without theory" critique followed these two students of Wesley Mitchell throughout the course of their long collaboration.[2]

The purpose of this chapter is to review methodological controversy surrounding the National Bureau during the period when Mitchell was director of research, which was the backdrop for "measurement without theory" charges brought against Friedman and Schwartz.[3] The focus of the chapter is primarily on Mitchell's own work on business cycles, but we also consider Frederick Mills's work on price behavior, which was meant to complement the business-cycle project. Although the chapter does not provide exhaustive coverage of the National Bureau's programs over its first quarter century, it sufficiently reveals the history of the "measurement without theory" issue surrounding the National Bureau business-cycle project.

We begin by examining Mitchell's business-cycle volumes and reactions from reviewers. Then we consider Mills's *The Behavior of Prices* and its critics. In both cases the aim is to identify the methodology presented explicitly in the Mitchell and Mills texts. In reviewing the critical reactions we attempt to reveal some of the more important

---

[1] For example, see Thomas Mayer's favorable review of Friedman and Schwartz's *Monetary Trends* (1982).

[2] The methodological chicken-and-egg question of which comes first, theory or measurement, and the question of where the marginal value of effort is higher, have remained difficult and contentious issues for economists since the advent of systematic collection of data. Recent developments in macroeconomics have generated renewed interest in National Bureau methods of business-cycle analysis and have brought to the foreground once again these issues. See, for example, Sargent and Sims (1977), Neftci (1986), Prescott (1986), King and Plosser (1994), and Simkins (1994).

Robert Eisner (1989) made the relationship between theory and measurement the theme of his 1988 American Economic Association presidential address. The issue as he put it was, how can economists know what they are talking about? Eisner opened his address with a reference to Koopmans's review of Burns and Mitchell that reflects the conventional wisdom that Koopmans's critique was on target. Yet the balance of Eisner's message – that the marginal product of economists' effort is high for compiling and synthesizing data – was closer in spirit to the emphases of the National Bureau tradition than those of the Cowles Commission.

[3] Mitchell served as director of research from 1920 until 1945.

elements in the contextual backdrop from which "measurement without theory" issues arose. The critical reaction to Mitchell's work culminated with Koopmans's review of *Measuring Business Cycles*. As part of the contextual background, we will also consider the methodology of the Cowles Commission econometrics program.

### Mitchell's business-cycle analysis

The first edition of *Business Cycles* was published by the University of California Press in 1913, just after Wesley Mitchell left the Berkeley faculty for Columbia University, which was to be his academic home for the remainder of his career. The book has three parts: Part I contains a review of then extant business-cycle theories, a review of the history of business crises, Mitchell's depiction of the organization of modern economies and his method of analysis; Part II contains detailed statistical data series for four countries for the 1890–1911 period; and Part III contains the bulk of Mitchell's analysis of cycles. A new, reworked edition of Part I was published by the National Bureau in 1927 as *Business Cycles: The Problem and Its Setting. Measuring Business Cycles* (1946) was an update of Part II, with Arthur Burns as primary author. Mitchell planned to redo Part III but, fearing toward the end of his life that he would not complete the project, consented to a new but mostly unchanged edition, published by the University of California Press in 1941.[4] At the time he died in 1948 Mitchell had made some headway on this revision; the result was published posthumously by the National Bureau as *What Happens During Business Cycles* (1951).

Mitchell characterized his method as "analytic description," which involved systematic and extensive use of statistical data to develop and test theory. He saw business cycles as complex processes that impose on the investigator the burden of acquiring extensive factual knowledge before any useful analysis is possible. He thought the conventional approach was flawed because it put theory too much ahead of facts. Yet Mitchell did not spurn the theories that he reviewed in Part I of the 1913 volume and in the 1927 volume. Indeed, he explicitly used them. What he considered their flaw was that each in and of itself had inadequate empirical foundations and was woefully incomplete. He thought the source of this flaw was the idea that one needs a more or less complete theory before one can know what facts to look for or how to interpret them. This idea, which Mitchell saw as a

[4] *Business Cycles and Their Causes.*

shortcoming, would become a theme of Koopmans's methodology. Mitchell contended that "the more thoughtfully one considers the relations between these two phases of knowing [the apprehension of facts and conception of theories], the less separable they become" (1927, p. 59, n. 2).

Mitchell set up the presentation of his approach to business-cycle analysis in the 1913 volume in a way that is useful to reproduce at length:

Beveridge ascribes crises to industrial competition, May to the disproportion between the increase in wages and in productivity, Hobson to over-saving, Aftalion to the diminishing marginal utility of an increasing supply of commodities . . . Fisher to the slowness with which interest rates are adjusted to changes in the price level.

One seeking to understand the recurrent ebb and flow of economic activity characteristic of the present day finds these numerous explanations both suggestive and perplexing. All are plausible, but which is valid? . . . Each may account for certain phenomena; does any one account for all the phenomena? Or can these rival explanations be combined in such a fashion as to make a consistent theory which is wholly adequate?

There is slight hope of getting answers to these questions by a logical process of proving and criticizing the theories. For whatever merits of ingenuity and consistency they may possess, these theories have slight value except as they give keener insight into the phenomena of business cycles. It is by study of the facts which they purport to interpret that the theories must be tested.

But the perspective of the investigation would be distorted if we set out to test each theory in turn by collecting evidence to confirm or to refute it. For the point of interest is not the validity of any writer's views, but clear comprehension of the facts. To observe, analyze, and systematize the phenomena of prosperity, crisis, and depression is the chief task. And there is better prospect of rendering service if we attack this task directly, than if we take the round about way of considering the phenomena with reference to the theories.

This plan of attacking the facts directly by no means precludes free use of the results achieved by others. On the contrary, their conclusions suggest certain facts to be looked for, certain analyses to be made, certain arrangements to be tried. Indeed, the whole investigation would be crude and superficial if we did not seek help from all quarters. But the help wanted is help in making a fresh examination into the facts (1913, pp. 19–20).

The distinction that Mitchell made between his and the conventional approach suggests that the issue was one of emphasis and orientation rather than an either/or choice between theoretical and atheoretical, or a priori and a posteriori, approaches. His approach was different because its primary focus was on the concrete phenomena to be explained rather than on the extant theory.

There was an evolution of Mitchell's views on causality, which is evident through the various editions of *Business Cycles*. In the 1913 edition Mitchell was not at all self-conscious about writing on the causes of business cycles. He directed readers who desire a quick reading on the causes of cycles to the final chapter, which includes a section entitled, "Diversities Among Business Cycles and Their Causes." His review of the history of business-cycle analysis in Chapter 1 suggests nonetheless that he saw causal problems in traditional methods. From the economic crisis of 1825 through the remainder of the nineteenth century, students of the phenomenon developed a number of plausible theories of business cycles. They typically identified a single causal factor that disturbed the economic equilibrium. *The* cause of each crisis was taken to be the event that precipitated the crisis – its genesis. The theories traced out the cause–effect chains emanating from the disturbance, proceeding from the crisis's beginning to its end. As Mitchell became increasingly self-conscious about causal analysis, he took this unidirectional, unicausal explanation to be its archetype.

Mitchell defined the aim of his work as developing "a descriptive analysis of the cumulative changes by which one set of business conditions transforms itself into another set" (1913, p. 449).[5] Because he thought of business cycles as cumulative processes, he expected that a complete theory would be out of reach: "Business history repeats itself, but always with a difference" (1913, p. 449). This was for two reasons. First, because every individual phase (such as prosperity or depression) is the cumulation of an indefinitely long history, pursuit of a complete explanation leads to an infinite regress. Second, because each phase has its own uniqueness, there is a necessary trade-off between completeness and generality in a theoretical account.

In the 1927 revision of Part I of the 1913 volume, Mitchell pondered the role of causality in business-cycle analysis. He questioned whether in light of the complex interdependence of the institutions and processes from which he saw business cycles arising, there could be scientific warrant for a search for causes. Part of the problem was that which he discussed in the 1913 volume – the association of causal analysis with identification of a single disturbing cause. But rejection of unicausal explanation need not imply rejection of causal analysis altogether. Mitchell had developed another concern. At the time, philosophers were suggesting that in scientific explanation, mathe-

---

[5] There was a trend at the time toward framing the problem in terms of cyclical phenomena rather than discrete crises. See Mitchell (1913, ch. 1, especially p. 5).

matical functions *replace* causal connections.[6] For example, Bertrand Russell wrote that "the law of gravitation will illustrate what occurs in any advanced science. In the motions of mutually gravitating bodies, there is nothing that can be called a cause, and nothing that can be called an effect; there is merely a formula" (1917, p. 194). The following passage suggests that Mitchell was influenced by this philosophical climate:

As our knowledge grows wider and more intimate, our attitude toward the discussion of causes undergoes a subtle change. When we have accounted in causal terms for each stage in a lengthy series of actions and reactions, we find that our analysis deals with many causes, each one of which is logically indispensable to the theory we have elaborated. On reflection, we see the application to our work of the old contention that the idea of causation has pragmatic, rather than scientific, warrant. . . .

In the progress of knowledge, causal explanations are commonly an early stage in the advance toward analytic description. The more complete the theory of any subject becomes in content, the more mathematical in form, the less it invokes causation (1927, pp. 54–5).

Mitchell's concern with the role of causality also reveals a sensitivity to a not inconsequential limitation of the new reliance on empirical statistical material – that the statistics could not in themselves reveal any causal mechanism. Mitchell was well aware of the pitfalls of spurious correlation and *post hoc ergo propter hoc* explanation. This created something of a quandary for him. He saw causality as an extrascientific metaphor, but nevertheless one that is useful in accounts of cyclical behavior.

In business-cycle theory, the transformation from causal explanations into analytic description is being hastened by free use of statistical materials and methods. What time series can be made to show are functional relationships. We are always reading something into statistics, when we assert that the process represented by one series exercises a causal influence upon the process represented by a second series. Yet a stiff refusal to employ causal expressions in the detail of our investigation might often hamper us. In the present stage of our knowledge, we can probably make more rapid progress toward attaining insight into business cycles, by using the thought-forms of daily life than by trying to express ideas at which we are grasping in the form which may ultimately prevail (1927, p. 55).

[6] Mitchell's teacher Thorstein Veblen traced an evolution of the scientific use of causal analysis from final cause to efficient cause to process cause. But he thought the urge to *replace* causal relations with mathematical functions to avoid the anthropomorphism of causal imputation was futile. See Veblen (1906, 1908).

A shift in perspective about which Mitchell was unambiguous was toward greater attention to processes. In various terms, this interest in dynamics was an interest in discovering transmission mechanisms.

## Theory and measurement: Mitchell's reviewers

Mitchell's reviewers, especially those writing about the 1927 volume, were predisposed to look for the assigned roles of theory and evidence because of his association with institutionalism and statements he made that were critical of neoclassical theory. Some of his writings in the 1920s, especially "The Prospects of Economics" (1924) and his American Economic Association (AEA) presidential address (1925), presented quantitative economics as an alternative to neoclassical theory. His 1924 presidential address came at a time when there was considerable concern about neoclassical theory, quantitative analysis, and institutionalism.

Mitchell began his speech on a conciliatory note: "It is a cheering evidence of progress that no such futile disputation (a new Methodenstreit) seems to be in progress or in prospect" (1925, p. 1). He ended similarly: "In the thinking of competent workers, the two types of analysis (quantitative and qualitative) will cooperate with and complement each other as peacefully in economics as they do in chemistry" (1925, p. 12). But in between and throughout much of the address his message was not so reassuring to those he elsewhere referred to as "representatives of theory":

"There is little likelihood that the old explanations will be refuted by these [quantitative] investigators, but much likelihood that they will be disregarded. . . . If my forecast is valid, our whole apparatus of reasoning on the basis of utilities and disutilities, or motives, or choices, in the individual economy, will drop out of sight in the work of the quantitative analysts, going the way of the static state. . . . The literature which the quantitative workers are due to produce will be characterized not by general treatises, but by numberless papers and monographs. . . . Books will pass out of date more rapidly. The history of economic theory will receive less attention" (1925 pp. 5–7).

Paul Homan included a chapter on Wesley Mitchell in his 1928 survey, *Contemporary Economic Thought*. He considered the question of whether Mitchell's 1913 edition of *Business Cycles* was a case of theory guiding empirical analysis or a case of theory made anew from empirical observations. He also considered the relations of Mitchell's work to conventional business-cycle analysis, in particular, Alfred Marshall's theory and methodology. Homan concluded that Mitchell set out to gather and analyze data without reference to any particular theory and to then let the data suggest the theory. But he thought Mitchell was not completely successful in doing so, for he used Veblen's theory of a money economy to screen the data. Mitchell's Veblenian test of the relevance of data was their bearing on business profits.[7]

Homan wrote that Mitchell's problem was different from that of Austrian marginal utility theory and Marshall's value theory, but "the introductory chapters of *Business Cycles* cannot be intelligently read without perceiving that they rest upon a groundwork of ideas incompatible with any of the variant statements of orthodox economic theory" (1928, p. 401). He believed that, within Mitchell's scheme, money or the pursuit of money income took the place of a neoclassical utility–disutility calculus. He thought that another difference resided in Marshall's belief that quantitative analysis would serve the function only of gauging the intensities of already known forces operating in the economy. Mitchell, on the other hand,

does not . . . look for any statistical measurement of the force of motives, nor think it desirable that quantitative analysis should be subordinated to any preconceived analysis of the forces at work. He wishes quantitative analysis to address itself strictly to the objective phenomena at hand, supported by whatever analysis of unmeasurable forces is relevant to the particular problem (1928, p. 431).

Although Homan interpreted Mitchell's quantitative work as derived from Veblen's vision of a money economy, and incompatible with Marshall's conception of the relationship between quantitative analysis and value theory, in another respect he found Mitchell more compatible with Marshall than with Veblen.

It is not a little curious that the most eminent of our economic workmen in the field of minute analysis of statistical data should be so heavily indebted to an impressionistic cosmic philosopher like Veblen, who heroically distorts facts and shows no evidence of commerce with figures. Mitchell's work is of the sort that would have pleased Marshall. One thinks of a certain resemblance between them in the union of moral and scientific interest in their problems, and in the scientific precision of their methods (1928, p. 436).

J. M. Clark (1931) assayed Mitchell's contribution to business-cycle analysis, considering both the 1913 and 1927 editions together, in Stuart Rice's *Methods in Social Science*. Clark was most interested in

---

[7] See Veblen (1904). Homan's evidence for his interpretation was that Mitchell's chapter "The Economic Organization of Today" precedes the data and its analysis in the 1913 text.

causality. He called attention to "a decided kinship with the type of theoretical approach originated by Walras and used at present by Cassel, insofar as they substitute the idea of a multitude of interacting functional relationships for that of single or ultimate 'causes' but Mitchell, of course, does not follow them in focusing attention on the conditions of a theoretical equilibrium in these relationships" (1931, p. 669). He saw Mitchell (following Veblen) substituting matter-of-fact causality for "disturbing causes" that push the economy away from a "normal" equilibrium. The result was, on the one hand, an "analytic description" of cycles not drawn from any one theory and, on the other, an account within which the cycle itself is normal in contradistinction to the normality of equilibrium analysis. Clark gave Mitchell more credit than Homan for allowing the data to determine the theory.

Frank Knight reviewed Homan's *Contemporary Economic Thought* for the *Quarterly Journal of Economics* in 1928. In discussing Homan's chapter on Mitchell, Knight took as his main theme the relation between the new quantitative economics and traditional economics. He concluded: "But when Mr. Homan ends his essay on Mitchell with the assertion that the latter's work 'proceeds within a general framework of ideas not consonant with the general ideas of (Marshall),' I can only register emphatic disagreement – in the face of a surmise that Professor Mitchell himself may endorse the statement" (1928, p. 137). On the more general point of the new and old economics, Knight's opinion was the same; where Homan saw an impasse between the new and the old, Knight saw none. He thought that the actual work of the "insurgents" was more conservative than their claims for it: "The discontinuity between the 'newer' and the 'older' economics is imaginary, and largely a reflection of the human frailty (however important as an incentive) of overestimating one's own uniqueness and originality" (1928, p. 137).

Joseph Schumpeter made a major point of the consonance between Mitchell's 1927 edition and Marshall's *Principles* in his 1930 *Quarterly Journal of Economics* review. Schumpeter's reading of Mitchell's methodological message was that Mitchell was not brushing aside existing theory to start anew from raw facts. Schumpeter even found in Mitchell's book something Mitchell had predicted would become extinct – a systematic treatise.

Now, inasmuch as we have before us the work of one of the leading figures of the scientific world of economics and of a leader who has, in former years, often betrayed some displeasure at the state of our science and our ways of dealing with its problems, both in toto and on a number of well-defined headings, it seems but natural, and hardly unfair, to ask what the outstanding features are, which could be pointed to as constituting or implying fundamental differences in results or horizons, and whether the presence of such differences spells revolution or evolution. It is natural, in trying to answer this question, to think of that mighty structure which, tho battered in places by the impact of newer methods and results, still stands broadly in the background of much, if not most, of the best work of our day – Marshall's great treatise (1930, pp. 153–4)

In Schumpeter's mind there was a "difference in aim and character" between Mitchell's business-cycle analysis and Marshall's *Principles*. Whereas Marshall was intent on building the engine for analysis, Mitchell was not primarily interested in that enterprise and conceived of theory more as a store of generalizations from facts than as an engine. But Schumpeter insisted that Mitchell neither would nor could proceed in his work without theory – theory,

which is not an unscientific or provisional substitute for facts, but an instrument – spectacles, so to speak – needed in order to discern the facts.

This being the case there is a great difference in emphasis, and yet no epistemological gulf between Mitchell and Marshall; not even between Mitchell and Marshall's fifth book (appendix included) (1930, p. 155).

Taking a retrospective view after Mitchell's death, Arthur Burns, himself a devotee of Marshall, wrote in the introduction to *What Happens During Business Cycles* that "Mitchell's economic outlook was thoroughly Marshallian. Had he lived to finish this book, he would have inscribed on its title page Marshall's motto: 'The many in the one, the one in the many'" (1951a, p. viii). Burns called attention especially to Mitchell's use of the Marshallian theme of the importance of time and compared Mitchell's "normal" with the classical "normal." Both were devices of abstraction used to separate effects of complex causes and to analyze new concrete situations. According to Burns, the important difference between Mitchell's business-cycle analysis and traditional business-cycle analysis was that Mitchell gave closer attention to more detailed data, thereby substituting "fact and measure" for "impressionistic judgments."

Burns's judgment that Mitchell's analysis did not represent a break from Marshallian economics was seconded by Harold Somers, who reviewed the posthumous revision of Part III of *Business Cycles*, along with four other business-cycle studies, for the *Journal of Economic History*. Three of the studies were from the National Bureau; the fourth was Jan Tinbergen's *The Dynamics of Business Cycles*. Somers wrote that Mitchell's "progress report" cleared up several misconceptions regarding the National Bureau approach, including that it is not intended to determine causal relations and that it does not make use of theory such as that of Walras and Marshall. Somers saw evidence in the five studies of a rapprochement among the historical, theoretical, statistical, and econometric approaches.

### Mills's *The Behavior of Prices*

Frederick Mills's *The Behavior of Prices* was published in 1927, the same year as Mitchell's first National Bureau business-cycle volume. The book contains virtually no methodology or posturing about old and new economics. From the start Mills settled into his workmanlike task of finding statistical relations among wholesale commodity prices and seldom strayed from this focus. But owing to Mills's associations with Mitchell and institutionalism, the book provoked highly negative reviews.

Mills's statement of purpose is summarized in only six pages at the book's beginning and two pages at its end. He characterized the book as the first report of a larger study of individual prices and the price system. His objective was twofold: to develop statistical measures to describe the behavior, and to find "principles of order" in prices. In the first half of the book, he dealt with measures of the behavior of individual prices and in the second half, with prices in combination (the price system). With its primary emphasis on charting facts in statistical form, the book bears a marked similarity to Part II of Mitchell (1913) and to Burns and Mitchell (1946). Mills stated in conclusion that he had not attempted to present or support any specific thesis. He claimed to have made but little progress toward the ultimate goal of understanding prices:

The present investigation and those which have preceded it in this field have gone only a little way in the search for principles of order among the variations within the price system, but there have been revealed numerous interrelations and uniformities, and there have been found many clues to other regularities (1927, p. 439).

Mills also made clear that he shared Mitchell's understanding that the marginal value of economic fact finding was high because little was known of the facts of prices and the price system.

### Mills's critics

Writing in the *Quarterly Journal of Economics* (1929), Jacob Viner evaluated *The Behavior of Prices* solely on the basis of its contribution to economic theory, laying aside any questions about the quality of the statistical description. The closest he came to any sort of praise for the book was saying that it provided abundant raw material for theorists.

He found no direct contribution to theory, or use of theory, in the book. Viner thought it fair to look for theory because Mills made statements about "seeking principles of order," "reduc(ing) masses of facts to understandable terms," and the "price system." Viner took these references to mean that Mills's objective was more ambitious than simply providing raw material for other theorists.

On these grounds Viner condemned the book. He argued that Mills made no direct contribution to theory, and could not have done so, because he did not bring theory to the data. He saw Mills's technique just as Koopmans would later see Burns and Mitchell's – as "empirical trial-and-error methods, unaided by hypothesis." Without a priori theory Mills could not know what questions to ask of the data or what he had found in the data. Mills's data consisted almost exclusively of prices, and of a restricted set of prices at that. No account was taken of nonprice (or nonwholesale price) factors that influence the behavior of wholesale prices. Mills studied price behavior without aid from the "connecting tissue" of demand and supply functions.

For price theory as such, the immediate harvest from this elaborate investigation seems scanty. The main significance of its results for theory may perhaps consist in its new and empirical basis for scepticism as to the wisdom of reliance on empirical trial-and-error methods, unaided by hypothesis; and its unintended contribution to a revived faith in the usefulness of price theory in explaining the relations of prices to each other and to other economic factors (1929, pp. 349–50).

Despite this condemnation by one of the preeminent theorists of the day, there was considerable opinion that Mills's book was a watershed for economics – so much so that the Social Science Research Council (SSRC) convened a conference in May 1939 to gauge its significance. The proceedings volume (Bye, 1940) includes reprints of Viner's review and another by Bruce Mudgett, a ninety-page critique prepared expressly for the meeting by Raymond Bye, a seventy-five-page response by Mills, and the transcript of a roundtable discussion.[8] This was the second research methods appraisal sponsored by the SSRC. The purpose was to examine state-of-the-art social science research to identify and evaluate standards in the various fields – "to shed light on the different ways which scholars have devised in seek-

---

[8] The conferees were Bye, Viner, Mudgett, Mills, M. A. Copeland, A. F. Hindrichs, E. S. Mason, W. C. Mitchell, O. C. Stine, T. O. Yntema and, from the SSRC Appraisal Committee, E. G. Nourse, F. W. Coker, A. M. Schlesinger, and W. S. Thompson.

ing to distil truth from the observed phenomena of human beings associated in society" (Nourse, 1940, p. x)[9].

Bye stated at the outset of his critique that he was not responding solely to *The Behavior of Prices* but to some of Mills's other writings (1930, 1935) and to his association with institutionalism via his affiliation with Mitchell and the National Bureau.

Although Mills does not appear definitely to have labeled himself such, it is fairly evident that he is a member of the institutional school of economists. This is revealed, not only by the methods which he employs in *The Behavior of Prices*, but more clearly by the confession of faith which he has made in certain of his other writings. In view of the fact that he is closely associated with Wesley C. Mitchell in the work of the National Bureau of Economic Research, this is rather to be expected (1940, pp. 10–11).

Bye certainly might have made other associations. For instance Mills was a trained statistician; his concern with the "price system" bears a certain similarity to the general equilibrium school; and Mills himself saw a kinship of his work with Henry Schultz's demand function estimates and acknowledged Schultz's assistance with preliminary manuscripts. But of these contexts within which the book might have been read, Bye considered institutionalism most appropriate.

*The significance of his work consists in the fact that he has attempted a new approach to the study of the price system differing fundamentally from that of traditional economists.* Other workers have applied statistical methods to price analysis, but, for the most part, they have sought to apply existing theories to their data, or to give quantitative precision or inductive verification to those theories. Mills deliberately avoids building upon neoclassical foundations. . . . It is a bold and interesting attempt to apply new methods to the central problem with which economists for several generations have been concerned, in the hope of reaching scientific generalizations of an entirely different character from those which have hitherto been developed. With the exception of Mitchell's exhaustive, life-long analysis of business cycles, it is perhaps the most ambitious, constructive undertaking upon which any institutionalist has thus far embarked (1940, pp. 13–14, emphasis in original).

With institutionalism thus in place as the backdrop, Bye viewed Mills's approach as a revolutionary alternative to the methodological individualism and static theory of the neoclassical school, including its general equilibrium branch. But in Mills's book Bye saw the revolution stumbling, a judgment made partly on Mills's own grounds and partly on neoclassical grounds. Bye found the analysis incomplete and

[9] The first such exercise was an evaluation of Thomas and Znaniecki's *The Polish Peasant in America and Europe* (1918).

overly abstract in that only wholesale prices were considered and the price system was separated from other facets of the economic system. He also found it overly holistic in treating the price system as something other than the sum of its parts. Furthermore, by not making use of neoclassical concepts such as equilibrium, Mills had limited his results to generalizations that were of little help in understanding the behavior of prices.

Mills would not accept the assertion that his book was part of an institutionalist research program. He wrote, "I am afraid that I must disclaim the honor, not least because I do not know what responsibilities it entails" (1940, p. 112). He also denied that it was the product of strict empiricism, and suggested that Bye was confusing the presence or absence of a theoretical framework with the presence or absence of specific concepts or premises. "Indeed, when 'theory' means to one a particular body of doctrines, research guided by other concepts is by definition nondeductive" (1940, p. 117). And Mills claimed that his objectives were more modest than building a new economic theory. He contended that the real differences between his approach and that favored by Bye were in the issue of methodological individualism, in the choice of how much theoretical detail one requires before doing empirical work, and in his opposition to nineteenth-century-style theoretical "system building."

## The Cowles Commission program

During the 1940s there developed a distinctively neoclassical alternative to National Bureau empirical methods in the Cowles Commission[10] approach, or what came to be known as "econometrics." The Cowles Commission was organized in 1932 in Colorado Springs. In founding the organization, Alfred Cowles wanted to promote economic research on financial markets. Some of the early work was in this area, but the commission's programs quickly turned toward mathematical economic theory and statistical analysis. From its inception there was a close relationship between the Cowles Commission and the Econometric Society, which was established two years earlier. In 1939 the commission moved to the University of Chicago, and the next year the first Cowles monograph on statistical analysis of time series was published. The momentum of research in mathematical economics and theoretical statistics picked up when Jacob Marschak

[10] For extensive histories of the Cowles Commission's role in the development of macroeconomic econometrics, see R. J. Epstein (1987) and M. S. Morgan (1990).

joined the commission as research director in 1943. For the rest of that decade the mission of the Cowles Commission was to develop statistical methods for simultaneous equation estimation.

The scholars – economists, statisticians, and mathematicians – whom Marschak brought to Chicago conceived of their work as an extension of Jan Tinbergen's pioneering efforts at macroeconomic modeling. They sought to develop probabilistically based econometric methods for use with structural systems of difference equations such as Tinbergen's business-cycle models.[11] There was a headiness among the Cowles staff born of their confidence that at the commission were assembled the best minds for developing the best scientific practices. They expected these practices to yield solutions to economic problems such as the business cycle, and to allow rational economic planning.

In the 1930s Tinbergen built some of the first dynamic macro-economic models of the Dutch economy (1937) and the U.S. economy (1939). Tinbergen conceived of business-cycle analysis as the search for dynamic relations between causes and effects that occur in time. His approach was to work with a "complete" system of difference equations, a system with the same number of equations as unknowns. He thought such business-cycle models should be determinate, with full specification of the causal factors. They should be complete in the sense of representing the structure of the entire economic system. He conceived of the structure as including proximate causes and deeper causes and their effects, definitional relations, and technical and institutional connections. Along with Mitchell, Tinbergen considered traditional business-cycle models incomplete inasmuch as they tended to highlight the role of a single causal factor. He thought the dynamic properties of the time lags between causes and effects should be specified. But Tinbergen realized that full completeness, in the sense of complete realism in a model's representation of business-cycle relations, was not possible. So although his models were intended to represent the entire economic system, they were stylized. Some of the variables were treated as exogenously determined outside the system. Tinbergen thought the final form that a model would take depended on a process of iteration between theory and evidence. "One cannot know *a priori* what variables are necessary and what can be neglected in the explanation of the central phenomena that are under consider-

---

[11] See Hildreth (1986, appendix II, pp. 132–5) for a list of Cowles Commission residents from 1939 to 1955, the year the commission left the University of Chicago for Yale University.

ation. It is only during the actual work, and especially after the statistical verification of the hypotheses, that this can be discovered" (1937, p. 9).

Trygve Haavelmo's "The Probability Approach in Econometrics" (1944) became a key element of the Cowles vision of macroeconomic econometrics. Haavelmo had been influenced by Jerzy Neyman and Abraham Wald, pioneers respectively in probabilistically based statistical tests and decision theory.[12] The distinguishing element of Haavelmo's approach was his conception of the nature of economic theory. He argued that economic theories should be thought of as hypotheses about stochastic processes. The purpose of statistical work was not to measure observed phenomena, and by extension the underlying reality of deterministic economic relations, or to adjust data to bring them into conformity with theory known to be true. It was instead to use observed data to make inferences about the underlying reality. For testing inferences he advocated test procedures developed by Neyman and E. S. Pearson, and now known by their names.

Another important emphasis in the Cowles approach was a concern for simultaneous equations bias. Haavelmo wrote on this statistical problem (1943), reviving an issue that had been largely dormant since the 1920s. The problem arose in situations quite common in economics, where an effect was the outcome of two behavioral functions. For example, in the economic theory of any market, price and quantity were jointly determined by demand and supply functions. Ordinary least squares estimation of one or the other functions produced estimates with biases that were potentially quite large relative to the true coefficients. This led to the research at Cowles on the problem of identification. The perceived solution was to estimate both functions simultaneously. During the 1940s Cowles econometricians developed maximum likelihood methods of simultaneous equations estimation.

### Koopmans versus Vining

Koopmans's review of Burns and Mitchell pitted the Cowles Commission vision of economics against that of the National Bureau. Koopmans elaborated on what he meant by measurement without theory:

The approach of the authors is here described as empirical in the following sense: The various choices as to what to "look for," what economic phenomena to observe, and what measures to define and compute, are made with a minimum of assistance from theoretical conceptions or hypotheses regarding

[12] See Morgan (1990, p. 242).

the nature of the economic processes by which the variables studied are generated. . . .

Burns and Mitchell do not reveal at all in this book what explanations of cyclical fluctuations, if any, they believe to constitute plausible models or hypotheses (1947, p. 161).

Koopmans failed to acknowledge that the Burns and Mitchell volume was only one part, and not the theoretical part, of a three-part study.[13] But this oversight is less important if we regard his review as not simply criticism of this one book but of National Bureau methods. Koopmans thought that, "the examples given illustrate the authors' scientific 'strategy,' in which measurement and observation precede, and are largely independent of, any attempts toward the explanation of economic fluctuations" (1947, p. 166). Furthermore, "Fuller utilization of the concepts and hypotheses of economic theory (in a sense described below) *as part of the processes of observation and measurement* promises to be a shorter road, perhaps even the only possible road, to the understanding of cyclical fluctuations" (1947, p. 162, emphasis in original).

Koopmans had something definite in mind with his reference to the dearth of theory in Burns and Mitchell. "The tool-kit of the theoretical economist is deliberately spurned. Not a single demand or supply schedule or other equation expressing the behavior of men or the technical laws of production is employed explicitly in the book, and the cases of implicit use are few and far between" (1947, p. 163). By not beginning with a formal theoretical model with structural equations depicting behavior, institutional rules, and laws of production, Burns and Mitchell had in effect not consulted economic theory at all. In failing to frame their discussion of randomness in terms of joint probability distributions, they had in effect not used statistical analysis.

The absence of formal theory was responsible for two different flaws, according to Koopmans. First, Burns and Mitchell were left without a guide for discerning what to measure or knowing what they had measured. Without a formal theoretical structure they could not know if they were making the most efficient use of the data in isolating the most important phenomena. Second, and equally important, they were unable to articulate the type of quantitative explanation that could provide reliable guidance for policy making. Any regularities they found would likely be complex results of a number of structural relationships. Because of their complex makeup, and with-

[13] The three-part structure had been set in the 1913 volume.

out information about the structural determinants, these regularities would be unreliable vehicles for explanation or prediction.

The National Bureau approach was defended by Rutledge Vining (1949). He argued that formal theory is a limited vehicle for learning about economic phenomena and that its advocates often paid no more than lip service to fact gathering:

Koopmans doesn't give his hypotheses specific economic content. He discusses the mathematical form that the model should (or must) take; and suggests the kind of content it should have in very general terms, such as "the behavior of groups of economic agents," "underlying human responses," "knowledge of man's behavior and its motives." But apparently all he has to insist upon at present is the mathematical form, and from his discussion it appears not unfair to regard the formal economic theory underlying his approach as being in the main available from works not later than those of Walras. . . . In a sense, these are the only problems that have been attacked by this entire line of development – the problem of statistical estimation that would be presented by the empirical counterpart of the Walrasian conception. Add to Walras the simple notion of lagged effects (if it is not already there) and certain devices of the nature of the difference equation, and the problem is wholly statistical as contrasted with economic (1949, pp. 79–80).[14]

Vining used Haavelmo's (1944) four stages of quantitative economic problems – construction of tentative theoretical models, testing theory, estimation, and prediction – to distinguish the two different approaches to business-cycle analysis. He pointed out that Burns and Mitchell were working at stage one. Koopmans erred in presuming that Burns and Mitchell *were* beyond stage one and that they *should be*. Koopmans's criticisms might have validity but only for work in stages two, three, and four. Burns and Mitchell's book, however,

purports to be a work of discovery and hypothesis-seeking, and it is not clear at all what meaning should be given to "efficiency" in this context. Statistical efficiency is an attribute of an estimation and testing procedure rather than of a procedure of "search," and problems of statistical efficiency may be trivial, or almost so, in the prospecting and probing phase of the development of the understanding of a phenomenon (1949, p. 78).

Vining suggested that business-cycle analysts who blithely skip over stage one should consider fields such as microscopy in biology, whose practitioners do not rely on formal theoretical models but who nevertheless use theoretical premises and produce valuable knowledge. "When we think of the enormous body of factual knowledge digested

[14] Mitchell himself portrayed the organic unity of the National Bureau's empirical studies as an embodiment of Walras's vision, but one dictated by empirical realities rather than by mathematical considerations. See Mitchell (1945, pp. 36–7).

and systematized in other fields of variation and the meagerness of our own results from efforts to systematize, are we quite ready to leave Haavelmo's first problem and launch into the last three problems in estimation theory?" (1949, pp. 82–3).

## Conclusion

In looking back on the methodological controversy over the National Bureau approach to business-cycle analysis, we find that the exchanges were vivid and sometimes acrimonious but not always easy to pin down in terms of issues and differences. For instance, though Haavelmo's 1944 article was a compass for the Cowles program, Vining used the same article in defense of the National Bureau. No doubt the passion in the charges and countercharges was in part the result of product differentiation campaigns. The two organizations vied for funds from the same foundations.[15] Each set out to develop a program with a distinct identity. The organizations' stated purposes ("exact and impartial determinations of facts" for the National Bureau and "advancement of economic theory in its relation to statistics and mathematics" for Cowles) are reflected in different emphases in the work of Mitchell and Mills and of Koopmans.[16] Likewise, there were clear differences of emphasis between the National Bureau approach and the approach favored by Viner and Bye. Yet the differences were more subtle than "measurement versus theory," unless of course one takes the position that the only theory is neoclassical theory or, alternatively, formal probabilistically based theory. A common plank in both programs was the integration of statistics into economics to facilitate empirical analysis, so they could have been seen as complementary. Likewise they shared the view that social control over aggregate economic activity was necessary and depended on scientific progress in economics.

This difficulty in pinning down the issues and differences is also the result of a fact of intellectual life prominent in current literature on economic methodology, as well as in literary criticism and philosophy: Context is vitally important to both the writing and reading of papers and books. Yet writers' and readers' contexts are never exactly the same, and they are to one degree or another hidden from view.[17]

[15] See Epstein (1987, p. 64).

[16] However, the Cowles Commission logo contains the motto "science is measurement."

[17] The reference is of course to the rhetoric movement in economics, decon-

Only portions of Mitchell's and Mills's contexts as writers can be seen in *Business Cycles, Measuring Business Cycles,* or *The Behavior of Prices,* but locating their contexts is essential for appraising their work. So their critics inevitably read into their books more than was literally contained in them. Much of the early controversy over National Bureau statistical analysis was a struggle to establish this context.

In the early critiques of Mitchell's and Mills's work the institutionalist challenge to neoclassical theory was foremost on readers' minds. This challenge cannot be found in the bare bones of *Business Cycles* or *The Behavior of Prices,* but it can be seen in Mitchell's AEA presidential address (1925) and "The Prospects of Economics" (1924), or in the two articles by Mills (1930, 1935) alluded to by Bye. In the 1920s and 1930s National Bureau statistical economics appeared, from the outside at least, to be an element of the institutionalist challenge. Mitchell appended a brief statement to the SSRC roundtable transcript expressing frustration at what he judged a rather meager outcome from the evaluation of Mills's *The Behavior of Prices:*

I thought, and still think, that the differences of opinion relate not so much to scientific issues as to what the other side really thinks. Specifically, the men who regard themselves as representatives of economic theory seemed to believe that the men they thought of as representing statistical inquiry hold that economic theorizing is altogether futile. The statisticians repudiated with emphasis the view imputed to them. What I do not know is whether their repudiation was believed or will be remembered.

Similarly, some statisticians seem to think that economic theorists ascribe small value to the contributions made by statistical work. If so, the professions of men like Viner and Bye should dispose of the imputation. But once again I am not sure that the people inclined to make such charges are adequately impressed by the repudiations (1940, pp. 299–300).[18]

Both sides contributed to the ambiguity over just how much old baggage was being jettisoned by the new economics. Mitchell himself, for example, could slide into and out of an "extreme" position within the text of a single paper. Yet although the debate over National Bureau methods can appear as an argument in search of differences,

structionism in literary criticism, and hermeneutics in philosophy. See Hammond (1992a) for a study of Friedman's methodology that explores the development of context.

[18] The importance and slipperiness of context is evident in a remark from Knight's commentary on a paper Mills gave at the 1929 AEA meeting: "In his references to the older, classical approach to economics, Professor Mills' words have a general tone of dismissal which is more sweeping than his explicit statements" (Knight, 1930, p. 35).

the evolution of their program and that of the Cowles Commission clearly proceeded on different tracks. Development of measurements and data in the context of "concrete problems" such as the business cycle continued to be the distinctive feature of National Bureau work through the Friedman and Schwartz era. The Cowles approach likewise continued to be distinguished by an overriding concern with formal characteristics of models. By the end of the 1940s, work at Cowles on estimating structural macroeconomic models was virtually at an end. Lawrence Klein, whose *Economic Fluctuations in the United States, 1921–1941* (1950) represented the most important tangible product of their effort to estimate simultaneous equations macroeconomic models, left Cowles in 1947. Thereafter work at Cowles was redirected to mathematical economics.

Mitchell's 1924 prognosis about the future of quantitative analysis proved to be mostly wrong outside the National Bureau, for formalized neoclassical theory became established as the dominant paradigm. The less formal and more data-intensive National Bureau approach of Mills and Mitchell remained much on the edge of the mainstream. It was carried forward into the 1950s by Friedman and Schwartz, among others working at the National Bureau.

# CHAPTER 2

# Origins of Friedman's Marshallian methodology

## Introduction

Despite the large influence of Milton Friedman on economists', public officials', and the public's understanding of the role of money in business cycles, his analysis has always been considered suspect on theoretical grounds. At least it has been so considered by economists outside the ambit of the University of Chicago. The Cowles Commission "measurement without theory" charge against National Bureau analysis dogged Friedman through the 1960s in persistent requests by critics that he write down his theoretical model.[1] "Money and Business Cycles" (1963a) and the *Monetary History* (1963b) were widely regarded as important contributions to the empirical record of evidence on money and income and to historical analysis, but they were regarded as incomplete and suspect because of the absence of a satisfactory theoretical model. Eventually Friedman responded with two models in *Journal of Political Economy* (JPE) articles "A Theoretical Framework for Monetary Analysis" (1970b) and "A Monetary Theory of Nominal Income" (1971b). Four critiques of these models were assembled in a 1972 JPE symposium on "Milton Friedman's Monetary Framework" (reprinted in Gordon, ed., 1974). The critics (Karl Brunner and Allan Meltzer, James Tobin, Paul Davidson, and Don Patinkin) were unanimous in judging that Friedman's model(s) was not sufficient to account for his empirical results and for received monetary theory.

A decade later Friedman and Schwartz published the final volume from their National Bureau monetary factors in business cycles project, the long-awaited *Monetary Trends in the United States and the United Kingdom* (1982). Once again the "measurement without theory" charge was brought against their work. This time the attack came

---

[1] Friedman's "The Quantity Theory of Money – A Restatement" (1956b) contained an explicit theoretical model but one that was not presented in terms of the popular IS–LM framework. Thus there remained the perception that he did not have a theoretical framework.

from a different direction. The earlier critics of "Money and Business Cycles" and *Monetary History* undercut Friedman's analysis with the charge that genuine *economic* theory was missing. The reaction to *Monetary Trends* by David Hendry and Neil Ericsson (1983, 1991) was that genuine *econometric* theory was missing. In both this and the earlier form, the "measurement without theory" charge carried the implication that because Friedman and Schwartz failed to approach their empirical analysis with appropriate theory, their "measurement" was not adequate measurement of the things that matter. In other words, measurement without theory is not even measurement!

Friedman used methodology as well as theory and evidence in responses to critics of his monetary analysis. His judgment at the time of the JPE symposium, as well as several years later at a follow-up conference at Brown University, was that communication between himself and his critics was difficult because they had different research methodologies. Responding to Tobin, he wrote:

The alternative [explanation for the failure of communication] that now appeals to me is that the difficulty is a different approach to the use of economic theory – the difference between what I termed a Marshallian approach and a Walrasian approach in an article I wrote many years ago (Friedman 1949b, reprinted in Friedman 1953c). From a Marshallian approach, theory is, in Marshall's words, "an engine for the discovery of concrete truth." . . .

From a Walrasian approach, "abstractness, generality, and mathematical elegance have in some measure become ends in themselves, criteria by which to judge economic theory" (1974b, pp. 145–6).

In response to Patinkin, he wrote:

A more fundamental reason for Patinkin's emphasis on long-run "neutrality," the interest rate, and the real balance effect, and for his slighting the short-run context of most of my framework is that Patinkin, even more than Tobin, is Walrasian, concerned with abstract completeness, rather than Marshallian, concerned with the construction of special tools for special problems (1974b, pp. 159–60).[2]

Friedman dated his development of the two categories, Marshallian and Walrasian analysis, with his 1949 article, "The Marshallian Demand Curve." However, his use of the categories can be traced further back in his writings, to his 1941 review of Robert Triffin's *Monopolistic Competition and General Equilibrium Theory*.

---

[2] Friedman retained use of this theme in comments on a paper by Tobin and Buiter at the Brown conference. See Friedman (1976, p. 311).

Friedman and Schwartz did not use the Marshallian–Walrasian labels in their response (1991) to their latest critics, Hendry and Ericsson, but they used another theme first seen in Friedman's writings in the 1940s. The Hendry and Ericsson critique was concerned not with his and Schwartz's economic theory but with their use of National Bureau methods for extracting information from economic time series. This econometric critique elicited a response containing a methodological theme that Friedman first used in a 1940 review of Jan Tinbergen's *Business Cycles in the United States of America*, a review Friedman wrote while on the research staff of the National Bureau. This theme is that the real test of an equation or technique for deriving equations is whether it can explain data other than those used in its derivation.

Friedman and Schwartz also used one of Friedman's favorite Marshallian principles in answering Hendry and Ericsson, though without the label as such. This is that the success of a theory can be judged only with reference to the purpose to which it is put, and the purpose is not a once and for all representation of reality; theory is an engine for analysis of concrete problems. This point arose in regard to the question of the exogeneity of money. Friedman and Schwartz wrote:

Hendry and Ericsson put much emphasis on "concepts of exogeneity," listing four distinct concepts, and stating: "In no case is it legitimate to 'make variables exogenous' simply by not modeling them." . . . We do not sympathize with such commandments. In our view, exogeneity is not an invariant statistical characteristic of variables. Everything depends on the purpose. In economic analysis, it may be appropriate to regard a variable as exogenous for some purposes and as endogenous for others (1991, pp. 41–2).

This chapter identifies the origins and substantive content of the methodology Friedman has used over a half century in critiques of other economists' work and in defense of his own. The focus is on Friedman's earliest writings on methodology, which were important background for "The Methodology of Positive Economics." Methodologists have devoted great effort trying to interpret and typecast the argument of that essay. Most have given either little or no significance to Friedman's self-identification with Marshall's economics and methodology. No doubt this is because he did not make the Marshallian category prominent in the essay and because many methodologists have not looked beyond the essay for evidence of Friedman's methodology.[3]

---

[3] See Hammond (1990, table 14.1, p. 195). Notable exceptions to the rule that Friedman's methodology has been examined separately from his economics are

Friedman has written much more on methodology than the one essay. Throughout his career he has used a handful of methodological principles to support his "positive economics," to criticize the work of others, and to explain difficulties of communication with his critics. Most of these principles can be found in his writings prior to "The Methodology of Positive Economics," a period when he was especially active in methodological commentary.[4] In this chapter, I follow the lead of methodologists who have sought to identify the essentials and typecast Friedman's methodology – but with two important differences. The first is that I rely primarily on Friedman's writings before the essay. The second is my concern for the historical origins of Friedman's methodology to understand the relationship between his methodology and his economics.

Evaluation of the 1953 methodology essay has been dominated by methodologists, specialists in the application of philosophy of science to economics. Their typecasts have thus been drawn mostly from philosophy. Friedman was never a methodologist in the same sense as many of the individuals who have written on his essay. His methodology has always been drawn directly out of particular problems of economic analysis. His work in methodology and in economics is a vestige of an earlier time, before the division of economics into specialties, with methodology relegated to a place outside the boundaries of the main fields. This fact has been concealed by the inordinate attention given to Friedman's 1953 essay, where the ties to economic issues are more obscure than in his other writings. An additional factor bearing on the interpretation of Friedman's methodology is that by nature he is an "economist as economist" (to paraphrase James Buchanan, who referred to his and Friedman's teacher Frank Knight as "economist as philosopher").[5] He never developed an interest in philosophy of science. Given the prominence of philosophy of science

---

Hirsch and de Marchi (1990) and Hoover (1984, 1988). Hoover uses the Marshallian–Walrasian dichotomy to distinguish Friedman's monetarism from the monetarism of new-classical economics.

[4] *Essays in Positive Economics* (1953c) includes four chapters in addition to "The Methodology of Positive Economics" (1953a) with substantial methodology, which were reprints of earlier articles. "Lange on Price Flexibility and Employment: A Methodological Criticism" (1946) and "Lerner on the Economics of Control" (1947) are together under the heading "Comments on Method." "The Marshallian Demand Curve" (1949b) and "The 'Welfare' Effects of an Income Tax and an Excise Tax" (1952d) make up the "Price Theory" section of the book.

[5] Buchanan wrote of Knight that he was "the economist as philosopher, not the economist as scientist" (1968, p. 426).

in the secondary literature on the 1953 essay, it is no surprise that Friedman abstained from participating in debate over its interpretation, restricting his written commentary on methodology to debates about substantive economic issues such as theory and evidence of money's role in business cycles.

When Friedman put a label on his methodology, it was Marshallianism. Though he did not use this label in the 1953 essay, he used it regularly over a half century, and it is the best descriptor for his methodology.[6] It is particularly apt because essential parts of Friedman's methodology are rooted in issues concerning Marshall's economic theory. Another component, concerning the role of empirical analysis, comes from Friedman's early experiences at the National Bureau of Economic Research. In this chapter, I examine the roots of these two components of Friedman's methodology as they are found in his early writings, and consider their relationship to one another. The next section of the chapter examines the roots of the Marshallian component, and the section that follows shows the importance of Friedman's early experiences at the National Bureau and his associations with National Bureau personnel at Rutgers and Columbia University for his methodology. In the final section, I consider the compatibility of these two elements of Friedman's methodology.

### Marshallian roots: monopolistic competition

In late 1940 Friedman wrote a two-page review of Robert Triffin's *Monopolistic Competition and General Equilibrium Theory*. Friedman was at the time a visiting professor at the University of Wisconsin, having just left New York where from 1937 to 1940 he was a member of the research staff of the National Bureau and part-time lecturer at Columbia University. His review of Triffin's book, published in the relatively obscure *Journal of Farm Economics*, marks the beginning of Friedman's public articulations and arguments for Marshallian methodology. The review was not the first published methodological piece by Friedman. That was his *American Economic Review* (AER) review of Jan Tinbergen's *Business Cycles in the United States of America, 1919–32*,

---

[6] The other label that comes to mind for his methodology is "the methodology of positive economics," from the title of the essay. But this label fails to distinguish Friedman's views from the dominant competing views about how to do positive economics. It also draws attention to a relatively unimportant component of the 1953 essay – his distinction between positive and normative economics. Friedman did not make this distinction, nor did he cite J. N. Keynes, from whom he got the distinction, in early drafts of the essay. See Hammond (1991).

published six months earlier. The Triffin review is important because it contains a response to Triffin's methodological attack on the economics of Alfred Marshall. Furthermore, for the next half century Friedman returned repeatedly to the categories laid out by Triffin – Marshallian and Walrasian analysis – to define his methodology.

Examination of Triffin's book reveals that he set up the categories much as Friedman would later use them. Triffin attempted to break the ties between the theory of monopolistic competition and Marshallian analysis and to reorient this theory of market structure within Walrasian general equilibrium analysis. In so doing, he argued that Marshall's concept of "industries," which Edward H. Chamberlin transformed into "groups," should be dropped. Friedman argued that if Marshallian industries have no place in monopolistic competition it is the latter that should be dropped. Though the content of the economic issues changed, Friedman returned again and again throughout his career to the theme of the relative usefulness of Marshallian analysis and the relative uselessness of Walrasian analysis. He taught Marshall's economics at Columbia while on the National Bureau staff in the late 1930s and at Chicago after returning there as a member of the faculty in 1946. He told students in his Economics 300a course at Chicago in the late 1940s that,

Marshall's "Principles" viewed contemporaneously, i.e., as if he were writing today instead of a century ago, is still the best book available in economic theory. This is indeed a sad commentary on the economics of our time. Marshall's superiority is explained primarily by his approach to economics as contrasted with the modern approach ("Lecture Notes 'Price Theory,'" undated, p. 1).

The theme is prominent in a number of his publications, including "The Marshallian Demand Curve" (1949b), "Leon Walras and His Economic System" (1955), and in responses to critics of his monetary analysis. In publications where he made less or no explicit reference to Marshall, such as the 1953 essay on methodology and the review of Oscar Lange's *Price Flexibility and Employment* (1946), he nonetheless made use of the Marshallian principles that he first defended in the review of Triffin.

Robert Triffin completed his Harvard Ph.D. dissertation seven years after the appearance of Joan Robinson's *The Economics of Imperfect Competition* (1933) and Chamberlin's *The Theory of Monopolistic Competition* (1933). Though already the subject of much discussion, monopolistic competition was still a new concept when Triffin set out to write his dissertation. What was less new, with origins in the nineteenth century neoclassical revolution, were two distinct traditions in economic theory, Marshallian analysis of "particular equilibrium" and Walrasian analysis of "general equilibrium." Marshallian analysis tended to be the favored approach among English-speaking economists. Alfred Marshall was the foremost personality in the dominant British academic institution for economics in the nineteenth and early twentieth century. American economists were drawn naturally to Marshall because of the common language and culture and the long and rich history of British economics beginning with David Hume and Adam Smith. In continental Europe, particularly among French-speaking economists, the general equilibrium approach of Leon Walras was more popular. This was part of a general inclination toward rationalism, in contradistinction to the Anglo-American empiricism.

Triffin thought the potential for progress in economics via the new theory of monopolistic competition was limited by its roots in the Anglo-American Marshallian tradition.

Something might be gained if we could approach the problem from a new angle and escape from the particular tradition and methodology within which the discussion has proceeded so far. A way of achieving this is clearly indicated. Monopolistic and imperfect competition theories have been evolved in the United States and in England alike along the lines of the theoretical tradition dominant in both countries: the particular equilibrium economics of Alfred Marshall. What we might well do now is to restate the whole problem in terms of the Walrasian, general equilibrium system of economic theory, so much more influential in economic thought on the continent of Europe (1941, p. 3).

Triffin realized that the "gravitational center" of Marshall's economics was the industry. He saw monopolistic competition in its Anglo-American form shifting the center inward to the firm by what was essentially an expansion of the scope of Marshall's theory of pure monopoly. Both monopolistic competition and monopoly theory dealt with the equilibrium of the individual firm rather than a group of firms, the industry. To Triffin this represented a step toward the gravitational center of Walrasian economics – equilibrium in terms of external interdependence. He thought it appropriate that Chamberlin had taken a step in this direction with his new theory and that the next step would be from the local situation of the firm or industry to the "whole economic collectivity."

For, if the firm, rather than the industry, is taken as the basic unit, there arise, as in general equilibrium theory, conditions of equilibrium *external* to the firm. Consideration of the general interdependence of the economic system is, however, still limited by the new theorists to the group or industry, rather than extended, as in Walrasian economics, to the whole economic collectivity. . . .

. . . As for the "industry" or "group," it could only appear to general equilibrium theorists as a far too timid substitute for a fuller recognition of the generality of economic interdependence throughout the system, permeating all the "industries" composing the collectivity as well as all the firms composing any one of these industries (1941, pp. 9–10).

Triffin did not expect the gains from trade between monopolistic competition and general equilibrium theory to go in one direction only. The gain for general equilibrium would come from dropping the standard assumption of perfect competition in favor of Chamberlin's "large group" and from establishing a clearer formulation of the requirements of equilibrium.

I will allow Friedman and George Stigler to inform us about what they found objectionable in Triffin's book rather than summarize its contents myself.[7] But I will close this brief sketch of the book with another quotation from Triffin that provides a strong hint of why the book made a lasting impression on Friedman and Stigler. Triffin wrote:

The appearance of monopolistic competition assumptions has been a new step in the historical process of purification and formalization of economic theory. The analysis loses in content, while gaining in generality. The sales curve of the firm, e.g., is no longer considered perfectly elastic: it may assume any and every degree of elasticity. A clear understanding of this evolution helps us to recognize the respective claims and domains of both "institutional" and "theoretical" economics. It is hoped that our analysis may contribute to such an "appeasement" by making our theory of value logically more satisfactory, while at the same time emphasizing the need for factual investigations in the choice of our assumptions. Empirical research should take the place of the conventional notions often presented as answers to our questions in the stage of general theorizing (such as the concepts of free, closed, restricted entry); it should fill up some of the famous empty boxes of Dr. Clapham.

On the other hand, we shall find that an increasing number of situations elude the grip of the traditional weapons of pure economics. This raises the question whether we should not, reversing the historical process of growing

---

[7] A word of explanation as to why I make use of Stigler's writings on monopolistic competition in addition to Friedman's. George Stigler was both critic and consumer of Friedman's methodology. He read and made important critical comments on early drafts of Friedman's 1953 methodology essay, where Friedman's concern with monopolistic competition is more prominent than in the published version. (See Hammond, 1991.) Friedman identified the theory of monopolistic competition as the most important example of economics based on misguided methodology (1953a, p. 15), but it was Stigler (1949) who wrote an extended critique of this new theory. Most significantly, Stigler concluded his critique with a summary of methodological principles from Friedman's then unpublished essay.

generalization just mentioned, enlarge the present box of assumptions of pure theory so as to enable us to tackle these cases; again, the required assumptions should be chosen on an empirical basis, and a price will have to be paid in the form of a lesser generality for the ensuing analysis (1941, pp. 15–16).

One can see in this passage two approaches to economics that lie on either side of Friedman's – formalized theory and "institutional" economics. Over his career, Friedman has had methodological opponents on both sides. His Marshallian approach is opposed to both tendencies – to the mathematization of theory that removes it from contact with actual institutions and to the dismissal of the "engine of analysis" that neoclassical theory provides. Friedman's argument that the "pure" theory of mathematical economics and "atheoretical" institutional economics were cut from the same methodological pattern has the flavor of paradox.[8] Are these two programs not antithetical to each other? Pure theory is the most general and most abstract economics, whereas institutional economics is the most specific and concrete. Triffin's book goes a long way toward explaining how Friedman came to view these tendencies in what are apparently different directions as having common origins. For it was Triffin who initially put the two seemingly disparate research programs together by making an institutionalist-style call for empirical analysis to choose assumptions for theory that is "purified."

Friedman's book review is very brief. He praised Triffin for providing new clarity about the implications of monopolistic competition and the meaning of monopoly, oligopoly, and other forms of firm interdependence. He noted Triffin's conclusion that "monopolistic

---

[8] See, for example, his discussion on p. 53 of "The Methodology of Positive Economics" (1953a). A passage that was dropped from the published version of the essay reads:

The fallacious notion on which I have placed so much emphasis, that hypotheses can be tested by the "realism" of their assumptions independently of the accuracy of their predictions, has had far reaching consequences in economics. The desire for descriptive realism which this belief so greatly strengthened indirectly fostered mathematical economics, with its emphasis on Walrasian general equilibrium analysis as an escape from the *ceteris paribus* of partial equilibrium analysis; it explicitly motivated monopolistic competition analysis and explains its popularity; it encouraged emphasis on arithmetical rather than economic considerations in all branches of economic analysis; it was the battle cry of institutionalism and the closely related emphasis on extensive statistical studies of economic phenomena; it is a major source of the naive yet recurring notion that the progress of positive economics depends critically on the progress of psychology; it has been manifested most recently in the belief that a theory can be tested by asking questions of consumers, producers, and the like (1952c, p. 46).

competition furnishes no tools for the analysis of an industry; that there is no stopping place between the firm at one extreme and general equilibrium at the other" (1941, p. 390). That is to say, there is no place in monopolistic competition for Marshall's "industry." Friedman found this conclusion "inescapable." But the implication drawn by Triffin, that Marshall's industry concept should be jettisoned to purify the theory, was not inescapable for Friedman.

The reviewer deduces that monopolistic competition adds little to our box of tools other than a refinement of Marshall's monopoly analysis. The most important problems in the real world relate to "industries," though admittedly the exact content of an "industry" depends on the problem under investigation. The fact that we state a problem in terms of a particular "industry" is likely to mean that the differences among the products of the members of the industry are less important, *so far as the specific problem is concerned,* than the similarities. For these problems, we must continue to employ the Marshallian tools, until better ones are invented. In doing so, we shall be using them for the purpose for which they were designed (1941, p. 390, emphasis in original).

Friedman introduced themes in this brief review that he would return to in subsequent defenses of Marshallian analysis – that economic theory should address concrete problems and that the adequacy of a theory must be judged in terms of success in using it to understand the problem for which it is designed. This meant that "elegance" and "generality," attributes held in esteem by devotees of the general equilibrium approach, were of secondary importance. Friedman praised Marshall's supply and demand curves not for their elegance but for what they offered toward understanding real world problems. He claimed that Marshall's interest was not with a world of pure competition but "with the kind of competition that prevails in the real world" (1941, p. 390).[9]

The entire discussion in the review foreshadows arguments Friedman would later make in the 1953 methodology essay. For example,

[9] It is important to understand that Friedman's objection to Walrasian general equilibrium theory was to its empirical emptiness, not to its attention to interrelations between markets. In "The Marshallian Demand Curve" he wrote:

A demand function containing as separate variables the prices of a rigidly defined and exhaustive list of commodities, *all on the same footing,* seems largely foreign to this [Marshallian] approach. It may be a useful expository device to bring home the mutual interdependence of economic phenomena; it cannot form part of Marshall's "engine for the discovery of concrete truth." The analyst who attacks a concrete problem can take explicit account of only a limited number of factors; he will inevitably separate commodities that are closely related to the one immediately under study from commodities that are more distantly related (1949b, p. 469, emphasis added).

in the essay Friedman wrote: "Viewed as a body of substantive hypotheses, theory is to be judged by its predictive power for the class of phenomena which it is intended to 'explain.' Only factual evidence can show whether it is 'right' or 'wrong' or, better, tentatively 'accepted' as valid or 'rejected'" (1953a, p. 8). In both the review and in the essay, Friedman presumed that economic theories are constructed for the purpose of explaining specific concrete problems in the "real world." Long after he wrote the essay, in a 1988 interview with me, Friedman said:

There's no doubt that Chicago was distinctive, and has been ever since. The real distinction was not making price theory the focal point of the graduate curriculum. That isn't the real distinction at all. The fundamental distinction is treating economics as a serious subject versus treating it as a branch of mathematics, and treating it as a scientific subject as opposed to an aesthetic subject, if I might put it that way. . . . The fundamental difference between Chicago at that time and let's say Harvard, was that at Chicago, economics was a serious subject to be used in discussing real problems, and you could get some knowledge and some answers from it (Hammond, 1992b, p. 110).

In the 1953 essay, Friedman suggested that monopolistic competition was the most important example of the mistaken notion that descriptive realism of assumptions is an appropriate test of theory. "The development of this analysis was explicitly motivated, and its wide acceptance and approval largely explained, by the belief that the assumptions of 'perfect competition' or 'perfect monopoly' said to underlie neoclassical economic theory are a false image of reality. And this belief was itself based almost entirely on the directly perceived descriptive inaccuracy of the assumptions rather than on any recognized contradiction of predictions derived from neoclassical economic theory" (1953a, p. 15). Further along in the essay, without any specific reference to Triffin, he defended Marshall's use of "industry" and "product" concepts. "Marshall took the world as it is; he sought to construct an 'engine' to analyze it, not a photographic reproduction of it" (1953a, p. 35).

George Stigler's University of London lecture "Monopolistic Competition in Retrospect" (1949) reads as an expansion of Friedman's three-page book review. It also contains an important reference, perhaps the earliest published reference, to Friedman's then unpublished methodology essay.

Stigler's strategy was to develop an "internal" critique of Chamberlin's version of monopolistic competition, showing that it founders on its attempt to focus on the diversity of firms and products while retaining the shade of Marshall's "industry" in the "group." He then considered Triffin's "purified" version of the theory and made a Friedman-like argument that Triffin's emphasis of "realistic" assumptions leaves the theory incapable of explaining the problems encountered in the real world. It is significant that Stigler did not extend his criticism to Robinson's imperfect competition, only to Chamberlin's and his student Triffin's. Robinson's work appeared not to be revolutionary, despite her rebellious language. She did not break with (Marshall's) traditional neoclassical economics. Chamberlin by comparison was a true revolutionary.

There were two parts to Stigler's criticism of monopolistic competition. The first, his "internal" criticism that he applied to Chamberlin, follows from his question, "did Chamberlin develop from this viewpoint a logically consistent theory of economic events?" (1949, p. 14). The second, which we can call the "Friedman criticism," for it followed form with Friedman's critique of Triffin, is an "external" criticism. It follows from another question, "does a theory incorporating this viewpoint contain more accurate or more comprehensive implications than the neo-classical theory?" (1949, p. 14)

The "internal" criticism hit on three components of Chamberlin's theory that are incongruent with his underlying vision of complex diversity: the "group," the "uniformity" assumption, and the "symmetry" assumption. In Chamberlin's words, "the group contemplated is one which would *ordinarily* be regarded as composing one imperfectly competitive market: a number of automobile manufacturers, of producers of pots and pans, of magazine publishers, or of retail shoe dealers" (Stigler, 1949, pp. 14–15; Chamberlin, 1946, p. 81, emphasis in original). Stigler concluded that "we are left with the strong impression that the Marshallian industry has reappeared and we do not understand its new role, for our new picture is one of diversity" (1949, p. 15). Stigler then quoted Chamberlin on the "uniformity" assumption: "We therefore proceed under the heroic assumption that both demand and cost curves for all 'products' are uniform throughout the group" (Stigler, p. 16; Chamberlin, 1946, p. 82). He pointed out that this assumption obliterates the diversity among "products" that is supposed to be at the core of the analysis. Unless the products are homogeneous, there can be no meaning in uniform costs and demands. What Stigler labeled the "symmetry" condition was Chamberlin's assumption that any adjustment in price or "product" by a single firm has negligible effects on any other firms. Two additional assumptions that violate the basic premise of diversity that lay at the core of monopolistic competition are that there is no complementarity between products and that the monopolistically competitive market structure does not extend to resource markets.

Having begun with the purported diversity of real world markets, Chamberlin leaves readers in the end, by Stigler's assessment, with something very close to a Marshallian industry. Triffin realized this and proceeded to remove the group from the theory. In the new purified form that Triffin envisioned for monopolistic competition, the theory has nothing to say about the interdependence of firms, for demands and costs are functions of every price in the economy. Perversely, in Stigler's view, Triffin considered the barrenness of this generalized theory an advantage.

Dr. Triffin does not fail to draw the conclusion that monopolistic competition has nothing to say of the interdependence of firms; this silence is indeed hailed as an advance over the Marshallian theory (p. 189). The basis for this claim deserves our attention. Dr. Triffin visualizes the discipline as composed of two very different types of studies: the "general pure theory of value"; and the investigation of concrete economic problems – for example, the New York housing problem. . . .

I would emphasize the separateness of these two types of economic analysis in Triffin's view of economics: there is neither substitution nor complementarity between the general theory and the specific economic investigation. The theory has nothing to learn from the study of specific problems because these problems are so diverse that no single inductive generalization is possible. Conversely the study of specific problems has nothing to gain from the general theory, for the theory can provide no apparatus to raise relevant questions, to indicate relevant types of facts, or to guide the economist in handling the facts to reach useful conclusions.

This is a fundamentally mistaken role to assign to general theory. The study of economic theory is not defensible on aesthetic grounds – it hardly rivals in elegance the mathematics or physics our sophomores learn. The theory is studied only as an aid in solving real problems, and it is good only in the measure that it performs this function. Dr. Triffin's advice is fundamentally to give up theory, "to tackle each problem with due respect for its individual aspects." Chamberlin's picture of reality has finally led, when consistently followed, to the familiar reaction: *ad hoc* empiricism (1949, pp. 21–2).

Stigler compared Triffin with an artist who sets out to paint a picture of the typical skyscraper but, when faced with the diversity in size, shape, and other attributes of actual skyscrapers, decides that it is best to leave the canvas blank. "Dr. Triffin should have been warned by the Walrasian theory of general equilibrium he sought to generalize. This theory proved to be relatively uninformative, even when it had as many equations as unknowns; it was not likely to gain in usefulness when the unknowns were multiplied and the equations reduced" (1949, pp. 22–3).

Stigler closed with a set of methodological principles the interpretation of which he credited to Friedman.

The purpose of the study of economics is to permit us to make predictions about the behaviour of economic phenomena under specified conditions. The sole test of the usefulness of an economic theory is the concordance between its predictions and the observable course of events. Often a theory is criticized or rejected because its assumptions are "unrealistic." Granting for a moment that this charge has meaning, it burdens theory with an additional function, that of description. This is a most unreasonable burden to place upon a theory: the role of description is to particularize, while the role of theory is to generalize – to disregard an infinite number of differences and capture the important common element in different phenomena.

But this line of argument grants the ungrantable: it is often impossible to determine whether assumption A is more or less realistic than assumption B, except by comparing the agreement between their implications and the observable course of events. One can but show that a theory is unrealistic in essentials by demonstrating that its predictions are wrong.

Should monopoly or competition be used to analyze the New York housing market? The answer is: both. If we are interested in the effects of rent ceilings and inflation, the theory of competition provides informative predictions. If we are interested in why one location rents for more than another, the theory of monopoly may be an informative guide. Different theories, each with its particular assumptions, can be applied to the same phenomena to answer different questions (1949, p. 23).

Stigler continued this application of Friedman's methodological principles by arguing that support for Chamberlin's monopolistic competition is based on the mistaken notion that if the assumptions of competitive theory are descriptively unrealistic, the theory's implications must be wrong. This, as he had argued, confuses descriptive and analytical relevance. He suggested that the real contribution of the new theory would be refinement in the old theory of monopoly, a genuine contribution, though not the revolution for which Chamberlin, Triffin, and their supporters hoped.

### National Bureau roots: empirical analysis of business cycles

The 1930s saw the birth of Keynesian economics and econometrics, which would become wedded into the dominant macroeconomic approach of building large-scale macroeconometric models, replacing "business-cycle" analysis virtually everywhere except at the National

Bureau. The first large-scale econometric model of the U.S. economy was Jan Tinbergen's (1939) model using data for 1919 through 1932. This was published as the second of two volumes Tinbergen prepared for the League of Nations.[10] Tinbergen's work in modeling the U.S. economy represents a critical juncture in the history of economic analysis.[11] He produced the first macroeconometric model, and his would become an archetype for later generations of models. Tinbergen used an explicit general equilibrium framework, beginning with an analytical skeleton with a linear equation for each variable to be explained. His approach was explicitly causal and aimed for full specification of the causal factors. He built into the model a dynamic potential for cycles by including lagged values among the right-hand side variables. We saw in Chapter 1 that Lawrence Klein and other economists at the Cowles Commission considered their work a continuation of Tinbergen's.

Tinbergen did the League of Nations study shortly after publication of Keynes's *General Theory*, but he made scant use of Keynesian concepts. Keynes himself was a severe critic of Tinbergen's econometric approach. In his famous review (1939) of Volume I of Tinbergen's study, Keynes argued for a highly restricted role for econometrics. He thought the techniques were useful only for measurement and criticism of theories, not for the discovery and development of hypotheses. So although Tinbergen's approach proved later to be a seemingly ideal vehicle for Keynesians to estimate and test macroeconomic theory, Keynes himself gave it little currency.

The more important point is that, as Morgan (1990) noted, traditional business-cycle theory, including Mitchell's work, was a much larger part of the context for Tinbergen's League of Nations project than Keynesian theory. In Volume I of his study, he used Gottfried Haberler's *Prosperity and Depression* (1937), also a League of Nations project, as his main source for extant business-cycle theories. Haberler completed his book in the summer of 1936 and made only passing footnote references to the *General Theory*. So Tinbergen's model of the U.S. economy grew out of business-cycles analysis, not out of Keynes's *General Theory*. But it stood at the juncture from which Keynesian analysis would take over from business-cycle analysis.

If Tinbergen's model was an important contribution to business-cycle/macroeconomic analysis, it was also an important part of the

[10] The first volume, *Statistical Testing of Business Cycle Theories*, was a statistical evaluation of existing business-cycle theories.

[11] I draw from Morgan (1990) in discussing Tinbergen's work.

emerging discipline of econometrics. Econometrics had broad origins in statistical analyses of business cycles and demand and supply curves in the 1920s and 1930s. As the field evolved, it came to be the product of a union of formal statistical theory and formal economic theory.[12]

Friedman was in a favorable position from which to evaluate Tinbergen's book; few other economists at the time had experience as broad as Friedman's in mathematics, theoretical and applied statistics, and business-cycle analysis, the areas from which Tinbergen's econometric model was drawn. Friedman was involved in work on estimations of demand functions the year (1934–35) he was research assistant to Henry Schultz at the University of Chicago. He studied business cycles under Arthur Burns at Rutgers (1931–32) and Wesley Mitchell at Columbia (1933–34) and later became directly involved in the National Bureau projects. He was working there when he wrote the review of Tinbergen's book. In between his undergraduate and graduate studies and his stint as a member of the National Bureau research staff (1937–40), Friedman worked as an economist/statistician on consumption studies for the National Resources Committee. He received extensive graduate training in mathematics (at Chicago) and theoretical statistics (at Chicago, Columbia, and the Department of Agriculture Graduate School), a level of training that was unusual for economists in the 1930s. At the time he read Tinbergen's book, Friedman had published two theoretical statistics articles and was collaborating with W. Allen Wallis on a statistics textbook.[13]

Yet when econometrics and Keynesian macroeconomics swept through the economics profession, the business-cycle approach of Friedman and his colleagues at the National Bureau was swept to the side. Friedman, who retained his National Bureau affiliation and the business-cycle framework for his monetary analysis after taking a faculty position at the University of Chicago in 1946, was considered throughout his career to be working outside standard econometrics.

Friedman's chief criticism of Tinbergen's model was that the equation estimates were chosen after a search for specifications that produce high correlation coefficients. Because of this the standard tests of statistical significance were invalid. Tinbergen relied on person power in the 1930s to produce his estimates, instead of the computer power that is used now, but Friedman's point is exactly the same point

---

[12] The third part of the union was to be probability theory (see Haavelmo, 1944), but there is still some controversy over the actual role played by the theory of probability in econometric analysis. See Lail (1993).

[13] They did not finish the book.

made more recently in Edward Leamer's often-cited article, "Let's Take the Con out of Econometrics" (1978).

The source Friedman chose to cite to indicate the nature of the problem and the way around it was his teacher and supervisor at the National Bureau, Wesley Mitchell. Mitchell discussed the pitfalls of correlating raw and transformed time series in his 1927 volume, *Business Cycles: The Problem and Its Setting*. Friedman's remedy for Tinbergen's problem was the remedy Mitchell suggested, testing the predictive value of the equations with data other than those used in their derivation.

He carried out such a test using a small set of annual data on corporate net income for 1932 through 1937. From this test Friedman concluded that the predictive power of Tinbergen's equation for net income was unimpressive, as the correlation between the actual and predicted levels of net income (0.66) would be exceeded by chance in more than ten percent of random samples. This was by Friedman's admission a modest test, primarily because of the very small set of data. Another data problem that Friedman pointed out for Tinbergen's study was that it was based on annual rather than quarterly data. A concern with the quality of data was one of the hallmarks of National Bureau work during Mitchell's era and continued to be for Friedman and Schwartz's monetary factors project.

Friedman indicated in concluding the review that although he did not think Tinbergen's methods were adequate for testing business-cycle theories, he thought they were useful "for deriving tentative hypotheses about the nature of cyclical behavior" (1940a, p. 660). This distinction between developing and testing theories of business cycles, and differences over where the marginal product of research effort was higher, would remain important at the National Bureau into the early 1950s. It is especially evident in exchanges between representatives of the National Bureau approach (Vining, 1949, and Burns, 1951b) and the Cowles Commission approach (Koopmans, 1947, and Marschak, 1951). Friedman used it in portraying the different status of static relative price theory and static monetary theory and business-cycle theory in his 1953 methodology essay and in early drafts of his interpretation of Mitchell's business-cycle theory (1950).

The distinction is also prominent in Friedman's 1951 comment on Carl Christ's tests of Klein's simultaneous equations macroeconomic model. Klein's model was a direct descendent of Tinbergen's. Friedman applauded Christ and the Cowles Commission for putting simultaneous equations models to empirical tests with data other than those used to derive the models. Christ had followed Friedman's suggestion and included among his tests a comparison of the model's predictive power against a naive model which predicts no change in the values of the endogenous variables. The simultaneous equations model failed this test.

Friedman noted that other simultaneous equations models had failed empirical tests, and asked the question, how do we proceed from this point? One path was to proceed with building and testing simultaneous equations models. Another was to do research on the individual sectors of the economy. Friedman argued that so little was known about dynamic processes that the potential payoff from building large-scale models was not great. What was required was knowledge of the dynamics within individual sectors of the economy – knowledge of leads and lags, intertemporal relations among phenomena, and the mechanisms that transmit impulses. This was knowledge that neither static relative price theory nor static monetary theory could provide. And from Friedman's National Bureau perspective, it was a task that placed a premium on observation and measurement. This is indicated by Friedman's remark that the important work is "analysis of parts of the economy in the hope that we can find bits of order here and there and gradually combine these bits into a systematic picture of the whole" (1951b, p. 114). One does not examine mathematical equations to find "bits of order"; one examines data.

### Conclusion

The hallmark of Friedman's methodology is Marshallianism. With this label he set his views apart from the Walrasians'. In the 1940s the differences in the two methodologies were recognized, and as we have seen, they were not Friedman's creation. As time passed, the Walrasian approach ascended to a position of dominance in both micro and macroeconomics, with the virtues of the general equilibrium approach and mathematical qualities of elegance and generality taken for granted by most economists. All the time, Friedman remained committed to the Marshallian approach. He also continued to use the Marshallian–Walrasian categories for methodological comparisons, while others ceased to think of methodological issues in those terms. Whereas the precepts of the Walrasian approach to economic analysis were taken for granted by most economists, the emerging specialized field of economic methodology was dominated by philosophy of science categories. Commentators identified Friedman's methodology in terms taken from that literature – terms such as Popperian, positivist, or instrumentalist.

Friedman's work in monetary economics and his commentary on contemporary macroeconomics throughout his career bear the distinctive marks of his National Bureau associations. These marks were first in evidence in his review of Tinbergen's business-cycles study. Unlike many of his colleagues at the National Bureau in the 1940s, including his mentors Arthur Burns and Wesley Mitchell, Friedman had the requisite knowledge and experience in theoretical and applied statistics to be on the forefront of the econometric revolution in business-cycle analysis. But he was critical of the direction the Cowles Commission research took the revolution, judging that the National Bureau approach had greater potential for producing and testing hypotheses about the dynamics of business cycles.

The primary precept Friedman insisted on for business-cycle analysis was empirical testing of hypotheses with data other than those from which the hypotheses are derived. This is a point on which there was no difference in principle between Friedman and the Cowles Commission researchers. But the failure of the simultaneous equations models to pass the empirical tests brought into prominence an important methodological difference. Friedman thought the surest route to knowledge of dynamic business-cycle phenomena was through empirical analysis of individual sectors of the economy. The Cowles Commission view was that mathematical completeness was required as an indispensable first step toward knowledge. In this respect the Cowles Commission approach was Walrasian.

Friedman's National Bureau approach to business-cycle research and his Marshallian methodology are not inconsistent with each other. Regardless of whether the problem at hand was macroeconomic or microeconomic, Friedman believed that economists should break problems into their constituent parts, that they should give primary attention to concrete problems, and that observation and measurement were more important than mathematical elegance and completeness. He believed the ultimate test of theories was their capacity for predicting data other than those from which they were derived.

Friedman was critical of both microeconomic and macroeconomic work being done from the general equilibrium approach. His methodological critiques of monopolistic competition and econometric model building in the 1940s and early 1950s were closely connected to his perception of the state of economic knowledge. He thought that Marshall's value theory and the Cambridge version of the quantity theory of money provided confirmed knowledge of relative price, quantity, and price level statics. But he thought there was little confirmed knowledge of the dynamics of prices and quantities in business cycles. This perception was a premise of all that Friedman wrote on methodology in the 1940s and 1950s. It placed him in a conservative position with regard to contemporary developments in microeconomics, and in what was coming to be viewed as a scientifically unsophisticated position in regard to developments in macroeconomics. In a culture that equated mathematical elegance and completeness with scientific precision, Friedman never fully escaped the perception by fellow economists that his business-cycle work was scientifically unsophisticated.

# CHAPTER 3

# Origins of the monetary project

## Introduction

This chapter is a history of the beginnings of Friedman and Schwartz's monetary project. Our purpose in considering this history is to provide another important piece of the background for Friedman's debates with his critics. It gives a picture of the presumptions and expectations Friedman brought to the project. The chapter that follows extends the history through the 1950s into the 1960s to examine issues of causality in Friedman's analysis that arose within the National Bureau.[1]

What began in 1948 as a three-year project eventually stretched over a third of a century and was brought to a close with the long-delayed publication of *Monetary Trends* in 1982.[2] When he and Schwartz embarked on their investigation of money in business cycles, Friedman was less than two years into his tenure as Professor of Economics at the University of Chicago. By the time *Monetary Trends* was published, he had retired from the University and moved west to California five years before. The first joint publication by Friedman and Schwartz did not come out until 1963; they worked together intensively for fifteen years before publishing a major product from their efforts.

There were three publications from the project before Friedman and Schwartz's "Money and Business Cycles" in 1963. Two of these were articles written by Friedman, "The Demand for Money: Some Theoretical and Empirical Results" (1959b) and "The Interpolation of Time Series by Related Series" (1962b). The third was Phillip Cagan's "The Demand for Currency Relative to Total Money Supply" (1958).

---

[1] The history of Friedman and Schwartz's project is not intended to be complete, inasmuch as the coverage is determined by the theme of this book.

[2] Friedman and Schwartz have each continued their research on monetary economics to the present, and have jointly answered critics as late as 1991, but the active part of their joint NBER project was concluded with *Monetary Trends*.

The Friedman–Schwartz National Bureau project cannot be separated entirely from Friedman's Workshop in Money and Banking at the University of Chicago. These were the twin parts of Friedman's personal research project. From the beginning of his endeavor in monetary economics, he identified his research program as a *cooperative* endeavor between the National Bureau and the university. Part of his original concern was to preserve for himself an escape from the National Bureau's restrictions on public policy debate, restrictions that were intended to ensure "scientific" neutrality.[3] Friedman did not intend to remain neutral on policy questions. But the Chicago side of the project was much more than a means for escaping the National Bureau restraints. For one thing, Friedman spent very little time at the National Bureau. During terms when he was teaching, he was in Chicago. When he was not teaching, he worked at the family cottage in New Hampshire. With Anna Schwartz in residence at the National Bureau offices in New York, they worked separately, connected by telephone and the U.S. Post Office.

Friedman began the Workshop in Money and Banking in the 1951–52 academic year, and thereafter a coterie of Chicago graduate students wrote dissertations on topics generated by Friedman and Schwartz's work. The first product of the workshop was the collection of essays by Friedman and four graduate students published as *Studies in the Quantity Theory of Money* (1956a). So although the focus in this chapter is on the joint work of Friedman and Schwartz, the complementary relationship between their research and Chicago Ph.D. dissertations should be kept in mind.

The teamwork approach to research at the National Bureau was carried over to Friedman's workshop at Chicago.[4] Within the National Bureau, teamwork came naturally as a virtual necessity borne of the kind of labor-intensive empirical work that was the Bureau's distinc-

---

[3] In a resolution adopted in 1926 and revised in 1933 and 1941, the board of directors were charged with responsibility for ensuring that the work of the National Bureau was carried out in a "scientific and impartial manner." The board screened proposals for research projects and completed manuscripts. Completed work would not be published unless it was approved by each member of a special manuscript committee drawn from the board of directors or by over half the full board membership and two-thirds of those who cast votes.

[4] Friedman remained inclined toward collaborative work throughout his career. One thinks as well of Friedman's writing with Rose Friedman on political economy, with Simon Kuznets in the National Bureau project on professional incomes that became Friedman's Ph.D. dissertation, and with Allen Wallis and L. J. Savage on choice theory.

tion from its very beginning. The research workshop concept that spread first throughout the Economics Department and Graduate School of Business at Chicago and then through economics departments at other universities far and wide is directly due to Friedman's influence and at one remove to the National Bureau.

## Background for the project

When Friedman was invited by Arthur Burns in 1948 to become director of a National Bureau study of monetary factors in business cycles, he knew very little about the history of banking and financial institutions prior to the Federal Reserve's creation in 1913, a bit more about monetary institutions under the Federal Reserve system, but he had extensive knowledge and experience with National Bureau techniques of business-cycle analysis. He acquired this knowledge initially in Wesley Mitchell's course on business cycles at Columbia University as a graduate student in 1933–34. He also worked as a staff member at the National Bureau from 1937 until 1939, though not specifically on business cycles.[5] In the 1940–41 academic year, Friedman taught his own course in business cycles at the University of Wisconsin (Economics 176). Lecture notes and tests from Friedman's course provide an indication of a portion of the background knowledge Friedman brought to the National Bureau's Monetary Factors in Business Cycles project seven years later. The primary texts for the course were two volumes by Mitchell – Business Cycles (1913) and Business Cycles: the Problem and Its Setting (1927) – and an unpublished manuscript of the Burns and Mitchell volume, Measuring Business Cycles (1946). Friedman's lecture notes and tests for the course make no mention of Keynes's General Theory, but it is clear that Friedman devoted considerable attention to underconsumption theories of the cycle.[6]

Friedman introduced the subject of business cycles to his University of Wisconsin students with a "state of our knowledge" judgment. He said that after fifty to sixty years of intensive study of cycles economists "know something about [their] nature and characteristics but little or nothing about causation or control" (1940b). Much of the analysis of business cycles that had gone before was not statistical in its approach, Mitchell's work was one of the exceptions to this generalization. Friedman judged that the lack of knowledge of causes and cures

---

[5] Friedman served as secretary of the Conference on Research in Income and Wealth.

[6] The set of materials from the course that are in the Friedman Papers is not complete, so we do not know for sure that he did not discuss The General Theory.

of business cycles was primarily because the intellectual problem was severe; developing an understanding of business cycles was exceedingly difficult. Ignorance was not due to lack of attention to the phenomenon. He stated his goals for students in the course as learning what business cycles are; considering some explanations for them, though "not with [a] view to getting real dope – but to get [a] better idea of causal relations"; and obtaining a historical view of the problem of control of cycles (1940b).

Friedman raised the issue of whether the Great Depression signaled a structural shift in business cycles, a shift toward secular stagnation. His hunch was that the 1929–36 experience was not unique. It compared with the depression of the 1890s and earlier depressions of the 1870s and 1840s. However, Friedman cautioned the students that this question could not be answered with confidence just yet because if there had been a structural shift in 1929, there was only one cycle's worth of postshift data; that was not sufficient for the statistical analysis necessary to support the assertion.

Friedman's course was a "hands on" experience for students. He gave them time series for commodities and other economic indicators and asked them to date the cycles. He discussed such practical measurement issues as how to distinguish true from false turning points, allowing for seasonal adjustments, and how either to choose a specific cycle (the best candidate being employment) or to aggregate specific cycles, to produce a measure of the "business cycle." Friedman expressed a preference for bypassing what he thought was the hopeless task of defining the "normal" course of economic activity and thereby identifying the business cycle as a departure from normalcy. He favored confining the definition of the business cycle to strictly observable characteristics of data series.

Despite his expressed preference for bypassing the issue of normalcy, Friedman's discussion of the nature of the business cycle, together with his remarks about "causes and cures," was suggestive of the power of the metaphor of the business cycle as a malady in the body economic, and in this sense as "abnormal." Yet, though human illness is considered abnormal, it is also recognized as a universal element of the human condition. Likewise Friedman stressed that for a significant stretch of history, business cycles had been a fact of life in Western economies. He explained to his students Mitchell's hypothesis that business cycles are endemic to economies in which the use of money has reached an advanced state.[7]

[7] Though he came to believe that adherence to a monetary growth rule would

The final examination that Friedman gave on January 30, 1941, is built around issues that he would take up again in the late 1940s and that would continue as points of dispute with his critics over the span of his career. This exam also brings to mind a distinguishing feature of Mitchell's approach to business-cycle analysis, in that it is centered on the business cycle itself rather than on any particular "named" theories of the cycle. Though particular theories and theorists are in the background, not a single reference is made in Friedman's exam to Fisher, Wicksell, Keynes, or for that matter Mitchell. The four essay questions from the exam are given below:

1. One device proposed for mitigating the severity of cyclical fluctuations is the concentration of governmental expenditures on public works in depressions, the extra expenditures at such times to be financed from surpluses accumulated during prior periods of prosperity, from borrowing, from the creation of new money, or from current taxes. Under what conditions, if any, would you recommend the adoption of this proposal? If adopted, what method of financing would you endorse? Justify your answers in detail. Discuss both the merits and demerits of the proposal and of the various methods of financing. Discuss also the observed features of cyclical fluctuations that make the proposal appear strategically desirable or undesirable.

2. "The business cycle in the general sense may be defined as the alternation of periods of prosperity and depression, of good and bad trade." Discuss.

3. Distinguish between "a theory of business cycles" and a "description of the cyclical process." What characteristics would an adequate cycle theory possess?

4. Does the fact that there has not yet been developed an adequate cycle theory known to be consistent with the observed course of cyclical fluctuations mean that there is no basis for judging the desirability of governmental measures designed to mitigate cyclical fluctuations? Does it mean that society is condemned either to inaction or to irrational intervention? Give the reasons for your answers (1940b).

Two and one-half years after the monetary project began, Friedman published a review of Mitchell's business-cycle analysis (1950). No doubt having the Cowles Commission depiction of Mitchell's work as "measurement without theory" in mind, Friedman reviewed Mitchell's early work on monetary economics (for example, 1904) and the several *Business Cycles* volumes to identify his contributions to economic theory. Given Mitchell's distinctive and unorthodox style, separating his theory from his description was not easy.

---

mitigate business cycles, Friedman never had confidence that the business cycle could be eliminated altogether. In 1992 Friedman stated that he thought the business cycle would always be with us. See W. F. Buckley (1992).

Careful study of Part III of Mitchell's 1913 *Business Cycles* induces in me both exasperation and admiration. It induces exasperation, because numerous significant theoretical insights are so carefully hidden under the smooth, casual-sounding exposition of descriptive material. . . . It induces admiration, because the theoretical insights are there after one pierces their protective coloring and are significant and profound and because the summary of empirical evidence on business cycles is so thorough, so thoughtful, and so well organized (1950, p. 478).

Friedman identified an emphasis on dynamics as a critical theme running through all of Mitchell's work. The phenomenon of business cycles was inextricably bound up with adjustments through time. So "The Real Issue in the Quantity Theory Controversy" (1904) in Mitchell's mind was how changes in money bring about changes in prices. Friedman saw Mitchell thinking in terms of a paradox, one that has the distinctive flavor of Friedman's own Marshallian paradoxes.[8] Mitchell asked how it could be that what appeared to be the most important factor for long-run movements in prices, money, seemed to play such a small part in some of the shorter-run movements that together comprise the long run? Friedman found his answer in the 1927 *Business Cycles* volume:

Time . . . is of the utmost consequence in considering the relations between prices and "the quantity of money." Relations which hold in long periods do not hold in short ones. Nor are all short periods alike; what is true in certain phases of business cycles is not true in all phases. Yet most of the seemingly contradictory statements which fill the long controversy over this problem can be reconciled when put in their proper relation to time (Mitchell, 1927, p. 138; Friedman, 1950, p. 474).

The implication for analysis within the quantity-theory framework was that for the short run the elements of the equation – money, velocity, prices, and quantities – should be dated. Payments in one period are typically for goods delivered in another period. For the longer run, dating is not important.

From Mitchell's emphasis on the dynamics of adjustment, Friedman drew the conclusion that the key ingredient of Mitchell's theory of business cycles was lags in adjustment. For the most part but not completely, Mitchell rejected the option of building his theory around the idea of "disturbing causes" intervening on an equilibrium. Likewise he mostly set aside ideas of fundamental instability to develop a

---

[8] See for example Friedman's discussion (1953a, pp. 36–7) of whether the cigarette industry should be treated as if it were competitive or monopolistic.

theory of self-generating business cycles characterized by the presence of lags.

In an appendix to his article on Mitchell, Friedman presented what he termed a "free rendering" of Mitchell's theory of business cycles in mathematical equations. He claimed that apart from differences in language and other facets of presentation, Mitchell's theory contained all the key components of the various important modern theories. The other theories were simpler than Mitchell's, but not for a good reason, for their simplicity was not the outgrowth of empirical testing. "The only criteria to which they appear to have been subjected are, first, whether they are logically complete and attractive and, second, whether they are capable of producing cyclical movements whose broadest and most general features are like those observed" (1950, p. 488). In this judgment we can see clearly the distinctive emphasis on substantial and systematic empirical analysis that Friedman shared with Mitchell.

## Anna J. Schwartz: The beginning of a collaboration

Friedman's initial contact with Anna Schwartz with regard to the monetary project was in a March 3, 1948 letter. This letter was the beginning of an extensive correspondence between the two economists. Friedman and Schwartz were almost always separated by considerable distance: he in Chicago or New Hampshire (and later Vermont) when he was not traveling and she in New York at the National Bureau offices. Occasionally they got together when Friedman traveled to New York for National Bureau or other business; they also talked by phone. But by far the bulk of their communication was by letter. Friedman recently reflected that this was a particularly productive way of collaborating, for writing to one another forced them to think carefully about whatever problem they happened to be working on and to use the time devoted to their collaboration efficiently.

Schwartz joined the National Bureau research staff in 1941. She worked on series of monthly estimates of demand and time deposits and currency since World War I for several years before Friedman became involved. With the aid of a research assistant, Elma Oliver, she completed a series for currency covering 1917 through 1944 and published it as National Bureau Technical Paper 4 (1947). In 1948 she was involved in work on the companion deposit series. Friedman's close friend since graduate school at Columbia and National Bureau staff member, Moses Abromovitz, sent him a copy of a memo Schwartz prepared on problems encountered in estimating deposits.

The first step Friedman took in embarking on the project was to become sufficiently acquainted with the data sources and materials to make an assessment of the relative importance of the problems Schwartz identified in the memo. He spent several days in New York in April 1948, as they began making plans for their work together. After he returned to Chicago, Schwartz sent him her 1942 evaluation of a National Bureau collection of national bank data, suggestions of possible additions to the data series, a memorandum by Arthur Burns on how to deal with bank call-date data, and a set of abstracts of annual reports of the Comptroller of the Currency annotated by Professor James Angell of Columbia University. Aside from a few other data series in Schwartz's files at the National Bureau, this was the raw material with which Friedman and Schwartz began their project.

Schwartz brought to the project not only firsthand acquaintance with the available data but also a considerable knowledge of the history of American banking institutions. She sent Friedman a reading list covering the banking system before and after the Federal Reserve, remarking that the literature on American banking was generally pretty deadly, but he would acquire less misinformation from the readings on her list than from others.

Friedman's comparative advantage was in theoretical analysis, hers in historical, so his initial contribution was to make assessments of the theoretical appropriateness of the data on hand and to suggest new series that they might develop. One of his first suggestions was that they put together a data series on government obligations held by individuals, businesses, and private banks. In proposing this series he explained the theoretical rationale for it. His idea was to shift the theoretical focus from the standard emphasis on the effects of monetary and credit conditions on businesses' production and investment decisions to their effects on households' consumption decisions. Schwartz responded with a request that he clarify for her his thinking on theoretical matters such as the role of banks in the transmission process of monetary effects, the role of government obligations as net wealth, and whether private obligations such as the surrender value of life insurance policies should be treated analogously with government obligations. Friedman said she could get an idea of his thinking from his 1948 article, "A Monetary and Fiscal Framework for Economic Stability," and then he took her questions one by one and answered them. Thus began the protracted ongoing discussion between Friedman and Schwartz, and later including others, most notably Phillip Cagan, about the theoretically appropriate measures of money and monetary phenomena.

The published version of "A Monetary and Fiscal Framework for Economic Stability" to which Friedman referred was based on a paper he presented at the September 1947 meeting of the Econometric Society. As he told Schwartz, the article provides a good indication of his perception of the nature of business cycles, prospects for their mitigation, and theoretical underpinnings of business-cycle analysis at the time they embarked on the monetary project. Friedman's proposal was designed to eliminate private creation and destruction of money in the banking system and discretionary control by the Federal Reserve. This was to be accomplished by requiring 100 percent reserves behind bank deposits and total monetization of Federal budget deficits and surpluses. The Federal budget would in turn be balanced at full employment (or an "attainable" level of income). Thus monetary policy would be folded into fiscal policy for which there would be a "rule" rather than "discretion." Budgetary balances would change automatically in a countercyclical direction over the business cycle.

Friedman identified price rigidities and lags in response as the two fundamental problems involved in business cycles and as the key determinants of the success of his or any other policy proposal designed to mitigate the cycle. He evaluated his proposal's likely performance in comparison with status quo discretionary policy under both actual conditions (rigidities and, he surmised, considerable lags) and ideal conditions (flexible prices and minor lags). Throughout, he stressed that his evaluation was based only on conjectural evidence about the lags. He believed that it was crucial for understanding the business cycle and designing countercyclical policies that systematic empirical evidence on lags be produced.

One could reasonably expect smaller fluctuations than currently exist [under his proposal]; though our ignorance about lags and about the fundamental causes of business fluctuations prevents complete confidence even in this outcome. The lag between the creation of a government deficit and its effects on the behavior of consumers and producers could conceivably be so long and variable that the stimulating effects of the deficit were often operative only after other factors had already brought about a recovery rather than when the initial decline was in progress. Despite intuitive feelings to the contrary, I do not believe we know enough to rule out completely this possibility (1948b, p. 254).

Friedman divided the total policy lag into three parts: the recognition lag, the action lag, and the effect lag, foreshadowing John Culbertson's (1960, 1961) argument about how work on lags should be approached. (See Chapter 5.) He argued that under his proposal the recognition lag would be virtually nonexistent, whereas with discretionary policy, inadequate forecasting capability made the lag considerable. He conjectured that the action lag was a problem under both policies, and for discretionary policy its length depended on the type of action taken. It was most likely shortest for monetary policy, longer for changes in taxes, and longest for changes in government expenditures on goods and services.

He also judged that the effect lag was significant for either monetary or fiscal policy, and its length varied by type of action taken. Friedman's expectation was that the order of length of the effect lag was the reverse of the order for the action lag; shortest for changes in government expenditures, and longer for changes in taxes and monetary policy instruments. However, he recognized that his conjectures were just that. "We have no trustworthy empirical evidence on the length of this lag for various kinds of action, and much further study of this problem is clearly called for" (1948b, p. 256).

On the whole, considering all three parts of the lag, Friedman ventured the estimation that his proposal would reduce the effective size of the lag.

This analysis, much of which is admittedly highly conjectural, suggests that the total lag is definitely longer for discretionary monetary or tax changes than for automatic reactions, since each of the three parts into which the total lag has been subdivided is longer. There is doubt about the relative length of the total lag only for discretionary expenditure changes. Even for these, however, it seems doubtful that the shorter lag between action and its effects can more than offset the longer lag between the need for action and the taking of action (1948b, p. 257).

The theoretical discussion to which Friedman referred Schwartz is found in the section of his article that explores the operation of his policy proposal under ideal conditions of price flexibility and inconsequent lags. The key idea was the wealth effect of a change in the net stock of the community's assets. Citing Pigou (1943, 1947) and Patinkin (1948), Friedman explained how a decline in the price level with an unchanged nominal stock of money increases net wealth held as money and other government debt. This reduces the propensity to save and increases the propensity to consume. The expansionary effect is reinforced by automatic reductions in tax revenues, increases in transfer payments, and under his proposal, increases in the nominal money stock, providing what Friedman called "defense in depth" against changes in aggregate demand.

Friedman applied through the University of Chicago to the Rockefeller Foundation for funds to provide research assistance and supplies for the Chicago end of the project. The National Bureau was to cover the great bulk of the cost, for transportation and computation, most of which would be handled there. He encountered problems from the start, for the foundation turned down his request on the grounds that this was a National Bureau project; funding could rightfully be expected from the NBER. For Friedman this was distressing news quite apart from not getting the funds, for he felt strongly that the project should be identified as a *cooperative* endeavor between the University of Chicago and the National Bureau. As noted earlier, he wanted to preserve freedom from National Bureau restrictions on engaging in controversial policy issues. Friedman saw essays such as "A Monetary and Fiscal Framework for Economic Stability" as part of his personal research program, and it was unlikely this sort of material could be published under the auspices of the National Bureau. He had already experienced the frustrations that could arise from the bureau's publication vetting process with his Ph.D. dissertation. Publication of *Income From Independent Professional Practice*, coauthored with Simon Kuznets, was held up for four years because of objections from the National Bureau board of directors to certain conclusions in the study.[9] Friedman was aware at the outset of the monetary project that an important part of what he wanted to do with regard to money would not pass through the National Bureau's filter, so it was important to have an independent component of the project.

Meanwhile Friedman spent the summer of 1948 reading through the list Schwartz had provided on the history of American banking and monetary institutions, working on the organization of the study, and making plans for construction of additional data series. Later in the year he began doing preliminary analysis of the data on hand. From his reading Friedman drew two important conclusions that they would later develop over the course of the project: (1) the Federal Reserve had on balance been a destabilizing force over the period of its existence and the United States might well have been better off had the Fed not been created and (2) there was a great deal to be learned from the pre-1913 era both about money in business cycles and about the effect of Treasury operations on economic activity.

In several documents that Friedman prepared for the university, the National Bureau, and the Rockefeller Foundation in 1948 and through the summer of 1949, he indicated detailed plans for the study. It would cover the United States since the Civil War primarily, though from the very beginning he contemplated using foreign data

[9] See "Director's Comment" by C. Reinold Noyes, pp. 405–10, in Friedman and Kuznets (1945).

to test conclusions drawn from the U.S. data. It was to have three main components:

(1) the behavior of monetary and banking phenomena during cycles in general business – the establishment of empirical regularities in amplitude, timing, and the like; (2) the relation between the cyclical behavior of monetary and banking phenomena and the cyclical behavior of other strategic economic activities – for example, the relationship between the timing of monetary changes and changes in prices, production, etc., the cyclical role of the banking system in capital formation; (3) the causal role of monetary and banking phenomena in producing cyclical fluctuations, intensifying or mitigating their severity, or determining their character ("Brief Statement of Plan . . . ," undated, p. 1).

Friedman thought that if the effort was successful, this analysis would produce conclusions that would

contribute to . . . a comprehensive theory of the generation of cyclical fluctuations. Such conclusions would also bear directly on the question whether control of the quantity of money or of its distribution can contribute to mitigating the severity of cyclical fluctuations, and if so, what the relative possibilities, advantages, and disadvantages of different kinds of monetary policy are ("Organization, Scope, Present Status . . . ," undated, pp. 3–4).

As the third component of the study reveals, Friedman did not embark on the project with an idea that the framework for analysis would be noncausal. For several reasons he might have. In the first place, he was a close student of Mitchell's work and, as we have seen in Chapter 1, Mitchell toyed with the notion that the type of analysis he was developing was noncausal. Second, though there is no reason to believe that Friedman was sympathetic to Koopmans's "measurement without theory" charge against Burns and Mitchell, and every reason to believe that he was very much on the side of Burns and Mitchell, he might have at least taken away from the debate an idea that National Bureau analysis was "measurement without causality." Third, from their origins in biometrics there was a general sense that the statistical techniques of correlation and regression were means of estimating statistical relations without causal presumptions.

However, the documents that Friedman prepared to explain his intent as he set out on the project show clearly that his understanding of what he and Schwartz would be doing was using data and other evidence to sort out cause–effect relations in the business cycle. There is only one hint of any sensitivity to the idea that this might be an inappropriate way to conceive of the task, and this hint is a pretty thin thread. In a revision of the prospectus Friedman changed the third component from "the causal role of monetary and banking phenomena in *producing* cyclical fluctuations . . . " to "the causal role of monetary and banking phenomena in *stimulating* cyclical fluctuations" [emphasis added]. Though we cannot know what was behind this change, and there may have been very little, it is consistent with an attempt to avoid giving the impression that the monetary and banking phenomena are the *sole cause* of business cycles. This would be accordant with Friedman's insistence more than a decade later in responses to Culbertson and to Tobin that he did not think money was the sole cause of income changes, and also with Mitchell's explicitly multicausal view of self-generating business cycles.

There is comfort in Friedman's memoranda for researchers who find their projects becoming more involved and taking longer than initially projected. Friedman expected that the product of the monetary project would be "a monograph, perhaps preceded by a number of briefer reports presenting some of the initial results. In addition, a number of supplementary reports may be issued presenting in full detail some of the new or improved statistical series developed for the study" ("Organization, Scope, and Present Status . . . ," undated, p. 3). He expected the monograph to be virtually complete within three years, by the end of 1951!

### Initiation of the project: building the data set

The first order of business in getting the project started was to expand and add to the data series in the National Bureau files. Data were selected on the basis of three theoretical perspectives on money's role in business cycles, perspectives that overlapped with the distinction noted earlier between the production and investment and the consumption transmission channels but that were cut along a different plane. The first perspective was money's role as the medium of exchange, "the supply and rate of use of generally acceptable means of payment." The second was money's role as an asset, "the supply of assets easily marketable at virtually fixed nominal prices." The third was the role of banks as lenders and investors.

In a September 10, 1948 document, "Preliminary Plan for Compilation of Data for Study of Monetary Factors in Business Cycles," Friedman expanded the rationale for organizing the data and analysis in terms of these three categories. He suggested that money's role as the means of payment was the obvious point of departure. A means of payment is inevitable in a highly developed economy to settle debts created in the normal course of exchange, though the particular form of the means of payment varies over time and place. Friedman remarked that the boundary an economist draws around the set of assets considered to be "generally acceptable" as a means of payment is to an extent unavoidably arbitrary. For example, he said, on the New York Stock Exchange, credit balances from daily clearings rather than demand deposits or currency are used to settle debts. He pointed out that significance attaches to both the total quantity of the means of payment and to the interchangeability of its various forms. That the latter may be more important for understanding cycles was suggested by the apparent role of attempts by the public to change the form in which they held means of payment during the panic of 1933 and other "currency panics." Fractional reserve banking with different reserve requirements for different types of money means that an attempt on the part of the public to shift their assets from one form of money to another has implications not just for the composition but also for the total quantity of money.

On the other side of the equation is the rate of use of the means of payment, money's velocity of circulation. Historically, technical factors such as payroll schedules and the degree of business integration were accorded an important role in explaining velocity, but Friedman suggested that these are surface reflections of a more fundamental consideration, which is money's role as an asset. The limited role of technical factors in business cycles was evinced by the fact that in periods of serious monetary disorder, there is practically no limit to the velocity of circulation. The effects of technical factors are swamped by effects emanating from money's asset nature. Friedman thought that money's role as an asset was fundamental to episodes when the public tried to change the form in which they held means of payment.

Friedman's conclusion to his discussion of money's role as a means of payment foreshadowed the large effort he and Schwartz would make analyzing velocity empirically and developing the theoretical principles to undergird the analysis. As we will see in Chapter 5, John Culbertson criticized Friedman for not adhering to the classical theoretical principles of the quantity theory of money. To the extent that the classical quantity theory relied on technical factors to explain velocity, Friedman made plans early in the project to move away from that theory. "It is clearly of the first order of importance to measure as accurately as we can cyclical variations in the rate of use of the circulating medium. For an understanding of these variations, however, my conjecture is that we shall have to go beyond technical considerations to an investigation of 'money' as an asset" (1948a, p. 3). Friedman also thought money's role as an asset was more important than its medium of payment function as a guide for setting up the empirical analysis. This was because any object used as a medium of exchange must necessarily be held as an asset, because the essence of a monetary economy is the temporal separation of receipt and payment. "The use of the circulating medium as an asset imposed by this 'transactions demand' shades imperceptibly into its use, deliberately and with forethought, as a form in which to keep some part of the community's assets. Any satisfactory medium of payments inevitably has characteristics that make it an ideal reserve for unexpected emergencies or opportunities; its nominal capital value is fixed, so that nominal capital gains or losses are impossible" (1948a, p. 4). Continuing this discussion, Friedman explained the consequences of price level changes for the real value of a fixed nominal quantity of the means of payment.

Just as money's medium of exchange function is inextricably tied to its asset function, the asset function of the medium of exchange shades imperceptibly into the asset function of items that are not media of exchange. When Friedman was writing, bank time deposits and postal savings deposits were almost as readily available for settling debts and, along with the medium of exchange, had fixed nominal value. Friedman's other examples of assets that could be expected to substitute closely for media of exchange were Series E and F government bonds, the cash value of life insurance policies, and, a small step further removed, short-term government securities that are fixed in value.

No clear ordering of these or of the numerous other claims or evidences of debt can be made, since they differ from one another in many dimensions. An ordering by certainty of nominal value would differ from an ordering by rapidity of possible conversion into circulating medium proper. But it is clear that there is no sharp dividing line between "money" and "near-moneys" or between "near-moneys" and "securities proper." It is also clear that cyclical movements in economic activity will alter the relative desirability of the circulating medium as an asset, and that this will in turn react upon and affect the character of the cyclical movement. Any study which is to take account of the role played by "money" as an asset must clearly consider other assets as well; indeed from this point of view the arbitrary line between "money" and other assets might well be drawn at a different point than it is when the emphasis is on the function of money as a circulating medium (1948a, p. 5).

This passage makes clear that Friedman thought from the beginning of the project that the definition of money should be left fuzzy, more so than was traditional for economists who identified the medium of exchange function as the essential property of money. He also began the project with the notion of a two-way causal relationship between money and business cycles. The concluding part of the section of

Friedman's memorandum concerning money as an asset explains the theoretical significance of the total volume of net obligations of the government, considered by the public as part of their wealth. Friedman projected that data for the project would include both the composition and total volume of government liabilities.

With regard to the third component of the study, the lending and investing activity of banks, Friedman was willing to make the sort of a priori distinction that he argued was inappropriate in considering money's roles as medium of exchange and as asset. Although institutional arrangements tied the supply of media of exchange to the banking system's lending and investing activity and although this tie followed naturally from banks' role as borrowers on demand and lenders on time, Friedman argued that the connection was not necessary. He asserted that there could be and at times actually had been monetary systems in which lending and borrowing produced no effect on the quantity of the means of payment. Friedman's proposal (1948b) and an earlier one by Henry Simons and other Chicago economists (1933) for 100 percent reserve banking were intended to sever this tie.

Lending and investing activity have significance of their own for the business cycle apart from the direct tie with the quantity of money, for financial institutions that do not issue circulating liabilities compete with those that do. Friedman suggested that the question of how far to extend the study out into the web of financial institutions would have to be left unanswered until after the study was under way. At one extreme, including all lending and investing activity would be impossible and would not be justified if it was possible. At the other extreme, taking some account of lending and investing by banks was obviously necessary.

With the three overlapping theoretical categories as a framework, Friedman outlined the data that he expected the study to require. He preferred coverage back to 1860 if possible in order to include the Civil War; this would give three major wartime and postwar periods. In this preference Friedman's approach was unorthodox. Usually economists would omit wartime data on the grounds that wartime experiences are abnormal. Friedman's idea was that these data are similar to information from "crucial experiments" and not only should not be wasted but should be especially valued.[10] He envisioned the need for a special study of the 1914–18 era to check for a valid statistical link between the

[10] He made use of the wartime data, omitting the data from "normal" times, early in the project in writing "Price, Income, and Monetary Changes in Three Wartime Periods" (1952a).

pre– and post–Federal Reserve data. Other potential discontinuities were at 1879, when specie payments were resumed, and 1934, when the Federal Deposit Insurance Corporation was established. Friedman's preferred time unit was a month. Mitchell had only annual data for his 1913 volume, *Business Cycles*. Much of the banking data available to Friedman and Schwartz was only on a call date basis, for irregular points through the year when the Comptroller of the Currency or other supervisory agencies requested statements of condition from banks. Previous studies indicated the need for separate data for some of the series related to the means of payment and all series related to banks' lending and investing behavior for New York, owing to the extraordinary volume and character of financial transactions in that market. Likewise separation of data for central reserve cities, reserve cities, and country banks was thought useful. Ideally Friedman thought the data should cover all banks, but this was not feasible because of the difficulty of obtaining data for banks that were neither national banks nor members of the Federal Reserve. He anticipated special efforts to extend the coverage of the quantity and rate of use of the means of payment to nonmember state chartered banks.

Friedman gave a detailed list of the data series he expected to make use of under the three headings. The list is reproduced in the appendix. It is notable that he mentioned that although it was preferable to have separate series for assets that are generally acceptable means of payment and those that are not, this might not be possible for the full period they planned to cover, because prior to 1914, separate data were not collected. He did not discuss plans for interest rate series though he acknowledged their relevance to the study, explaining that all the series that might be relevant were being developed separately in another of the National Bureau Studies in Cyclical Behavior.

In another memorandum, "Outline of Work in First Phase of Banking Study: Cyclical Behavior of the Quantity and Rate of Use of Circulating Medium" (1949a), Friedman provided a statement of the status of the project in terms of what they knew three-quarters of a year after beginning. Preliminary investigation of the data on hand and other studies suggested the following empirical regularities:

(1) the quantity of circulating medium responds sluggishly to cyclical movements, skipping many minor movements and reacting to major movements only after a considerable lag; (2) this is true of both non deposit and deposit currency, though somewhat less so of deposit currency; (3) both seem to react sharply if late, in major movements; (4) the rate of use (velocity of circulation) of the circulating medium conforms positively, velocity increasing during expansion phases and declining during contraction. Such studies as have

claimed a more sensitive relation to cyclical fluctuations (e.g., those by Warburton) find it in deviations from trends and in particularly sensitive components of the money supply (1949a, p. 1).[11]

He noted the disparity between their empirical evidence and what was often presumed about behavior of money and velocity:

These general conclusions differ widely from the assumptions about the behavior of the circulating medium implicit in most qualitative discussions of the role of money in cyclical fluctuations. If valid they have important implications for the possible role of monetary factors in generating cyclical fluctuations and for the possible effectiveness of policies directed at promoting stability by controlling the volume of circulating medium (1949a, p. 1).

Friedman stressed that their results were tentative and that their primary objective for the immediate future was to test and give greater substance and precision to them. They would do so by testing for biases in the data, measuring cyclical patterns and leads and lags; testing for differences in response to major and minor movements; checking the regularity of response over longer periods; and studying cyclical movements if there were such movements in the composition of the total stock of means of payment.

He stated that he and Schwartz were picking up where Mitchell left off in Chapter VI of his 1913 *Business Cycles*. Their goals were the same as Mitchell's. The main difference in what they hoped to accomplish was that they would have data not available to Mitchell. It is noteworthy that Friedman and Schwartz chose to begin their study with the first of the three categories outlined in Friedman's memorandum on data requirements, money's role as the means of payment. Walter Stewart, chairman of the Rockefeller Foundation Board of Trustees, tried to persuade Friedman in the spring of 1949 to begin with the lending and investing activity of banks. Friedman was not swayed by the suggestion because, he told Stewart, many theories of the business cycle (especially theories that focus on fractional reserve banking) imply that the quantity of money reacts sensitively and conforms positively to the business cycle. Friedman himself was among those, including Henry Simons and the Chicago economists who prepared the 1933 memorandum on "Banking and Currency Reform," who believed that the fractional reserve banking system played an important role in business cycles. However, as indicated in his memorandum, the preliminary evidence that he and Schwartz put togeth-

---

[11] In early National Bureau documents, Friedman and Schwartz used the terms "deposit currency" and "non deposit currency" instead of "deposits" and "currency." The studies by Clark Warburton include (1945, 1946, 1948).

er did not confirm this hypothesis. Thus Friedman thought it was important to clear the issue up before proceeding to the other two components of the study. Furthermore, Friedman expected the analysis would not take long. He projected finishing work on the behavior of the quantity of money within eight months, by the end of 1949. As for the order in which they would take up the other two parts of the project, Friedman expressed no strong feelings in his discussion with Stewart. He indicated that he thought they might take up the lending and investing behavior of banks second and leave the role of money as an asset to the final stage.

At the end of 1948, the work Friedman and Schwartz had completed was confined mostly to assembling data for currency, checking deposits, what they referred to as minor forms of currency, and close substitutes for currency. They broke the analysis of the series into three periods: (1) December 1917 to the present, (2) 1914 to 1917, and (3) 1860 to 1914. Currency and deposit data were almost complete for period (1). The primary problems expected in building data for the earlier periods were obtaining currency holdings and interbank deposits for nonnational banks and separating demand and time deposits. There were no data available for the minor forms of currency and close currency substitutes. These included postal deposits, railway express deposits, traveller's checks, private money orders, and cashier's checks. Although Friedman expected their quantities to be negligible, in keeping with his empirical bent he judged that this fact should be established rather than merely assumed.

Nothing had been done for data on the brief period after the Federal Reserve's beginning, 1914 to 1917. For period (3), prior to the Federal Reserve, they had annual data on currency held by the Treasury and total currency held by banks and the nonbank public back to 1860 and monthly data back to 1880, but these needed to be carefully reworked to check and correct errors. Separation of currency into the portion in banks and the portion held by the public was an important and difficult task that remained to be done. The available evidence in Mitchell's 1913 volume and the Comptroller of the Currency Annual Reports suggested that up to forty percent of currency was held as vault cash and almost half of this in nonnational banks. Many of these banks were small and relatively weak, and Friedman expected that their behavior over business cycles might be markedly different from that of national banks. Friedman planned to make a study of the relative cash holdings of national and nonnational banks for selected states in order to gauge the possible bias in their data.

For bank deposits in the early period (1860–1914), there was the same problem as for currency; observations were irregular and for nonnational banks, no more frequent than annual. The problem was compounded by the fact that the series that was available, for "individual deposits," included both demand and time deposits. The most serious potential for error was again in the possibility that national and nonnational bank deposits behaved differently over the cycle. During a panic, depositors might switch from nonnational to national banks and between demand and time deposits. So the limitations of the data could conceal crucial changes in monetary holdings during recessions. As he did for currency, Friedman proposed testing for bias in the data with studies from selected states for which good reports were available.

## Conclusion

In June 1949 Friedman reported to T. W. Schultz, chair of the University of Chicago Economics Department, that the Rockefeller Foundation proposal was still pending. This meant that though the scope and definition of the project were taking shape conceptually, the project remained in a financially tenuous state.[12]

Through the first five years of the 1950s, efforts in New York and Chicago were largely devoted to the same task that dominated work in 1948 to 1949: building the set of data. In 1955 Friedman reported that Schwartz had completed series on vault cash in banks, currency held by the public, adjusted demand deposits, time deposits in commercial banks, time deposits in mutual savings banks, and U.S. Government deposits for 1907 to 1953. David Fand, working in the University of Chicago Workshop in Money and Banking, had finished estimates of components of the money stock outside national banks for 1876 to 1896. Phillip Cagan, also working in the workshop and at the National Bureau, was developing estimates of the supply-side sources of the money stock and preparing the series on hand for cyclical analysis. This involved separating privately and publicly created money and building a deflator for the money series.[13]

[12] Friedman and Schwartz did not receive Rockefeller Foundation funds for their project. However, Friedman's Workshop in Money and Banking at the University of Chicago received a three-year grant of $50,500 beginning July 1, 1954. This was extended through June 30, 1958, and again through September 30, 1959.

[13] Cagan's work culminated in his National Bureau monograph, *Determinants and Effects of Changes in the Stock of Money: 1875–1960* (1965).

These data-building efforts were laborious, but Friedman and Schwartz considered them a crucial component of their project. Their plans were for a monograph similar in type and purpose to Burns and Mitchell's *Measuring Business Cycles,* with a heavy emphasis on problems and techniques for measuring the phenomena of interest. The heavy investment in production of data was not merely a means to their analytical product, which was to be a cyclical and secular analysis of money, but also a final research product that would be of value to other economists. So by the mid-1950s, with most of their work since the project's inception devoted to building their data set, they were finally ready to shift attention to analysis.

Meanwhile, through the first half of the 1950s, the work of Friedman and his graduate students in the Workshop in Money and Banking was more analytical. Several products of this enterprise were published in 1956 as *Studies in the Quantity Theory of Money.* In addition to Friedman's "The Quantity Theory of Money: A Restatement," which developed a key portion of the theoretical framework for analysis of the monetary data with Schwartz, these included Cagan's classic study of hyperinflation, John Klein's exploration of the relationship between money and prices in Germany from 1932 to 1944, Eugene Lerner's study of inflation in the American Confederacy, and Richard Selden's analysis of income velocity in the United States.

Friedman's teaching apart from directing dissertations written in the Workshop in Money and Banking included courses in Business Cycles, Banking Theory and Monetary Policy, and Monetary Dynamics. In the spring quarter of 1952, monetary inflation was the central theme of Economics 432, Monetary Dynamics. Readings and lectures covered the theory and empirical evidence relating to

the process whereby changes in the stock of money produce their effect on prices and output or conversely, whereby changes in prices and output affect the stock of money; the role of the interest rate in inflation or, conversely, the effect of monetary changes on the interest rate; the role of exchange rates in monetary inflation as both cause and effect; the relative value of alternative simplified theories for predicting the course of an inflationary movement; the role and problems of governmental monetary policy in inflationary periods; empirical regularities in monetary inflations and hyperinflations (1952b).

As he did in the prospectus at the beginning of the monetary project, so also in course lectures Friedman presented monetary analysis of business cycles as an endeavor to sort out cause–effect relationships. This passage also makes clear that he was thinking in terms of two-way causal relationships.

Though completion of their National Bureau monograph was pushed back farther and farther, Friedman regularly published articles on monetary economics and stabilization policy in the early 1950s. There were several articles in addition to those we have referred to. Friedman along with other members of the AEA Subcommittee on Economic Stability published a report on "The Problem of Economic Stability" in the *American Economic Review* in 1950. He also published articles in 1951 on "Commodity–Reserve Currency" and "Comments on Monetary Policy."

The 1951 volume of the National Bureau's *Conference on Business Cycles* included Friedman's comment on Carl Christ's "Test of an Econometric Model for the United States," in which he compared the performance of that large-scale econometric model against a naive model that predicts no change in the values of the dependent variables from one period to the next. That article continued a line of criticism of large-scale macroeconometric models that Friedman began with his 1940 review of Jan Tinbergen's model for the United States. Both of the reviews give clear pictures of Friedman's Marshallian–National Bureau methodology and of his assessment of the state of economic knowledge at the time. He was critical of the macroeconomic model builders for presuming more knowledge than they in fact had about the dynamic process of economic change.

We do have a very well developed and, in my view, successful and useful theory of relative prices which tells us a great deal about relationships among different parts of our economic system, about the effects of changes in one part on its position relative to others, about the long-run effects of changes in technology, the resources at our disposal, and the wants of consumers. A theory of short-run changes in the economy as a whole must deal with many of the phenomena that are dealt with in price theory, and thus it is tempting to suppose that price theory substantially reduces the arbitrariness of a system of equations – enables us to narrow substantially the class of admissible hypotheses.

I believe that this is a serious mistake. Our theory of relative prices is almost entirely a static theory – a theory of position, not of movement. It abstracts very largely from just those dynamic phenomena that are our main concern in constructing a theory of economic change. . . .

The important point is that the existing theory of relative prices does not really help to narrow appreciably the range of admissible hypotheses about the *dynamic* forces at work.

Monetary theory, interpreted broadly, has somewhat more to offer. It is at least concerned with absolute prices. But even monetary theory, in its present state, is less useful than might at first appear. It too has typically been concerned with positions of equilibrium, with comparative statics rather than with dynamics – and this, I may add somewhat dogmatically, applies equally to Keynesian and pre-Keynesian monetary theories.

One cannot, of course, specify in advance what a workable theory of change will look like when it is developed. But I think it is clear that it will have to be concerned very largely with leads and lags, with intertemporal relations among phenomena, with the mechanism of transmission of impulses – precisely the kind of thing about which neither contemporary price theory nor contemporary monetary theory has much to say (1951b, pp. 113–14).

# CHAPTER 4

# Critiques from within
# the National Bureau

### From data to analysis

By the mid-1950s Friedman and Schwartz had assembled most of the basic U.S. data for their study. The core set of data they began with were monthly data on currency in the hands of the public from 1917 through 1944 (Schwartz and Oliver, 1947). In May 1954 Friedman reported in the National Bureau's annual report that they had extended this series back to 1907, the year of a severe banking panic that led directly to the Aldrich–Vreeland Act and appointment of the National Monetary Commission and ultimately to the Federal Reserve Act. They had also revised the series to account more accurately for the allocation of currency between public circulation and vault cash. They had produced a monthly series on commercial bank deposits from 1919 forward and were in the process of extending the series back to 1907. Comparable data for mutual savings bank and Postal Savings deposits were in the works.

A significant portion of their data compilation effort went toward the problem of estimating vault cash and deposits in banks that were not national banks (for the pre–Federal Reserve period before 1914) or members of the Federal Reserve system (from 1914 on), and converting irregular call-date data into monthly estimates. This involved interpolating to produce the "missing" monthly observations. One byproduct of this effort was that Friedman discovered a flaw in what were at the time standard procedures for using one series to interpolate between observations in another. Standard interpolation techniques involved choosing a related variable on the basis of a presumed relationship between it and the variable to be interpolated but not actually using information on correlation between the two. Friedman showed that in some cases straight-line interpolation produced smaller errors, and demonstrated how to combine straight-line, or mathematical, interpolation with interpolation by related series. Ten years later Friedman published a statistical piece that was the outgrowth of this work on the monetary series, "The Interpolation of Time Series by Related Series" (1962b).

69

In 1955 Friedman and Schwartz negotiated with Geoffrey H. Moore, associate director of research at the National Bureau, over plans for their published product. Friedman related his preferences to Schwartz in a letter he wrote in March of that year. He envisioned two volumes, one to present the data and the other for analysis. He envisioned the first volume in two parts,

In which Part I would be relatively brief, perhaps fifty or sixty printed pages and would present the estimates and analyze them to a rather limited extent. . . . Part II, which would be the body and the heart of the book, would be very much longer, and would contain the description of the preparation of the estimates. As I see it, this part is important for two reasons, first to provide the user of the figures with a description of how they were prepared, and second because many of the breakdowns obtained in the process of preparing the estimates are of value in themselves. . . . I certainly feel that it would be most unfortunate and most improper to have a volume which presented the figures but did not explain in fairly considerable detail how they were arrived at (MF to AJS, March 1, 1955).

Moore preferred an abbreviated discussion of the steps involved in building the data series.

Friedman and Schwartz continued to make and adjust their publication plans for years afterwards, with many changes and delays along the way. The twin volumes that they thought were near at hand in the mid-1950s, and which they thought would bring the project to completion, were not published as planned. The first volume, which was to present the basic data and their derivations, was delayed until 1970, when they published *Monetary Statistics of the United States: Estimates, Sources, and Methods.* A portion of what was to be the second volume, on cyclical analysis, was published in 1963 as a lengthy journal article, "Money and Business Cycles," and another portion, which began as an "analytical narrative" that was to serve as background for the more formal cyclical analysis, grew into their *Monetary History of the United States, 1867–1960,* also published in 1963.[1] At that time the planned analytical volume was still unfinished but had a title, *Trends and Cycles in the Stock of Money in the United States, 1867–1960.* Later on, in 1967, they split the volume into two: *Monetary Trends* and *Monetary Cycles.* As we know now, *Monetary Trends* was delayed much longer than they ever expected. Though a first draft that included analysis of trends along with cycles ("The Stock of Money in the United States, 1875–1955") was completed in 1957, and a second draft including trends and what came to be *Monetary Statistics* in 1966, the book was

[1] Friedman made several published reports of their results prior to 1963. See (1958, 1959b).

not finished and published until 1982. The principal holdup was from their 1967 decision to incorporate data from the United Kingdom along with the U.S. data. The other half of the original analytical volume, *Monetary Cycles,* was never finished. One of the ironic quirks of the history of the Friedman and Schwartz collaboration is that the volume they never completed was the one closest to the original title of their project, "Monetary Factors in Business Cycles."

### Two National Bureau critics

Most of the published criticism of Friedman and Schwartz's project did not appear until after their first major publications in 1963. However, in the course of their work through the 1950s and early 1960s, they received criticism from members of the National Bureau staff on some of the same issues that would later draw the attention of economists outside the National Bureau. In this chapter we examine criticisms from two National Bureau staff members who were involved in the project but, by virtue of their different positions on the National Bureau staff, in quite different ways.

Mark Wehle was an economics graduate student at Columbia who worked in the National Bureau's New York office as research assistant for Schwartz in the 1950s and 1960s. He completed his Ph.D. in 1964. The division of labor between Friedman in Chicago and Schwartz in New York was such that virtually all the statistical computation was done in the National Bureau's New York office under Schwartz's supervision. Wehle was responsible for doing much of this work.

Geoffrey Moore was the other critic. Moore graduated from Rutgers in 1933, a year after Friedman left for the University of Chicago. He took an M.A. from Rutgers in 1937 and a Ph.D. from Harvard in 1947. Moore joined the National Bureau research staff in 1939. In 1948, the year Friedman and Schwartz began their collaboration, Moore was promoted to associate director of research.

### Mark Wehle and choice of money measure

Wehle was a capable economist and something of a perfectionist. His interest in the theoretical foundations of Friedman and Schwartz's project went beyond what might have been expected of a graduate student hired to do computations, and the points he made to Schwartz in person and to Friedman by letter concerned key components of their approach. Most significantly, Wehle challenged the theoretical justification for their using the rate of change of the money stock, rather than its level, as the basic measure of money. This challenge was a preview of the published critiques made later by John Culbertson, J. M. Clark, Tobin, and Kareken and Solow. (See Chapters 5 and 7.)[2]

In 1957 Friedman and Schwartz were assembling a draft of the trends and cycles volume, "The Stock of Money in the United States, 1875–1955." Schwartz suggested to Wehle that he read it to look for internal inconsistencies and problems of exposition. After reading Chapter IV, on "Cyclical Behavior," in April 1957 Wehle wrote to Friedman and brought up two substantive points involving the choice between the level and rate of change of the money stock.[3] One con-

[2] Later, when their work was published, another issue would arise regarding the measure of money – which assets belong in the aggregate identified as money? Friedman and Schwartz chose M2, which included currency in the hands of the nonbank public and all deposits in commercial banks, including deposits that did not circulate as means of payment. Their choice of this broad aggregate drew criticism that they conflated the definition and identification of money. According to the various a priori approaches, the appropriate procedure would be to first determine what are essential characteristics of money (the definition) and then to identify the assets that have these characteristics (the identification).

[3] In writing the draft of Chapter IV Friedman presented time series for both the level and rate of change of the money stock. When Schwartz read his draft in March 1957, she noted some ambiguity about which of the series Friedman was referring to at several points in his discussion. One example was the following passage:

If permanent real income and permanent prices both conformed positively and synchronously to the cycle – and there is as yet no reason to suppose otherwise – and if the desired real stock of money were determined entirely by permanent real income and if the desired stock were equal to the actual stock, then the nominal stock would conform positively and synchronously as well. Yet one of our major findings is that it does not – it tends to lead at both peaks and troughs. Our analysis to date will somehow have to be altered and perhaps complicated if this result is to be incorporated in it (AJS to MF, March 27, 1957).

Friedman responded with what is likely his first written explanation of why he considered the rate of change the more appropriate measure:

It seems to me that the relevant timing is not of the stock, but of either deviations from a trend or rates of change. The reason is that all our measures of size of the cyclical movement take out intra-cycle trend, so all the preceding analysis is implicitly on trend adjusted data. For real income, I am under the impression that timing would be the same on trend adjusted or original basis. But as I write this I realize they may not be the same for permanent real income.

In any event, I do not really want to defend this paragraph. As I read over before sending you the material, I was rather unhappy, since it seemed to me I was explaining too much, that there was no room in this model for the leads and lags that play so

cerned Friedman's use of the rate of change as a means of detrending the levels series. Separating trends and cycles was standard procedure for National Bureau analysis of time series. Wehle argued that detrending by first differencing was an excessively violent technique, for ideally the trend adjustment should not affect the dating of cycles. Friedman and Schwartz had computed first differences of logarithms of the money stock. They fit a step function to this series and dated peaks and troughs of cycles in the step function.[4] The resulting dates did not coincide with dates for the unadjusted level series.

Wehle's second point was implicit in this argument about detrending, for it presumed that the series on the money stock level contained the primary data. Otherwise cycle dating for this series would not be given priority. Wehle thought the money stock level was the variable for which the quantity theory suggested a fundamental association with business cycles. He argued that the rate of change measure did not match the theoretical concept of money in the quantity theory. Wehle explained why he thought taking first differences of logarithms of money, to convert the series into rates of change, was a theoretically inappropriate way of measuring money.

Should not the stock of money, rather than its rate of change, be matched with physical output? It is true, as you say, that the flow of money per unit time is the thing to look at. But if we stand at a particular point in the economy and watch the flow of money against goods, will not the flow of money be proportional to the stock, rather than to the rate of change in the stock? (MW to MF, April 13, 1957)

Wehle asked Friedman if, with constant velocity, that is, with changes in the level of business activity being caused solely by changes in the money stock, a lower level of business would not involve a proportionately lower level of the money stock.

Wehle included in his letter the "circular flow" type diagram shown in Figure 1. The area inside the ring represents the stock of money, and with constant velocity the flow past point P would be proportional to this stock. The stock of money in the ring may grow because of additions through the small pipe that comes into the ring from the right and above. Wehle asked rhetorically, "Is there any reason to suppose that the rate of flow past P will be proportionate to this tiny

---

striking a role earlier, and so I inserted this paragraph, partly as a qualification to the reader, partly as a reminder to myself when I went over this again that the analysis was not satisfactory and needed some more thinking through (MF to AJS, April 5, 1957).

[4] The step function was used because of the high degree of variability characteristic of time series of first differences.

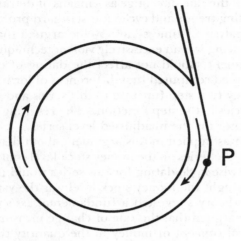

Figure 1

accretion?" He concluded that for evaluation of money flows, and for use of money flows to explain flows of expenditures, the appropriate measure was the money stock, that is, the stock of money inside the ring.

Wehle also indicated that although the rate of change measure was theoretically inappropriate for evaluating money's role in business cycles in the context of the quantity theory, if Friedman wanted to treat it simply as a leading indicator, this would be another matter. In this case he could see no objection to exploring the cyclical behavior of the rate of change in relation to reference cycles, for there would be no presumption of a cause–effect relationship between the measure of money and general business conditions.

Friedman did not respond to Wehle's letter until July. In the meantime Wehle pressed his objections with Schwartz. She told Friedman in May:

I have had some discussion with Mark on two points on which he challenges you, and you will be hearing from him on them as well as on some others that don't disturb me. He claims that we will not get by the reading committee with a first derivative series used as a way of eliminating trend. He has no objection to the use of a first derivative series as such, but the justification of its use on the ground that we thereby abstract from trend is not admissible. The reason is that a correction for trend ought not to affect the dating of cyclical turns; a first derivative series does affect dating. His other point is that it is false to draw an analogy between the first derivative of the stock of money and the current output of goods as a first derivative: what circulates against current output is the stock of money, not the change in the stock; what we discuss is the stock of money per unit of output, not the rate of change per unit of output. I have made a few starts at answering these objections, but don't seem to be able to follow through (AJS to MF, May 7, 1957).

In response Friedman told Wehle that he had been persuaded that his exposition in Chapter IV could be improved, but he did not think the substance was wrong. He drew an analogy between money and housing to illustrate why he considered the rate of change a theoretically appropriate measure. Conceptually there are two flows and one stock measure for both money and housing. For housing the stock is the stock of existing housing. This stock yields a flow of current services to people using the housing. Then there is also the flow of investment in new housing. Likewise, Friedman argued, at any point in time there is a stock of existing money. This stock yields a flow of services to people who hold the money. Additions to the stock of money that occur through the banking system are a flow of new money into the stock analogous to the flow of investment in new housing.

Friedman drew Wehle's attention to the stock measure and the second of the flow concepts. He argued that for secular analysis of either housing or money, the stock was appropriate but for cyclical analysis, the flow of new money or new housing was.

The main point, it seems to me, is that there are two kinds of components of national income. One is net investment, the other current services rendered by existing capital, human and nonhuman. As an example of the first, consider net new construction of houses. Now there is no reason why this should be proportional to the existing stock of houses. Further, what is important for cyclical purposes is not whether this is above or below zero, which is what tells whether the stock of houses is rising or falling, but whether it is changing, which is to say whether the stock of houses is rising or falling at a changing rate. Whether net new construction tends to be above or below zero is important for secular purposes; if it is at a constant value above zero, the stock of houses is rising secularly at a constant absolute or relative rate depending on how net new investment has been measured. This case carries over precisely to money. The stock of money is comparable to the stock of houses; the rate of change in the stock of money to net new construction; whether this rate of change is positive or negative is important for secular but not cyclical purposes; if it is positive, say, and a constant percentage, this would imply that money income is changing at a constant rate and would, so far as I can see, give no occasion for cyclical movements (MF to MW, July 6, 1957).

Friedman admitted that he had not made sufficiently clear in his chapter draft the distinction between the flow of monetary services from a given stock, which would be proportional to the stock, and the flow of new money into the stock, which would not. His approach to analysis of money and business cycles was based on the theoretical presumption that the latter flow was the more important measure.

Three years later Wehle raised questions about the role Friedman and Schwartz were assigning to interest rates in explaining the behavior of velocity in Chapter 12 of the *Monetary History*. This was just after Friedman published "The Demand for Money: Some Theoretical and Empirical Results" (1959b), in which he presented an empirical demand function that did not include interest rates.[5] In the article, Friedman explained the long-term secular decline in income velocity since the 1880s as the result of rising real income and the services of money being a luxury good. Income grew after World War II, but the trend in velocity turned up. Wehle sent Friedman a graph of commercial paper rates and income velocity that he thought lent support to the hypothesis that interest rates were responsible for the puzzling post–World War II rise in velocity.

Friedman's response to Wehle on the interest rate hypothesis provides a good view of his standard for judging empirically the adequacy of hypotheses; a relatively simple hypothesis should account for a broad range of experience. He noted that other people, such as Henry Latané (1954, 1960), John Gurley (1960), and James Tobin (1956), had discovered the same apparent relationship between interest rates and velocity. He explained that although in a *full* theoretical explanation of velocity, interest rates should undoubtedly be given a place, the key issue for him was the degree of their empirical relevance. The reason he was inclined to believe their role was relatively unimportant was that he had been unable to identify one quantitative relationship between velocity and interest rates that would explain both the postwar rise in velocity and the drop in velocity that occurred in the 1880s and early 1900s. The residuals from a regression of income velocity on real income for the earlier period were not highly correlated with interest rates, and the magnitude of the effect was too small to account for the rise in velocity after World War II.

Friedman also pointed out that theoretically one would expect the measured effect of interest rates to be greater over long periods than over short periods, for the same reason that one generally expects long-run elasticities to be greater than short-run elasticities. In the correlations of cycle bases he and Schwartz used to get long-run estimates, they were not able to obtain interest rate effects strong enough to account for the short-run cyclical behavior of velocity. Thus he

[5] He did however use interest rates to analyze residuals from the equation with permanent real income as the explanatory variable.

preferred to explain the cyclical behavior of velocity in terms of differences in measured and permanent income rather than interest rates. The permanent income hypothesis allowed greater conciliation between long-term and short-term behavior.

The principle revealed in Friedman's explanation, of requiring a preferably simple hypothesis to account for a large range of experience, is evident in other important ways in Friedman's work. As we have seen, the major reason for the long delay in the publication of *Monetary Trends* was that Friedman and Schwartz decided to include data from the United Kingdom in the study. They sought to expand their base of evidence for refining and testing their hypotheses. Another example is that in the 1950s one of the major initiatives by Friedman and his students in the Workshop in Money and Banking was to test the explanatory power of the quantity theory and the income–expenditure theory with data from a wide array of countries. In 1955 studies were under way for Canada, Great Britain, India, and Egypt, as well as for the United States.

This issue of the role of interest rates in money demand or velocity equations that Wehle was among the first to raise was to be one of the points of controversy between Friedman and his Keynesian and non-Keynesian critics. The published criticism on this issue originated in reaction to Friedman's "The Demand for Money: Some Theoretical and Empirical Results" (1959b). That article was a progress report on his project with Schwartz. Friedman did not include interest rates in the estimated money demand equation, from which critics inferred that he denied any effect of interest rates on desired money balances. The criticism carried over in reactions to the *Monetary History* and prompted Friedman's response in "Interest Rates and the Demand for Money" (1966).

Friedman disclaimed denying interest rates a role in money demand, despite their absence from his estimated equation. The confusion about whether he was or was not denying their role was sustained by his and Schwartz's methods. They did not work from an explicit Walrasian general equilibrium framework. The confusion this created among his critics is illustrated by two reviews of the *Monetary History* that Friedman quoted in his 1966 article responding to the critics. Harry Johnson wrote: "Moreover, this need for a general equilibrium model comprising the real and monetary sectors is what the Keynesian Revolution was about; hence to admit interest rates into the demand function for money is to accept the Keynesian Revolution and Keynes' attack on the quantity theory" (1965, p. 396). Allan Meltzer wrote in his review: "Had the authors systematically incorporated interest rates or asset yields as a determinant of velocity or of the money supply, they would have been forced to do what they had otherwise avoided doing, develop a more extensive analysis of the real system to supplement their treatment of the monetary sector" (1965, p. 420).

### Geoffrey H. Moore and credit quality

While Wehle, the research assistant, was challenging Friedman and Schwartz on these two points that later became important issues in the public controversy over their work, Moore, the associate director of research, was finding fault on other grounds. At the National Bureau there was a formal vetting procedure for publications, one that involved both staff's and directors' reading committees. The committees approved manuscripts before they were published under the National Bureau's imprimatur. From his position as associate director of research, Moore possessed more leverage to influence the structure and content of Friedman and Schwartz's manuscripts than either Wehle or outside critics. As they put finishing touches on a draft of the *Monetary History* in late 1961, Moore became concerned that Friedman and Schwartz were overstating the role of Federal Reserve miscues in causing the Great Depression and overlooking the effects of a decline in the quality of credit in the second half of the 1920s. Moore thought that a collapse of credit quality in the mid-1920s and a "long-wave" decline in construction activity were causes of the Depression and that there was little the Federal Reserve could have done to prevent it. Negotiations between Moore and Friedman and Schwartz over how they would treat the issues of credit quality and the Fed's culpability continued from late 1961 into 1963.

Moore's concern with credit quality did not originate with his reading of the *Monetary History* manuscript. From the start of their project in the late 1940s, Moore expressed interest in Friedman and Schwartz exploring the role of credit quality in business cycles.[6] In December

---

[6] Walter Stewart, who was chairman of the board of the Rockefeller Foundation when Friedman made his initial request for funds, also urged Friedman to give high priority to investigating the role of bank lending and investing in business cycles. Friedman related his negotiations with Stewart to Arthur Burns in a May 3, 1949, letter:

Stewart wanted to know why I had decided to start with the quantity of circulating media, and what general hypothesis underlay my interest in it. I noted that many theories about the role of monetary factors in business cycles implied that the quantity

1948, having read Friedman's memorandum, "Preliminary Plan for Compilation of Data for Study of Monetary Factors in Business Cycles," Moore suggested that they add a series on bank solvency. He wrote to Friedman that, "I feel confident that these figures reflect an important feature of business cycles" (GHM to MF, December 9, 1948). Friedman responded at the time that he thought this was a good idea, and they would add the series to the data they were going to collect.

There were several reasons that they might have followed Moore's suggestion and given serious attention to credit conditions. For one, Friedman's initial outline of the parameters of the project identified three areas for investigation: money's role as means of payment, money's role as an asset, and the provision of the means of payment by lending and investing institutions. Though their primary focus was on money, not lending and investing, it was natural to go some way toward consideration of credit markets as such because of the intimate connection between the money supply process and borrowing and lending. Banks and other financial institutions created money and money substitutes in the process of making loans. Another circumstantial reason to extend the scope of the monetary study to financial markets was that the National Bureau began two research projects on financial markets shortly before the monetary project got off the ground.[7] It would have been natural for Friedman and Schwartz to dovetail their study with these other studies, drawing on the data and analysis from them for use in the monetary study.

---

of money reacted sensitively and conformed positively to business cycles. In particular, this is true of theories which consider the fractional reserve system as a disturbing influence, in particular because of the effect under such a system of a change in the desires of the public as to the proportion in which it desires to divide its total cash between currency and deposits. I have myself felt this to be a significant factor and have been impressed by the fact that the data do not offhand conform to my own expectations. Further, I noted that this seemed a fairly straightforward job that would provide a highly important background for study of more complex relationships. We talked this over at some length, together with the problems arising in interpreting the data because of the absence of data for the non-national banks.

Stewart expressed the view that on the whole he would have preferred to have me start on the third item, namely, lending and investing activities of the banking system. It was his feeling that the banking system exercises its most significant cyclical influence through its lending and investing activities. I agreed that this might well be the case, and that the analysis of the lending and investing activities of the banking system should be an important part of the total study. I argued, however, that there was much to be said for cleaning up the quantity of circulating media first (MF to AFB, May 3, 1949).

[7] The Urban Real Estate Finance Project was initiated in 1945, and the Corporate Bond Project, a year later in 1946.

But these reasons could also be turned on their head. Monetary phenomena may overlap with lending and borrowing, but the two sets of activities are not identical. In terms of institutions and assets, the latter set is much larger. Friedman noted in his 1948 sketch of the monetary project that the choice of where to stop expanding the scope of a monetary factors study into financial activity was arbitrary, but as one moved away from institutions whose liabilities serve as means of payment or close substitutes, the connection between financial activity and monetary phenomena became increasingly tenuous. Moreover, the gains from division of labor would suggest that the analysts working in various National Bureau projects not allow the projects to fade into each other. If they did, the result would be unproductive repetition of effort and loss of focus.

In the end, Friedman and Schwartz opted for a narrower delineation of their project. They considered credit market activity primarily as it impinged on the creation and use of money. Friedman came to the project in 1948 with a belief that the money supply process ought to be divorced from the credit creation process. Though historically it turns out that most often the two were linked, this need not be the case. Friedman's view was that in the best of worlds there would be no link. This was the purpose of his 100 percent reserve requirement proposal that Friedman made at the Econometric Society meeting six months before taking on the National Bureau project.[8]

Friedman and Schwartz attached overriding importance in their explanation of the Great Depression to mistakes in monetary policy. Right or wrong, it was destined that many readers would recoil at such a simple and personal explanation of the momentous and devastating event that occurred from 1929 to 1933.[9] Moore used both his powers of persuasion and the power of his position to try to get them to consider the role a decline in credit quality in the late 1920s may have had in precipitating the Depression and tying the Federal Reserve's hands. He urged them to soften their harsh criticism of the Federal Reserve. Friedman and Schwartz yielded to Moore in considering the role of credit quality in their book, but they did not accept

[8] See Friedman (1948b).

[9] See Chapter 9. Friedman and Schwartz's explanation was personal in the sense that they assigned blame to the Federal Reserve Board for policy mistakes, and they argued that if Benjamin Strong, president of the Federal Reserve Bank of New York, had not died in October 1928, the likelihood of these mistakes would have been less.

his hypothesis. Nor did they make a substantial concession in their criticism of the Fed.

Years before, in the 1940s, Friedman's dissertation work with Simon Kuznets created a storm of controversy at the National Bureau. Publication of *Income from Independent Professional Practice* was held up for five years in part because of objections from the directors' reading committee to their conclusions about the role of the American Medical Association in restricting entry into the medical profession. In 1962 there were again rumblings of a delay and pressure to soften criticism of an important and powerful institution. Moore held up distribution of the manuscript to the directors because of what he thought was unnecessary and unjustifiable criticism of the Federal Reserve. He explained in a January 5, 1962 letter why he felt his delay of distribution of the manuscript to the directors was warranted.

I believe many other readers will believe that you have overstated the case for the potency of the Federal Reserve's action or inaction with respect to the monetary and financial difficulties during the Great Depression. I believe it would be wise to indicate – it is largely a matter of the tone of your writing rather than any particular statement – that the Fed may have been up against extraordinary factors emanating from speculation in all kinds of credit instruments during the latter 1920's and from the "long downswing" developing in construction and other investment processes. To say that they did not adopt the appropriate policies in the face of these developments (had they been aware of them) is one thing. To suggest as I think you do, that they were responsible for the entire "monetary debacle" and could have "readily stemmed and reversed" it at any time is another. The first kind of statement is likely to command respect and support, and be considered helpful with respect to the future problems that monetary policy may face. The second is likely simply to provoke debate (GHM to MF, January 5, 1962).

Friedman responded in much the same way he responded to Mark Wehle about the choice of a money measure. He conceded a deficiency in exposition but not in substance. He said that he believed that he and Schwartz had substantial evidence to support their conclusions about Federal Reserve mistakes and their effects and that it served no useful purpose to trim their argument to avoid embarrassment or loss of face for the Fed. He was not aware of convincing countervailing evidence to support Moore's alternative hypothesis about the quality of bonds. But Friedman promised that he and Schwartz would consider Moore's hypothesis in the manuscript and renew their effort to state their case in a way that would persuade Moore and other readers who might bring the same presuppositions to a reading of their book.

The argument that Friedman made in correspondence (January 9, 1962; February 13, 1962; and February 11, 1963) and later in Chapter 6 of the *Monetary History* to counter Moore's hypothesis was built from two distinctions – *ex post* versus *ex ante* events and will versus power to take actions to bring about or forestall events. He argued that an increase in the currency to deposit ratio and additional bank runs that took place after the initial wave of runs in 1930 made bad credit out of what otherwise would have been good credit, that is, turned *ex ante* sound credit instruments into *ex post* unsound instruments. Therefore the decline in credit quality was an *effect* of the monetary crisis rather than a *cause*. He also argued that the Federal Reserve had adequate power to shut off the downward spiral of bank runs, bank failures, and contractions of the money supply – power they lacked the will to use. The Fed had been created for the express purpose of preventing financial crises from evolving into liquidity crises, and, Friedman argued, they could have done so in 1930 and 1931 by providing cash to banks. But they simply lacked the will. Furthermore, not even their lack of will could be blamed on an *ex ante* decline in credit quality or on real forces such as a long downswing in investment. Friedman granted that speculation in credit instruments and real forces during the 1920s may have contributed to a severe contraction, but he argued that in no way did this make inevitable the "monetary debacle" that occurred. The Federal Reserve bore responsibility for this.

The argument between Friedman and Moore carried over to an exchange of letters concerning the press release the National Bureau was to issue to publicize the book. Moore wrote that he felt a statement in a draft of the release prepared by Friedman indicating that the Federal Reserve had power it did not use was too strong. Perhaps weary of the argument, he suggested that there was no point in continuing to debate the issue, for the charge Friedman and Schwartz brought against the Fed was "one of those unprovable propositions, likely to be inflammatory rather than enlightening" (GHM to MF, January 25, 1962). Friedman was not about to accept this point. He fired back a response (February 13, 1962) saying that theirs was not at all an unprovable proposition, and although they may be wrong, he thought that he and Schwartz had demonstrated that the Fed did have the power. He saw no reason to change his mind in the absence of evidence and arguments to the contrary.

Friedman and Schwartz made minor adjustments to the *Monetary History* text to respond to Moore's thesis about the decline in credit quality.[10] They included a discussion of credit quality and, mostly in long footnotes, considered four National Bureau publications that gave measurements of credit quality through the 1920s.[11] All four of the National Bureau studies found that there was a decline in credit quality in the late 1920s. This was indicated by the fact that bonds issued in the late 1920s had higher rates of default and foreclosure than those issued in the first half of the decade. For example, Hickman (1958) found that domestic bonds issued from 1920 to 1924 had default rates in the range of 2 percent to 30.3 percent (with an unweighted average from the yearly figures of 13.9 percent), whereas those issued from 1925 to 1929 defaulted at rates from 18 percent to 43 percent (with an average rate for the five years of 29.8 percent).

Friedman and Schwartz argued that Hickman's study and two of the others were marred by a failure to adequately separate changes in *ex ante* credit quality from changes in *ex post* quality caused by the contraction. They asserted that it could not be ruled out that the observed increase in default rates was due to the lower age of bonds issued closer to the Depression. Borrowers who issued bonds in the early 1920s had a longer period of economic growth and stability to build capital for servicing their debt than borrowers in the late 1920s. Thus apart from any difference in *ex ante* quality, debt from the latter period would be expected to experience higher default rates. Friedman and Schwartz argued that by not adequately ruling out this hypothesis with evidence from properly adjusted data, Moore and the other National Bureau analysts failed to provide grounds for believing that credit quality was a causal factor in bringing on bank failures and the Great Depression. The only concession they made to Moore's credit quality hypothesis was to allow that *if* there was a deterioration in the *ex ante* quality of credit in the latter part of the decade, this "may have contributed a mite to the banking collapse of the early thirties" but "not by making such a collapse inevitable or even likely, but by opening the way for mistakes in monetary policy and by making the monetary system more vulnerable to such mistakes" (1963b, p. 248).

### Conclusion

During the long gestation period of Friedman and Schwartz's study of money in business cycles, they encountered criticism from colleagues

[10] See (1963b, ch. 6, pp. 244–9; ch. 7, pp. 354–7).
[11] Mintz (1951), Hickman (1958), Behrens (1952), and Morton (1956).

in the National Bureau that anticipated controversies that would follow publication of their work. Their choice of the growth rate of the money stock rather than its level, their empirical analysis of velocity "as if" interest rates had no effect, and the role they assigned to monetary forces as the cause of the Great Depression were controversial within the National Bureau before they became controversial outside. Friedman's responses to Wehle and Moore were unwittingly rehearsals for responses to a long line of economists who objected to their empirical methods and conclusions on similar grounds. It turned out, however, that the research assistant's critique was more prescient than the associate director of research's.

Moore's criticism concerned Chapter 7 of the *Monetary History*.[12] Recall Moore's claim was that two important factors in precipitating the Great Depression were a "long downswing" in construction activity and a speculation driven decline in the quality of credit instruments. He thought Friedman and Schwartz gave undue importance to monetary policy mistakes. Subsequent critics repeated the construction activity hypothesis and blamed the recession on speculation. They also rejected Friedman and Schwartz's claim that inept policy by the Federal Reserve was a cause of the Depression. But theories of speculation and the Depression were related to the role of the stock market crash. The possible influence of an increase in the riskiness of credit instruments in the last half of the 1920s received scant attention. The most prominent critique of Friedman and Schwartz's hypothesis about the Depression after publication was made by Peter Temin (1976) (see Chapter 9). Temin's argument fit into the Keynesian–monetarist debate, which was at its apogee at the time, for he attributed the Depression to an autonomous drop in consumption expenditures. Where Moore had argued that there was little the Federal Reserve could do in the face of "extraordinary pressures" that prevented them from making the best policy choices, Temin argued that even the best monetary policy choices would have been inadequate to the task.

In subsequent literature where credit conditions were considered, and evaluations of the Depression came closest to Moore's concern, the quality of credit was not the issue. For example, Bernanke (1983) and Mishkin (1978) focused on the role of financial factors in propagating the Depression, not as exogenous causes. In the terms Friedman used to define his disagreement with Moore, these authors considered roles of *ex post* rather than *ex ante* changes in financial

---

[12] Published separately as *The Great Contraction* (1965).

markets. They also were not strictly concerned with credit quality. Mishkin considered the effects of changes in household balance sheets as part of the transmission mechanism for shocks from exogenous causes, and Bernanke considered an increase in the cost of financial intermediation that may have resulted from bank failures. Both studies supplemented Friedman and Schwartz's work rather than standing in opposition to it as Temin's and Moore's criticism. In his later work, Temin (1989) came part way around, at least, to the Friedman and Schwartz view that monetary forces proximately caused the Great Depression. He identified the cause as a continuing commitment to the international gold standard coupled with structural changes associated with World War I that rendered the gold standard unworkable.

Wehle touched a more fundamental issue for the entire project when he suggested that Friedman and Schwartz were using the wrong measure of money. His concern was repeated in several instances by prominent critics in the 1960s. Friedman and Schwartz's use of the money stock growth rate was in part the result of their following standard National Bureau practice of separating trends and cycles in time series. But their choice of this particular measure for detrending the data was a departure from practices of other economists. For example, in similar work on money and business cycles, Clark Warburton (1945, 1946, 1950) estimated a linear trend and expressed observations as deviations from the trend.[13]

Burns and Mitchell had also departed from standard practice. In *Measuring Business Cycles* (1946) they seasonally adjusted data, broke time series into specific cycles, and then converted observations within a cycle into percentages of the average value for the cycle. This had the effect of removing the trend between cycles while allowing it to remain within cycles. Their technique also amounted to a move away from a linear or smooth nonlinear trend to a flexible nonlinear trend. They were motivated to make this change by a belief that the choice of any technique for separating trends and cycles was necessarily arbitrary and that there was useful information in economic time series that could not be dichotomized into trend and cycle.

Friedman and Schwartz used Burns and Mitchell as their starting point and took the technique a step further, allowing for an adjustable

---

[13] In his 1945 JPE article, Warburton estimated a linear trend in income velocity for 1919 through 1943 by fitting a line through the 1923 and 1928 observations on expenditures on final products and the quantity of money. The 1946 and 1950 articles do not indicate how he estimated trends.

trend from observation to observation. They wrote in the 1957 manuscript, "The Stock of Money in the United States, 1875–1955":

. . . the very notion of a secular trend has a different meaning and theoretical significance for the money supply, expressed in nominal units, than for such physical magnitudes as population, the output of a commodity or a group of commodities, and the like.

For such physical magnitudes, one can conceive of the existence of a trend in the sense of the path that would be produced by the full working out of specified or specifiable long-term forces if these were not interrupted by random influences and by cyclical fluctuations in the economy as a whole. Moreover the trend can in these cases be regarded as a kind of moving stable equilibrium; a position to which the magnitude in question has a tendency to return when random influences or cyclical fluctuations produce perturbations. These conceptions may or may not be acceptable in the light of the evidence; it may be, as Burns and Mitchell suggest, that they involve a sharper separation between secular and cyclical forces than it is useful to make. But they are not on their surface implausible (1957, ch. V, pp. 11–12).

They continued this distinction by arguing that though a stable long-term trend might be appropriate for a commodity money, as for nonmonetary commodities, it would be inappropriate for a fiat money. Unlike commodity money or nonmonetary commodities, there was no self-equilibrating mechanism for a fiat money. Any trend there may be would be the product of decisions made by monetary authorities, and any departure from a trend would be corrected only by actions taken by the authorities.

Underlying Wehle's critique was a theoretical question of what the basic monetary factor was. Wehle objected to their rate of change measure because he thought the quantity theory specified the level of the money stock. Since this was what theory said was relevant, the timing of cycles should be obtained from this data, preserved in the detrending, and used as monetary cycles are compared to reference cycles.

Friedman's response to Wehle indicated his concern, stated elsewhere in his writings during the late 1940s and 1950s, that the quantity theory was satisfactory only for static analysis. Business cycles required dynamic analysis. In what he later labeled the "dimensional" consideration (1961), he argued that the flow measure of income should be matched with a flow measure of accretions of new money (see Chapter 5). In the 1957 draft manuscript, he and Schwartz made the argument as follows:

For both prices and money, what appears important for cyclical analysis is not their level in nominal units – this is purely a matter of convention – but changes in their level. To regard the "normal" or long-term background against which cyclical change is viewed as described by constant levels of either prices or money thus seems a less appropriate and less general analytical framework than to regard it as described by constant rates of change in prices and the stock of money, and the cyclical process as reflected in the changes in the rate of change.

This way of looking at money, moreover, seems conceptually comparable to the way we look at physical magnitudes during the course of a cycle. In respect of most physical magnitudes, we tend to center attention on the flow of output, not the stock in existence. The extreme example, and the one most strictly comparable with money, would be a physical good that lasts indefinitely. The stock of such a good at any point of time is conceptually comparable to the stock of money; the amount produced per unit time, to the rate of change of the money supply. More generally, of course, goods produced have a limited life, so that some output is required to maintain the stock, and services have a zero life, so that there is no meaningful "stock" corresponding to them. This is, of course, largely why we use output series in describing and analyzing cyclical movements. And it explains also why we seldom regard such series as first derivatives of some more basic stock series. Yet, analytically, this is what they are – they are flows *per* unit time to be compared to the flows of money *per* unit time, i.e., the rate of change of the money supply, rather than to the stock of money *at* any point in time (1957, ch. V, pp. 16–17).

# CHAPTER 5

# Post hoc ergo propter hoc: Part I

## Introduction

The earliest published charges that Friedman's empirical analysis of the relationship of money and income was based on spurious correlation were by John M. Clark and John M. Culbertson, a decade before the more famous *post hoc* critique of James Tobin (1970a). Clark shared with Tobin the view that money was less important than Friedman believed. Culbertson's views on the importance of money were closer to Friedman's. This makes his exchange with Friedman in the *Journal of Political Economy* especially useful, for it allows separation of methodology from Keynesian–monetarist doctrine. Aside from their sharing the critical theme that Friedman's conclusions were based on spurious correlation, Culbertson and Tobin appeared on the surface to have had little in common. The two economists held different views on the importance of money and they took different approaches to point out deficiencies in Friedman's analysis.

Tobin (see Chapter 7) wrote down "Keynesian" and "monetarist" models that produced simulated patterns of behavior in money and income that appear to be inconsistent with the models' structures. In his strict Keynesian model, money does not matter at all in the determination of income, yet temporally, money leads income. In the monetarist model, money is the cause of income; yet money follows income in time. His point was that one cannot infer the underlying structure of the economy from observed patterns of timing between the variables of interest; temporal priority does not necessarily indicate causal priority. Hence the charge that Friedman had stumbled into the *post hoc ergo propter hoc* fallacy.

Culbertson's approach was to assess the compatibility of Friedman's data with theoretical specifications of the money supply lag and with the quantity theory. His belief in the importance of money was much closer to Friedman's view than to Tobin's. Culbertson believed, in Irving Fisher's terms, that the business cycle was a "dance of the dollar." He believed in the causal efficacy of changes in the money supply and that the Federal Reserve bore responsibility for the depth of the Great Depression. Nonetheless, he found ample grounds for objecting to Friedman's empirical analysis of monetary policy lags.

For both Tobin and Culbertson, the *post hoc ergo propter hoc* critique was a rejection of National Bureau business-cycle methods and Friedman's Marshallian methodology. In the 1960s, to most economists outside the National Bureau and the University of Chicago, Friedman's work seemed to be methodologically both radical and naive. It appeared to contemporary critics as Burns and Mitchell's had to Koopmans, as "measurement without theory."

By 1960 Friedman and Schwartz had been working together for twelve years, but they had not yet published anything jointly. Friedman had used their empirical evidence on monetary policy lags in two appearances before the Joint Economic Committee of Congress (1958, 1959a) and in a series of lectures at Fordham University (1960). Their data on money and general business conditions, which had been put through the National Bureau processes for identifying specific and reference cycles, suggested that the lag between the peak in the rate of growth of the money stock and the succeeding peak in general business activity was on average about sixteen months and that between the troughs of the rate of money growth and general business, about twelve months. Over eighteen cycles that Friedman and Schwartz studied, the lags for peaks ranged from six to twenty-nine months and for troughs from four to twenty-two months.[1]

From this evidence Friedman drew the conclusion that a monetary growth rule was superior to discretionary policy.[2] Because of the length and the variability of the lags, discretionary policy actions would likely be mistimed and exacerbate inflations and recessions. This evidence, which Culbertson called Friedman's "lag doctrine,"

---

[1] Thomas Mayer (1958) estimated that for restrictive monetary policy, half the effect occurred by five months, and three-fourths by nine months from the change in credit availability. For expansionary policy, half occurred by seven months, and three-fourths by ten months. His estimate of the "compensation point," at which the effect of expansionary policy completely negated the effect of prior contractionary policy, was twenty-two months.

[2] Friedman explored theoretically the implications of lags for the effectiveness of countercyclical policy in two articles (1948b, 1953b) written around the time he and Schwartz began their project. His advocacy circa 1960 of a growth-rate rule offered a less radical change in actual policy practice than his earlier proposal for a 100 percent reserve requirement (1948b). Both had the same objective, to reduce destabilizing effects from portfolio shifts between different monetary assets and from monetary policy mistakes.

drew the *post hoc* charge from Clark and Culbertson, and later from Tobin and others.

## Clark on "new" and "classical" inflation

John M. Clark, who was one of Friedman's professors at Columbia University in 1933–34, published a study of inflation, *The Wage–Price Problem*, in 1960. The American Bankers Association's Committee for Economic Growth without Inflation commissioned the study because of growing concern that sound financial policies were not alone sufficient to achieve economic growth without inflation. They requested that Clark study nonfinancial sources of inflation.

Clark opened the book by making a distinction between "new" and "classical" inflation, a distinction that he based on differences in their causes. With classical inflation, prices are pulled up by excess monetary demand. With the new type, cost–push inflation, prices are pushed up by sellers in the absence of excess demand. Clark made a distinction between "causes" and "conditions" in identifying the new inflation, with exogeneity as the key attribute of causes. With cost–push inflation, the higher nominal volume of business activity is accommodated by "the elastic resources of our flexible credit system, this monetary expansion being an induced enabling factor, not an initiating cause" (1960, p. 1). Clark reduced the role of monetary changes to a mere condition rather than cause because the monetary system reacted to the wage pressure, notwithstanding his admission that monetary changes play a role by "enabling" inflation to occur.

Clark thought that cost–push inflation began to appear in the United States during or just after World War II. There developed not only a new cause of inflation but a new causal mechanism in the real sector of the economy. Clark claimed that most episodes of inflation since the war were in fact mixed cases, with elements of both demand–pull and cost–push. Appraising the community of fellow economists he found that "all but the most extreme advocates of the classical theory admit the importance of both kinds of forces" (1960, p. 4). These "most extreme" advocates were Friedman and his students at the University of Chicago. Clark singled out for special attention Friedman's 1959 testimony before the Joint Economic Committee, along with testimony in the same hearings by Friedman's former student Richard T. Selden.[3]

---

[3] Selden's Chicago dissertation on monetary velocity was completed under Friedman's direction in 1954.

Clark noted that as an identity, the equation of exchange has no causal content until a hypothesis is put forth regarding the independence and/or dependence of its terms, a hypothesis such as: M, V, and T are determined independently and they in turn determine P. Friedman and Selden attempted to convince the Joint Economic Committee that labor unions and administered prices had no effect on behavior of the price level. Clark picked for particular criticism Friedman's evidence on the relationship between peaks and troughs of the rate of change in money and the level of business activity. He interpreted Friedman as inferring from this evidence that money is causally prior to business activity. Clark considered this correlation entirely spurious. It was, he said, a mathematical artifact from Friedman's transformation of the data. Peaks and troughs in the rate of change of any series would lead levels of the same series or levels of another that was congruent with the first. So Friedman not only failed to establish causal priority for money over real economic activity; he also failed to establish temporal priority. His measurement of the lag was spurious.

Clark also made what must be considered a "seat of the pants" analysis of Friedman's data. He contended that Friedman's Chart 1 from the 1959 JEC testimony showed the *level* of money lagging business activity, with income velocity taking up the slack. Clark described Friedman's Charts 1 and 2 as correlating money and economic activity, but the correlation in the charts is only visual, not statistical. Chart 1, from which Clark drew the inference that peaks and troughs in the level of money lag behind peaks and troughs in income after 1943, gives in ratio-scale time series from 1869 through 1957. It appears that at most there is one, possibly two, peaks for money and money income and one trough for each from which Clark could draw his inference that the level of money lags business activity. Certainly he did none of the painstaking analysis of data that was common at the National Bureau for identification of peaks and troughs, and even if he had, his inference was from a very small portion of the series. We will see that Culbertson structured his critique the same way. He rejected Friedman's data as spurious measurement and then made use of the data to draw different inferences from Friedman's.

An important step in establishing a causal link between money and income was to show that "adaptive" changes in velocity do not negate the effects of money changes. As Friedman explained in his 1959 statement to the Joint Economic Committee, "conceivably such a change [in the stock of money] might be absorbed entirely in V, without affecting prices or output at all" (1959a, p. 608). The point of Selden's testimony was to explain the behavior of velocity, showing that it did not play this adaptive or passive role. Friedman submitted "The Quantity Theory of Money – A Restatement" as a technical paper to go along with his JEC testimony.[4] Selden and Friedman both reported that over the business cycle, velocity moved procyclically.

Clark rejected Selden's explanation, claiming that Selden had dismissed "adaptive" velocity changes on the grounds that the supposedly adaptive behavior could not be traced to any of the determinants of velocity included in his model. That is, Clark asserted that Selden rejected adaptive velocity on the basis of not having found it while systematically declining to look for it. Clark also accused Selden of taking *any* evidence of excess demand for goods and services as confirmation of the hypothesis that excess demand is the *only* cause of price level increases.

Friedman was preparing his JPE response to Culbertson's critique when Clark's book came out, and he sent Clark a preliminary draft, expressing hope that the paper would resolve their differences. Clark responded that he feared their differences remained. He reiterated his concern with Friedman's attaching "causal import to the (mathematically-inevitable) lead of a rate-of-change series over the total-amount series of a related quantity" (JM Clark to MF, March 31, 1960 [act. 1961]). With reference to Friedman's claim that he recognized two-way causality between money and income Clark said:

This recognition of a two-way causal relationship *would be* fine, *if* you acted on it in your actual treatment of the question; but in the remainder of your article you ignore it – as you and Selden do in your Congressional-Committee testimony which is aimed at discrediting a theory of two-way causal relationship. To this extent, Culbertson's attribution to you of the one-way theory which you here disclaim seems to me justified in terms of your actual treatment (JM Clark to MF, March 31, 1960 [act. 1961], emphasis in original).

Further on in the letter, Clark wrote, "I yearn for clarification of implied hypothesis as to causal relations," and "I remain skeptical as to whether your recognition of a two-way causal relationship is real, or a pro forma device for disarming criticism without allowing the recognition to affect your views in any operational way" (JM Clark to MF, March 31, 1960 [act. 1961]).

Friedman revised his paper and wrote again to Clark that he thought their quarrel over monetary accommodation of inflationary impulses from real sectors of the economy could be resolved by recognizing that Clark viewed the banking system as having a readily avail-

[4] This paper is Chapter 1 of *Studies in the Quantity Theory of Money* (1956a). Selden's "Monetary Velocity in the United States" is also a chapter in the volume.

able pool of funds so that an increase in business activity would automatically and directly produce an increase in money. His own view was that banks continuously equate margins so that the increase in business calls forth an increase in money only by raising interest rates and thus inducing banks to reduce their free reserves.

### Culbertson on the "lag doctrine"

John Culbertson, a professor at the University of Wisconsin and former staff member at the Federal Reserve, met Friedman in 1959 when he visited the University of Chicago to give a paper in the Money and Banking Workshop. Their correspondence indicates that this session was amicable and productive for both Culbertson and Friedman. Soon thereafter Culbertson submitted a critique of Friedman's analysis of lags in the effect of monetary policy to the JPE. The article led to an exchange between Culbertson and Friedman in letters and the journal that acquired a contentious edge, with Friedman accusing Culbertson of "casual theorizing" and "casual empiricism" and Culbertson accusing Friedman of "deceptively pretentious empiricism."[5] The fundamental dispute was over how economists should go about measuring causes and effects.

Culbertson (1960) addressed both the implications of Friedman's evidence on the money supply lag and the evidence itself. He disputed Friedman's policy conclusions on three grounds. First, "neutral" policy need not be identified solely with a fixed money growth rule. The operational rule might also be to fix interest rates or bank reserves. Moreover, definition of "neutral" policy is a matter for economic theory, and identification of an operationally neutral policy rule must await theoretical analysis of neutrality. Friedman's work provided no theoretical foundation for identifying neutral policy.[6]

Second, Friedman's evidence on the lag, taken at face value, vitiated his 1948 proposal for automatic stabilization. This was because the lag doctrine's real implication was not simply that *discretionary* policy is likely to be destabilizing but that *any anticyclical policy* will be. It matters not whether the monetary changes are discretionary or automatic so long as their effects are transmitted through the same channels. In either case the long and variable lag implies that the effects of changes in the money supply will be mistimed.

---

[5] The strong feelings on both sides carried over into Culbertson's 1964 review of the *Monetary History*, which is covered in Chapter 6.

[6] See Culbertson (1968) for extended discussion of policy neutrality.

Culbertson's third point was that the lag doctrine raises serious questions about the economy's capacity for self-stabilization. If financial adjustments are the self-stabilizing mechanism, and if the channels of their effects are the same as the channels for money supply changes originating in the Federal Reserve, the lag for self-stabilizing adjustments should be as long and variable as that for policy induced changes. So endogenous monetary changes could just as well be destabilizing as stabilizing.

Culbertson argued that the lag Friedman thought he found was very likely a mere mathematical artifact. His point was the same as Clark's. Friedman's monetary variable was a growth rate, and his economic activity variable was a level. For any smooth cyclical series, the peak in the variable's growth rate would precede the peak in the same variable's level. So *even if* the level of money and level of economic activity series were perfectly coincident (that is, there was no lag between the levels of money and economic activity) there would be a lag between the rate of change in money and the level of economic activity.[7] Furthermore, if a cyclical series was irregular, the lag between peaks in its rate of change and its level would be variable. Given the irregular nature of cycles in money and economic activity, it would be expected on entirely mathematical grounds that Friedman's data would show a variable lag between money and activity. Thus, his "measured" variable lag between cause and effect was nothing more than a mathematical artifact.

Culbertson also attempted to undermine Friedman's lag doctrine by offering a counterinterpretation of Friedman's data. He suggested that Chart 2 in Friedman's 1959 testimony before the Joint Economic Committee (1959a, p. 639) generally showed no lag between the rate of change in money and the *rate of change* in activity. For some cycles, there was even a negative lag (the rate of change in activity led the rate of change in money). On a *post hoc* basis, this evidence was inconsistent with the hypothesis that changes in the growth rate of money *cause* changes in the growth rate of economic activity.[8]

[7] Kareken and Solow made the same point against Friedman's analysis in a prepublication draft of their 1963 article at about the same time that Culbertson's paper was written and published. See Chapter 7.

[8] It is not clear from his article and the published record of Friedman's 1959 testimony to which he refers, how Culbertson came to this reading of Friedman's evidence. Friedman's chart included no series for rates of change in business activity, only shaded regions along a time dimension to represent business-cycle

Culbertson's second point in criticism of Friedman's evidence was that to get a meaningful estimate of the monetary policy lag, one must unravel the separate effects of the various forces acting upon economic activity. The lag should also be specified counterfactually as the time between a policy action and the departure of the effect variable from the path it *would have taken* had the policy action not been taken. He argued that for Friedman's evidence to fit this theoretical specification, it would be necessary for the change in money to be the *only* cause of economic activity. Otherwise what is seen as the lag between money changes and economic activity may be partially the result of other forces outweighing the effect of money. And, Culbertson argued, one would expect "other" forces to act in a systematic way, providing momentum early in business-cycle expansions and leading a shift toward contraction in the later stages of expansions.

Lastly, Culbertson claimed that Friedman's estimates depended on money being exogenous, with causation running from money to economic activity but not in the other direction. On this point, which became a key issue in Friedman's reply and Culbertson's rejoinder, Culbertson provided no elaboration in the 1960 article. He concluded his critique with the admonition that the proper way for Friedman to go about making estimates of the lag was to first identify the channels through which monetary changes have their effect and then to determine how long it takes the effect to begin through the various channels. Presumably the task of identifying the channels was for theory.[9]

Culbertson also made empirical judgments (apart from Friedman's JEC charts) that the "predominant direct effects" of monetary, debt-management, and fiscal policies occurred within three to six months. But, as Friedman noted in his reply, he presented no evidence in support of this assertion. In a 1959 *Journal of Finance* article, Culbertson used reports of Open Market Committee meetings to evaluate the Federal Reserve's success in adjusting policy to changes in economic conditions over the period of the Fed–Treasury Accord from 1951 through 1957. From this evidence he concluded that the Fed did a reasonably good job of diagnosing major business-cycle changes and responding appropriately (he judged that the Fed recognized major changes within a month or two of their occurrence) but that their

---

contractions. It is possible that the idea was from evidence in a prepublication draft of Kareken and Solow (1963).

[9] Mayer (1958) attempted to estimate the lag in a manner that accounted for channels of money's effects.

forecasting ability was not sufficient for fine tuning. He suggested that overall the postwar record could have been duplicated or improved had the Fed followed a policy rule of simply preventing procyclical movements in the money supply.

Whatever the other difficulties that would be involved in such an approach to policy – and surely there would be difficulties – you can see that it quite eliminates the need for predicting turning points. This approach would reflect the view that the changes in credit conditions that characteristically accompany changes in economic conditions reflect mainly forces naturally generated by the economy. . . . One advantage of the policy would be that it would direct attention to these forces and would combat the common error of attributing to the Federal Reserve everything that happens in financial affairs (1959, p. 159).

Culbertson's evaluation of Fed policy indicates how close his and Friedman's views were on practical policy questions. His policy suggestion was close in spirit to Friedman's constant-growth-rate rule. It also suggests that his analysis was open to some of the same criticisms he directed at Friedman. His analysis presumed the importance of causality in both directions between the money supply and economic activity. It further presumed that the endogenous procyclical changes in the money supply, as well as policy induced changes, have causal power and that he could distinguish between the two. Also, Culbertson's empirical judgments about the course of monetary policy and its effects were made without a fully specified structural model for counterfactual analysis.

### Friedman's response

Friedman took up the point of exogeneity at the outset of his response. He quoted from his 1958 paper submitted to the Joint Economic Committee the year before he presented them with the "lag doctrine":

The direction of influence between the money stock and income and prices is less clear-cut and more complex for the business cycle than for the longer movements. . . . Thus changes in the money stock are a consequence as well as an independent cause of changes in income and prices, though once they occur they will in their turn produce still further effects on income and prices. This consideration blurs the relation between money and prices but does not reverse it. For there is much evidence . . . that even during business cycles the money stock plays a largely independent role (1958, p. 249; 1961, p. 449).

Friedman and Culbertson were talking past one another. Culbertson made a point about what logic dictated that Friedman must believe for there to be an underlying theoretical model of the economic structure corresponding to his empirical measures. Friedman responded not in terms of the relationship between theoretical and empirical models but in terms of what he actually believed about the cause–effect relationship between money and income.

Friedman thought the feedback effects from income to money and back to income could be the reason for the long and variable lag. In his view, the "largely independent role" for money, not unidirectional causation, was crucial. This sort of gray empirical judgment was not compatible with the black and white theoretical specification of variables as exogenous *or* endogenous. For a critic such as Culbertson, who assigned responsibility to theory for sorting out causes and effects, "largely independent" money made no sense. Variables were either exogenous (causes) or endogenous (effects).

This would not be the only time that Friedman's assessment of causation in terms of degrees of independence frustrated critics who expected him to treat money as either exogenous or as endogenous. His Marshallian methodology did not fit into their boxes.

True to his empirically oriented method, Friedman cited evidence in support of the "largely independent" role of money. One type, which he claimed was *only suggestive,* was the tendency for money to lead rather than lag general business conditions. Most important was the history of specific episodes of monetary changes. This evidence revealed significant changes in the money stock that were not the automatic results of contemporaneous or prior business conditions. A third type of evidence was the fact (a fact being established by the various parts of the money study) that the empirically observed relationship between money and business was robust over different types of monetary arrangements. The evidential quality of this information was that different monetary institutional structures have different implications for the causal link from business to money, that is, for the transmission mechanism and the qualitative effect of impulses running from business activity to money. Yet these different structures have no implications for the causal link from money to business. Thus the robustness of the observed relationship between money and business over time and over institutional arrangements indicated that the predominant effect was from money to business rather than the other way around.[10]

---

[10] Friedman gave as an example the breakdown of the international gold standard and creation of the Federal Reserve at the time of World War I. Before the

Friedman offered three defenses of his use of the rate of change rather than the level of money. He labeled them dimensional, statistical, and economic. He argued that the mathematically inevitable relationship between turning points in the rate of change and level of series that are perfectly coincident in levels had no implications for determining whether there was an economic relationship between money and economic activity. That is, that there may be a mathematical relationship does not mean that there cannot be an economic relationship.

This is no doubt correct, but the possibility that what is found is a mathematical artifact of the data transformation presents a problem for drawing causal inferences from the data. The other evidence for independence of monetary changes thus became more important. The situation is akin to the inferential problems associated with use of the equation for gross domestic product,

$$Y = C + I + G + X,$$

and other identities as frameworks for analysis. The question can be put as to whether one is drawing causal inferences from the mathematically inevitable relationships or from other sources. Purely tautological relationships are not causal. Causality requires something beyond the identity, such as identification of sources of movement of the terms from outside the identity. Yet economic theories of cause and effect often are built on the skeleton of identities.

On the dimensional level, Friedman argued that investigating the relation between the rate of change of money and the level of business activity was appropriate because the transformation to rate of change turned the money variable into a flow, and this corresponded to the flow dimension of business activity. The money variable and business-activity variable then had the same dimension. He had rehearsed this defense in his letter to Wehle. (See Chapter 4.) Many economic categories, Friedman argued, can be treated either as stocks or flows, for example, inventories versus investment and housing versus housing services. "The imputed value of the services rendered by the stock of money is comparable to such income items as the rental value of land; the rate of change of the stock of money is comparable to such items

---

war, business expansions produced monetary contractions through balance of payments deficits. After the war the price-specie-flow mechanism was no longer operative, and business expansions produced monetary expansions through their upward pressure on interest rates and banks' borrowings from the Federal Reserve.

as residential construction, production of durable consumer goods, net investment in inventories, and so on" (1961, p. 452).

But these dimensional considerations were, in Friedman's account of his work, less important than the statistical and economic considerations. He interpreted Culbertson's argument for conceptualization of the lag as the time between a policy action and the point at which business activity begins to behave differently than it would have in the absence of the action as a statistical objection to the National Bureau method of comparing reference with specific cycles. He pointed out that the National Bureau's was one of the few tested methods for extracting information from economic time series.[11]

He contended that the crucial statistical problem was how to deal with trends. In particular, money normally grows during both reference cycle expansions and contractions. Superficially this might seem to indicate that there is no cause–effect relation in either direction. The clearest evidence that there is a cause–effect relationship emerges only after trends have been removed. The two most common ways of extracting a trend were to estimate it directly and express the series as deviations from the estimated trend or to use first differences of the series. Friedman favored first differences because this obviated the need to make choices of type or period for the trends.

He thought there were two "economic" reasons that made it particularly important in the case of money to allow for a trend and to do so via first differences. The first was that unanticipated money changes had bigger economic impacts than anticipated changes. A detrended money series could serve as a proxy for unanticipated changes in money. Secondly, since the creation of the Federal Reserve, there was nothing outside the political policy-making sphere to give anchor to any particular long-term trend in money. Most likely there were numerous short-term trends within post-1913 money series. Detrending by first differences obviated the need for estimating shifting trends.

Friedman accepted Culbertson's point that the conception of the effect of monetary policy and the lag in that effect involve a counterfactual hypothesis as to what the path of business activity would have

[11] Another method that Friedman had an interest in was cross-spectral analysis, a type of multiple correlation. He worked on this technique with John Tukey at the Institute for Advanced Study in the Behavioral Sciences in 1957–58 and with Jon Cunnyngham when he was a graduate student at Chicago in the late 1950s and early 1960s and then faculty member at Columbia. Henry Schultz, for whom Friedman worked as a research assistant in 1934–35, also had an interest in these techniques.

been in the absence of policy action. But, he argued, "the" lag cannot practically be identified because the effect does not happen all at once and may be cumulative. This meant that Culbertson's notion of the lag as the time lapse between the action and the point at which the target variable *begins* to behave other than it would have, captured only the front end of the effect. The lag should be thought of rather as some form of weighted average of the effect(s) as it is distributed through time.

On the matter of separating the effect of an autonomous change in money from the feedback effects, the difference between Friedman's and Culbertson's techniques can be interpreted as the difference between total and partial derivatives. Friedman's technique was based on a notion, with allowance for the problem of averaging over a distributed effect, of the total derivative of business activity with respect to money. Culbertson called for an estimate of the lag corresponding to the partial derivative.

Friedman also justified the National Bureau technique on the basis of the law of large numbers, that "other" effects cancel out. "In practice, we evade the explicit isolation of the effects of autonomous monetary changes by the usual device of relying on the averaging out of the effects of other changes, which is to say, we take the average relation between the actual changes in money and in income as an estimate of the relation to be expected between an autonomous change in money and the resultant change in income" (1961, p. 456).[12]

Returning to the question of what role the evidence on lags played in his research program, Friedman argued that however strong the evidence may be, it cannot be sufficient by itself. It must be complemented by "what we think we know about economic interrelationships" (1961, p. 462). This was an explicit denial of the *post hoc* and "measurement without theory" charges. Friedman responded to Culbertson's challenge to identify the channels of money's influence by outlining a theory of the transmission mechanism in which balance sheet adjustments play a pivotal role and interest rates are defined as the prices of sources of consumer and producer services relative to the services themselves. In this sketch Friedman identified some of the transmission effects one would look for in following Culbertson's method of estimating the lag, for example, the rental price of housing relative to price of houses. However, he rejected Culbertson's ap-

---

[12] From the context of his discussion, Friedman seems to have been thinking here of feedback effects rather than nonmonetary factors that influence business activity.

proach, arguing that the transmission is widely diffused over markets and time and that the relevant conception of the lag would have it ending not with the initiation of the effect but with some weighted average of it.

### Culbertson's reply

Culbertson reiterated the four main points of his criticism in an April 17, 1961 letter to Friedman, written after he read a draft of Friedman's JPE response. Culbertson clearly expected his article to convince Friedman that he was on the wrong track, for his letter shows disappointment with Friedman's refusal to yield in any substantial way. He tried in his letter, as in the article, to identify conceptually the lag relevant for countercyclical policy, and he responded to Friedman's suggestion that if one is being strict about the lag specification, it must be specified as distributed through time. To this end he suggested that Friedman consider an example of a policy choice, increasing the money supply by $300 per month for three months and thereafter holding it constant versus holding it constant throughout. He argued that the effect of policy is the difference in the behavior of income under these two choices. This effect can be decomposed into its direct and indirect components, and both are spread through time with the indirect effects continuing to infinity. For the policy maker, Culbertson suggested, the relevant lag is the time between the policy action and "the center or concentration point of the directly induced expenditures" (JM Culbertson to MF, April 17, 1961).

Policy makers must limit their attention to this effect (and this lag) because the indirect effects stretch out indefinitely and are intertwined with effects of other forces influencing income. Moreover, he argued, this lag is likely to be sufficient for countercyclical purposes because the indirect effects are probably minor in comparison with the direct effects, and at such time as they become problems, they can be addressed with a new policy action. Culbertson asked, "How would your approach be applied in such a setting?" (JM Culbertson to MF, April 17, 1961) He challenged Friedman to show how the cyclical peaks and troughs of the National Bureau method might be brought into this picture.

Culbertson raised another issue that brought into question not just the National Bureau method of estimating the lag but *any* method of doing so. He argued that there was no way to extract the empirical counterpart of a correct conception of the lag from past data because this would require that other things actually remain frozen when the policy action was taken and that the policy action not be endogenously related to the business cycle. Recall that in his JPE article Culbertson contended that the legitimacy of Friedman's approach required that money be the sole cause and be exogenous. The argument in his letter vitiated *any* attempt to estimate a lag because no one, Friedman not excepted, believes that the two conditions are met. They require nothing short of full laboratory control.

Culbertson explained further what he thought was the difference between autonomous and endogenous policy changes. The endogeneity he had in mind seems not to be the endogeneity of banks trimming their reserve positions in response to the increase in demand for loans that would typically occur during an expansion, but the endogeneity of policy makers reacting to the course of the business cycle, that is, countercyclical policy. If central bankers pursue countercyclical monetary policy, this makes the money supply endogenous, and the appropriately specified policy lag cannot be estimated. Whether one used National Bureau methods or regression analysis, there simply was no "raw material" for empirical determination of the lag.

Culbertson rejected Friedman's "dimensional" and "economic" justifications for using money's growth rate on theoretical grounds in his letter and his published response (1961). In the letter he asked:

But what does theory and general observation say, as to which of these two is the valid causative relation? Do we believe that $M = (OP)/K$ (where K is a variable that behaves systematically and is subject to explanation, and OP is the variable that we want to control), or does experience suggest that $\Delta M = (OP)/K$? Is the size of the money supply irrelevant to income determination; is it only its rate of change that matters? Could we have the same income with any absolute money supply, so long as the correct rate of change existed. This seems absurd, which implies that the relationship on which policy planning (and "lag" measurements) should be based is one between M and Y, or between $\Delta M$ and $\Delta Y$ (JM Culbertson to MF, April 17, 1961).[13]

He rejected Friedman's "statistical" defense as absurd, as any defense grounded in convenience would be. This reaction highlights the different methodological bents of Friedman and Culbertson. Friedman's defense of first differences to eliminate trend would have less appeal for someone whose interest was theoretical purity and who was less involved in the empirical work of estimating lags than for someone committed to a search for quantitative regularities.[14]

---

[13] See also Culbertson (1961, p. 469).

[14] Friedman told the Joint Economic Committee in 1958 that the purpose of his

Culbertson preceded Tobin by a decade in accusing Friedman of the *post hoc ergo propter hoc* fallacy. He argued that in taking the observed relationship between money and economic activity as manifestation of the causal relation, Friedman implicitly assumed that money changes are exogenous – that is, there are no feedback effects from income to money – and that money is the sole cause of changes in economic activity. He asserted that either of these conditions, feedback or "other" causes of economic activity, makes necessary a precise and specific theoretical specification for there to be any hope of extracting the causal relationship from data. This is very close to requiring a full specification of the causal structure before any estimation is done. But we have also seen that given these requirements and what he thought he knew about the causal relationships, Culbertson did not think there was any hope for accurate estimation of the lag. In his JPE rejoinder Culbertson referred to the growing literature, mostly from the Cowles Commission, on spurious correlation and the identification problem. It was there, in the seat of opposition to the National Bureau "empiricism," that Culbertson looked for progress.

## Conclusion

We have examined in this chapter two critiques of Friedman and Schwartz's empirical analysis of the role of money in business cycles, especially their attempts to estimate monetary lags. Several common features stand out in the criticism. Both Clark and Culbertson could use the *post hoc ergo propter hoc* charge as a critical device because they were not themselves attempting empirical evaluation of money's role in business cycles. If they had, it is likely that the charge could have been directed at them as well. Without controlled experiments no economist can get very far beyond correlation, and it is generally accepted that correlation does not prove causation. Friedman tried to find historical facsimiles of controlled experiments by assimilating data that spanned a broad range of institutional structures. He prefaced his evidence in support of his hypothesis of a largely independent causal role for money with a disclaimer that he did not believe that money was the sole cause of income changes or was itself insulated from "reverse causation." But Clark did not believe the dis-

---

estimates was to use scientific analysis to establish economic regularities on the basis of the historical record. See (1958, p. 180).

claimer was genuine, and Culbertson thought it logically incompatible with his use of the evidence.

The critics used the "identification problem" to rebut Friedman's empirical claims. Friedman's estimates, it was said, did not distinguish between changes in money supply and in money demand. Likewise, "demand–pull" theories of inflation applied to evidence on money or other demand-side variables tacitly assumed identification of demand and supply functions for goods and services, without actually providing identification. Clark and Culbertson also used the distinction between arithmetical and causal relations to counter Friedman's inferences. Friedman recognized, as anyone working with the equation of exchange or national income accounting identities should, that there is a difference between arithmetical and "economic" (read "causal") relationships. (See, for example, 1959a, p. 608.) But this distinction is much easier to make in principle than in practice.

Neither Clark nor Culbertson used empirical evidence of their own to rebut Friedman's claims, except for drawing contrary conclusions from Friedman's data. But their reinterpretation of his data was not a crucial component of the critiques. The key component was a principled theoretical rejection of Friedman's results. Friedman's susceptibility to the *post hoc* and spurious correlation charges was in no small part due simply to the fact that he was doing empirical work. In the macroeconomics community of the 1960s, that was actually quite rare.

# CHAPTER 6

# Reactions to the *Monetary History*

### Introduction

In the previous chapter we examined reactions to Friedman's analysis of monetary lags. In this chapter we examine three reviews of Friedman and Schwartz's *Monetary History*, the first monograph product of their collaboration. Publication of the *Monetary History* in 1963 marked an important and long awaited point in their research project. In the *Monetary History*, there is a much richer catalog of evidence on money's role in the economy than there is in Friedman's analysis of the lags. The three reviewers are James Tobin and John Culbertson, whose *post hoc ergo propter hoc* criticisms of Friedman's monetary analysis are covered in Chapters 5 and 7, and Robert Clower, whose review is notable for its methodological diagnosis of the conflict between Friedman and his critics.

### Tobin's review

James Tobin presented a version of his June 1965 AER review at the American Bankers Association Conference of University Professors at Princeton in September 1964. Friedman's written response for the conference remained unpublished.

Tobin's review was on the whole favorable, especially toward the book as a history of monetary policy. His primary concern was with the theoretical framework underlying and guiding the analysis and the associated assignment of causal roles. He was particularly concerned with their dismissal of interest rates as a factor in money demand and with what he considered an inclination to draw stronger conclusions about the power of monetary policy than the evidence warranted. Using the left-hand side of the equation of exchange (MV) to organize his comments, Tobin began with Friedman and Schwartz's definition of money, moved from there to their explanation of the determination of the money stock, and then went on to their evaluation of the behavior of velocity.

Tobin took note of Friedman and Schwartz's pragmatic approach to the definition of money. He suggested several factors that might have led to attention on aggregates other than currency plus total bank deposits and ways in which this could have impinged on their conclusions about the relationship between money and income. Tobin saw no problem with expediency as such, but he did with the way Friedman and Schwartz coupled indefiniteness about what is and what is not money with definite conclusions about the right amount or rate of growth of money. "Sometimes Friedman and his followers seem to be saying: 'We don't know what money is, but whatever it is, its stock should grow steadily at 3 to 4 per cent per year'" (1965, p. 465).

Tobin gave a summary sketch of Friedman and Schwartz's scheme for sorting out the "proximate determinants" of the money stock. They begin with a tautology

$$M = H \; \frac{\dfrac{D}{R}\left(1 + \dfrac{D}{C}\right)}{\dfrac{D}{R} + \dfrac{D}{C}}$$

and "breathe life into it" by tracing the behavior of its components over time. Though Tobin did not say so directly, "breathing life into it" indicates getting beyond the identity to a causal explanation. Friedman and Schwartz provided this on two levels. The first was that the breakdown of M into H, high-powered money; D/R, the deposit to reserve ratio; and D/C, the deposit to currency ratio, though it remains tautological, helps one understand which of the money stock's components account for its behavior. But as the term "proximate" suggests, this was only the first step. The second step was explanation of the behavior of the components. At this step, variables from outside the identity were brought into the picture. Tobin imputed to Friedman and Schwartz the view that for the most part the government controls high-powered money, banks control the deposit to reserve ratio, and the public controls the deposit to currency ratio.

Tobin claimed that for high-powered money Friedman and Schwartz were remiss in not considering differentials in the potency of changes in the money stock depending on the manner in which additions to the stock are created. If, as he argued, a given quantity of H is created through the exchange of existing Treasury securities (pure monetary policy), this will not be as expansionary as if it is created through government purchases of goods and services. What Tobin was saying, in the terms that came to characterize the debate over the relative power of monetary and fiscal policy, was that pure monetary policy is less powerful than monetary and fiscal policy together.

One of the highlights and most controversial parts of the *Monetary History* is the chapter on the Great Contraction (See Chapter 9). The Keynesian–monetarist dispute over the power of monetary policy comes through with force in Tobin's remarks on behavior of the deposit to reserve ratio (D/R) during this episode of monetary history. Friedman and Schwartz used total reserves, so changes in the ratio's value could reflect changes in the required reserve ratio, changes in banks' desired excess reserves, or changes in truly idle reserves. The deposit to reserve ratio peaked at 13.4 in 1929 and thereafter declined to 3.14 in 1940. By 1936, reserves in excess of the legal minimum were at $2.5 million, forty-two percent of the total. Reserve requirements were doubled in 1936–37, but excess reserves remained at eighteen percent of total. The issue was whether these excess reserves were truly idle or whether they were held by banks to satisfy their demand for liquidity. An estimate of demand for excess reserves was needed to determine the extent to which expansionary open market operations would have produced growth in the money stock and income. The practical problem was that the theoretically important variable, quantity demanded of excess reserves, could not be directly observed.

Friedman and Schwartz thought that the observed excess reserves were not idle, that the banks' demand curves were interest inelastic and shifted out because of their experience with bank runs and the Fed's failure to provide adequate cash in 1930–33. Tobin suggested the alternative Keynesian view that banks operated along a relatively flat demand-for-reserves schedule that reflected a paucity of profitable lending opportunities. He noted the negative correlation between high-powered money and the deposit to reserve ratio and imputed from the timing of reserve requirement changes and changes in D/R, and from near zero short-term interest rates, that causality ran from H to D/R. Tobin buttressed this argument with a reference to an empirical study by George Horwich (1963). Horwich found closer correlation in the 1930s between adjusted personal income (a proxy for loan demand) and the volume of bank earning assets than between effective bank reserves and their earning assets.[1] From this he concluded that causation more likely ran from loan demand to re-

---

[1] Effective reserves are total reserves adjusted for changes in banks' legal capacity to use them, e.g., for changes in reserve requirements.

serves, consistent with a Keynesian liquidity trap, than from reserves to bank earning assets and the money supply.

Tobin's criticism of Friedman and Schwartz's analysis of income velocity is especially notable, for he used one of their own methodological principles, that other things equal, the better theory is that which explains the broadest range of experience. Also in contrast to much of the criticism of Friedman and Schwartz's work, Tobin countered empirical evidence with empirical evidence.

He divided his remarks on velocity into sections on trend, cycles, and the stability and independence of velocity. Over the long term from about 1880 (according to Tobin, 1869 according to Friedman and Schwartz) until World War II, the trend of velocity was downward. Friedman and Schwartz explained this as the result of rising per capita income and the luxury status of services of money. However, after the war the trend was reversed and velocity increased. Their explanation for the reversal was that it was a response to enhanced expectations of economic stability. Tobin took issue with both explanations, of the downward trend and its reversal. To say that the services of money are a luxury (have income elasticity greater than one) is just another way of saying that income velocity declines with increases in income. This, according to Tobin, was dangerously close to being a tautological explanation. Nothing in their theory led them to expect the result. Moreover, the crucial variable, the income elasticity of the *services* of money, involved an unobservable. The explanation of the reversal of the trend after World War II was also based on an unobservable variable, and it was *ad hoc*. It violated the methodological dictate for unified explanation.

Tobin was critical of Friedman and Schwartz for spurning two alternative theories. On the one hand, in not giving the medium of exchange function any special significance, they isolated themselves from Fisherian explanations of long-term trends in demand for money that focused on changes in payments schedules, the share of income to total monetary transactions, and the like. Moreover they broke with this tradition within monetary theory without so much as a nod. Secondly, they declined to make use of an alternative (Keynesian) hypothesis that could explain a greater portion of the long-term velocity behavior through the effects of interest rates. Tobin presented regressions of his own to support the interest rate linkage. These indicated that after 1914 a simple trend explained fifty-one percent of the variation in velocity while short-term interest rates explained fifty-six percent and long-term rates forty-five percent.

The inclusion of either interest rate in a multiple regression lowered the size of the trend coefficient.[2]

For Friedman and Schwartz, money was a consumer good analogous to refrigerators, cameras, and other consumer durables. A stock of money yields its holder a stream of services that they left largely undefined.[3] The nature of money's services had no special significance any more than the nature of refrigerator or camera services. What makes money distinctive, in Friedman and Schwartz's framework, is that its supply is controlled by the government so that increases in demand do not call forth increases in the quantity supplied the way an increase in the demand for refrigeration services does. For Tobin, the primary service of money was convenience in making transactions, and its relevant cost was foregone interest on alternative assets. So from Tobin's perspective, Friedman and Schwartz's explanation of long-term trends in income velocity pushed the distinguishing function of money and one of the theoretically most appealing explanatory variables into the background.

Friedman and Schwartz found that velocity tended to move procyclically, which they explained via differences in measured and permanent income. Money demand depends on permanent income. During expansions, measured income moves ahead of permanent income, with the result that velocity rises. During contractions, the opposite occurs. Measured income falls below permanent income, and this brings reductions in velocity. Tobin suggested two alternative explanations of the behavior of velocity over the business cycle. On the one hand, if the cycle had nonmonetary origins and an endogenous money supply adjusted slowly, this would mean arithmetically that velocity would rise during expansions and decline during contractions. Tobin noted that Friedman and Schwartz gave narrative evidence showing that this was not the case for at least some occasions. The second explanation, which Tobin preferred, focused on interest rates. Procyclical interest rate movements would reduce desired money balances and create procyclical movements in velocity. This explanation was superior to Friedman and Schwartz's, according to Tobin, on both methodological grounds: It was consistent with both the cycle and trend evidence, and it did not require *ad hoc* adjust-

[2] Tobin also cited an empirical study of velocity by Latané (1960) in support of the interest rate hypothesis.

[3] Money could also be viewed as a capital good, and the same analysis would apply.

ments to theory in the face of anomalies such as the postwar rise in velocity.

Furthermore, Tobin pointed out that in using inflation expectations to explain money demand, Friedman and Schwartz went part way towards the use of interest rates. Why not go all the way? The relevant interest rate on money (which may normally be negative) is the difference in the explicit rate of return on money and rates of return on alternative assets. A priori, there should be complete symmetry between the effect of an increase in expected inflation and an increase in expected rates of return on liquid nonmonetary assets.

The third area in which Tobin challenged Friedman and Schwartz's analysis was the issue of stability and independence of velocity. This issue is central to the Keynesian–monetarist dispute. Tobin presented evidence from a univariate regression of $\Delta Y/Y$ on $\Delta M/M$ for 1869 to 1959 indicating that money supply changes explain thirty-one percent of observed changes in income. This left a lot of room for velocity changes to account for the behavior of income. But Tobin questioned even the thirty-one percent of the variation of income that was statistically explained by money, pointing out that those who assign little causal importance to money would not be surprised at finding a close statistical association. Money's variation could be the result of changes in income, as for example if the central bank followed a "needs of trade" rule, or money and income could be joint effects of something else, such as a change in demand for imports. "F & S's monetary interpretation of history requires not simply that monetary contractions and major business contractions are statistically associated, but two further propositions: Preventing monetary contraction would have prevented these business contractions, and nothing else would have done so. The authors require also, of course, the corresponding propositions regarding marked expansions of money income" (1965, p. 481).

Tobin gave Friedman and Schwartz more credit in this review than he would several years later in the *post hoc* piece for recognizing the two-way nature of money–income causality. He cited passages from the *Monetary History* and "Money and Business Cycles" where they distinguish the predominant direction of causality in short- and long-run and minor and major changes in income. But he complained that they were not content to make a good case for the claim that "money matters"; they slipped from there into the conclusion that "money is all that matters."

They have put to rout the neo-Keynesian, if he exists, who regards monetary events as mere epiphenomena, postscripts added as afterthoughts to the nonmonetary factors that completely determine income, employment, and even prices. But in their zeal and exuberance Friedman and his followers often seem to go – though perhaps less in this book than elsewhere – beyond their own logic and statistics to the other extreme, where the stock of money becomes the necessary and sufficient determinant of money income. Much as I admire their work, I cannot follow them there (1965, p. 481).[4]

### Friedman's response

Friedman divided his response to Tobin's review into two parts: misunderstandings and disagreement over minor details and deeper and more fundamental differences. The latter included differences over the relative stability of velocity and the multiplier, the channels of monetary impulses, the relative importance of wealth and substitution effects, and judgments about the relative importance of money–income causation in the two directions. Though there were these different dimensions of their disagreements, there was one unifying and consistent characteristic to them, according to Friedman. This was that their differences were about empirical generalizations rather than economic theory. Thus one could expect to narrow and perhaps even resolve the differences by seeking empirical evidence. Friedman went further than this and argued that their differences *were* being narrowed by the accumulation of empirical evidence. Friedman pointed out that his debate with Tobin was not confined to the material in the *Monetary History;* to understand their debate one should look beyond that particular book and Tobin's review of it. This broader field of dispute was, as we have seen, evident in portions of Tobin's review.

Friedman wrote that he agreed completely with Tobin's interpretation of the claim that money services are a luxury as simply another way of saying that velocity declines with income. He had confidence in this "first-order generalization" because the time-series and cross-section evidence were consistent. However, there was no theoretical reason a priori to expect this result from the data. To Tobin this was dangerously close to a tautology; to Friedman it was a genuine empirical generalization. Yet Friedman thought nothing of importance hung on the question of whether money's services are a luxury. He

---

[4] The references to "Friedman and his followers," "this book [and] elsewhere," suggest that Tobin's target in these comments was broader than the *Monetary History.* Friedman's controversial paper with David Meiselman, "The Relative Stability of Monetary Velocity and the Investment Multiplier in the United States, 1897–1958" was published in 1963 and circulated for several years before.

recognized that he and Schwartz shifted emphasis away from the transaction motive for holding money to the asset motive but thought this shift was justified by the large holdings of money in excess of what would be needed for bare-bones transactions purposes.

With respect to the postwar rise in velocity, Friedman stated that he and Schwartz regarded their explanation as tentative. "The problem at issue is really the variables that are important in the demand function for money. My only firm conclusion about that problem is that as yet we have a long way to go before we can be sure that we have a sufficiently tight explanation of the demand for money to allow us to use a single function for a period as long as a century and for both long-term trends and cyclical fluctuations" (1964c, p. 13).

On the matter of Friedman and Schwartz's focus on price level expectations to explain velocity's behavior during certain time periods and their exclusion of explicit interest rates on near-money assets from the analysis, Friedman said that he accepted Tobin's suggestion that the variable they used and the variables they omitted were parallel, that is, there is no better theoretical justification for including one than the other. Their reason for giving relatively little attention to explicit rates is that these do not change value very much over time, whereas expectations occasionally change radically.

Did Friedman and Schwartz believe that the stock of money is the necessary and sufficient determinant of economic activity? Tobin said that when they shifted their position from "money matters" to "money is all that matters," he could not go along. Friedman responded: "Neither can I, and I should very much appreciate it if Tobin would point out statements by us in this book or elsewhere that seem to him to be at that other extreme. We were aware of the danger of being misinterpreted in this fashion, and tried to go out of our way to reduce the danger to a minimum. Apparently, we failed, and often" (1964c, p. 16) After quoting three passages from the *Monetary History*, Friedman concluded, "I am hard put to see how we could have leaned over much further backward without toppling over" (1964c, p. 17). He then concluded his reactions to matters of "misinterpretation" and "minor differences on empirical matters" with a summary statement that was itself meant to clear the air on how just much he and Schwartz thought money matters:

We do hold the view that a substantial rise in the rate of change of the quantity of money over a short period is a necessary and sufficient condition for a substantial rise in the rate of change of *money* income; and that a substantial decline in the rate of change of the quantity of money over a short period is a necessary and sufficient condition for a substantial decline in the rate of change of *money* income (1964c, pp. 17–18, emphasis in original).

This is a clear statement that for substantial changes in money income over short periods, money growth is *the only* effective cause. What is left open is the matter of interpreting "substantial" and "short."

In Friedman's view the "deeper difference" between his and Schwartz's position and Tobin's was over the *relative importance* of forward and reverse causation (my terms) between money and income and the channels that transmit money's influence. He stressed that their differences, though major, concerned questions of degree and were capable of being closed with empirical evidence. They were not at bottom "theoretical" differences.

Tobin remarked that he thought it surely must be the case that money created through bank loans would have a larger effect on income than money created through bank swaps with the public of Treasury bills. Friedman responded, "It seems plausible to me too that there should be a difference but not at all obvious that the difference is quantitatively appreciable. Maybe it is. But how does Tobin know? What empirical evidence can he cite in support of what 'seems indisputable,' once someone disputes it? Surely the issue is an empirical one" (1964c, p. 19). He stated that his experience in doing empirical work on the money–income relation suggested to him that what matters is only the size of money increments, not how the money is created.

Tobin also compared the effect on employment and income of purchasing a million dollars worth of gold with the purchase of a million dollars worth of government securities, to which Friedman asked:

What is his evidence for this proposition? My tentative judgment is that the results will be so nearly identical that the difference will not show up in anything like the crude evidence we have. I base this on my empirical observation that changes in the quantity of money seem to bear the same relation to economic activity under very different sets of monetary institutions involving differences in the sources of the changes in the quantity of money. Maybe I am wrong, but surely it is not inconceivable I am right. How can Tobin be so dogmatic unless he had some empirical evidence? (1964c, pp. 19–20).

Friedman noted Tobin's judgment that "F & S's monetary interpretation of history requires not simply that monetary contractions and business contractions are statistically associated, but two further propositions: Preventing monetary contraction would have prevented business contraction, and nothing else would have done so. The authors require also, of course, the corresponding propositions regarding expansions" (1964c, p. 23).[5] This amounts to saying that monetary contraction (expansion) is both necessary and sufficient for business contraction (expansion). Friedman responded that this particular statement is incorrect as an interpretation of their views because it does not allow a distinction between mild and severe expansions and contractions. If the statement is restricted to severe fluctuations, then it correctly conveys their position. Friedman repeated that he and Schwartz were very careful in the *Monetary History* and "Money and Business Cycles" to make the distinction. They claimed that "money is all that matters" only in the transformation from mild to severe contractions and inflations.

Friedman considered this point a matter of misinterpretation, but one that led to a real and substantial issue with Tobin. Tobin's interpretation continued: "I believe that this amounts to saying that velocity is independent of the stock of money" (1964c, p. 24).[6] Friedman wanted to assert in the strongest terms that he did not believe velocity was independent of the stock of money. In fact he and Schwartz produced evidence showing that with velocity defined conventionally, as the ratio of current income to money, there is a systematic relationship. But, this relationship is qualitatively the opposite of that implied by Keynesian doctrines of the liquidity trap or interest inelasticity of spending. The association is positive over the cycle, and through secular inflations, it is initially inverse and then positive.

Friedman rejected the all or nothing identification of their differences implied by the liquidity trap doctrine or by Tobin's interpretation of his claim as "money is all that matters." He summarized his and Schwartz's view as that there is on average a strong linkage between money and income, but from one experience to another the strength is variable. Though this is markedly different from saying that money is all that matters, it is easy to see how Tobin would have been frustrated in attempting to nail down exactly what their belief about the relationships was.[7] But Friedman's characterization of the substance and the state of his views makes clear that at this point in his

---

[5] See Tobin (1965, p. 481).

[6] See Tobin (1965, p. 481).

[7] Tobin said in his rejoinder in the *post hoc* exchange, "I am continually perplexed by Friedman's propensity in professional debate to evade by verbal quibbling the responsibility and the credit for the characteristic propositions of 'monetarism' associated with his name" (1970b, p. 329).

research program he thought his knowledge of the precise mechanism by which money affects income was rudimentary.

### Culbertson's review

John Culbertson continued his methodological and theoretical critique of Friedman's monetary research program in a review article of the *Monetary History* for the *National Banking Review* (1964). This review so provoked Friedman that he threatened to sue Culbertson. The review is particularly interesting, for half of it is largely favorable, or at least favorable on one level. Culbertson, like Friedman and Schwartz, believed in the causal power of changes in the money supply, in the usefulness of monetary theory as a framework for macroeconomics, and in the Federal Reserve's responsibility for the severity of the Great Depression. On all three of these issues Culbertson proclaimed the *Monetary History* a success. He wrote:

It seems to me that the case for the orthodox monetary theory, as buttressed by the detailed evidence offered here, is unassailable. The authors demonstrate that generally — and surely in a number of crucial test cases — the behavior of the money supply reflected political, international, and institutional considerations, and thus the influence must be viewed as running from money to income (1964, p. 360).

With this affirmation of Friedman and Schwartz's history, what was there that was negative in the review? We get a hint very early when Culbertson says "This study, true to its title, is straight economic history" (1964 p. 359). Friedman and Schwartz described the book as a prologue to their planned "Trends and Cycles." Culbertson saw the work as history without theory. He thought Friedman and Schwartz's historical evidence lent support to orthodox monetary theory but that the evidence was in no way tied specifically to Friedman's own monetary theory. This became one of the themes of his review, that Friedman's monetary theory was unorthodox, and the *Monetary History* provided no evidence in support of his theory as opposed to orthodox theory.

Culbertson identified the central issue of the *Monetary History* as money's role as an independent causal agent. He argued that Friedman and Schwartz's conclusions, gleaned from their massive set of data — that money is closely associated with income and prices, that the relationship is stable, and that monetary changes often have independent origins — were generally correct and consistent with the quantity theory of neoclassical economists such as Irving Fisher and Alfred Marshall. He saw their history as counterevidence to Keynesian and other secular stagnation views that money matters hardly at all.[8]

Thus, the principal contest of ideas arising from this work is not one between orthodox monetary theory and Friedmanian innovations, but rather between orthodox monetary theory and the modern belief that the money supply is not an important causal variable. . . .

It seems to me, as is indicated below, that the antimonetary doctrines are untenable on their face and that the excellent and detailed review of the chronology of the Great Depression provided by Friedman and Schwartz may be what is needed finally to force a reconsideration of this whole period (1964, pp. 360–1).

The theoretical principle that Culbertson blamed for what he viewed in concert with Friedman and Schwartz as disastrous monetary policy during the Great Depression was the idea that the quality of credit is more important than the quantity of money. He saw this as the foundation of Keynesian analysis of the Depression.

However, this affirmation of Friedman and Schwartz's work as historians left him plenty room to criticize. "What this book supports is the basic premise of orthodox monetary theory and not specifically the Friedman version of monetary theory. Indeed, in some respects the interpretation embodied in this book is inconsistent with distinctively Friedmanian doctrines" (1964, p. 361). Like Tobin, Culbertson viewed the medium of exchange function as the heart of orthodox monetary theory. Furthermore, he argued, the crucial place of this function has been established by "a broad empirical review of the operation of economic institutions and behavior" (1964, p. 371). Friedman and Schwartz were right to be concerned to establish empirically the independence of monetary changes in order to determine the direction of causation. But, Culbertson argued, the supply of medium of exchange assets, whether in a commodity or fiat money system, is more independent of demand than the supply of time deposits and other short-term savings assets. These are subject to more feedback causation.

Culbertson contended that much of Friedman and Schwartz's discussion of the reasons for money's macroeconomic significance, that it is legal tender or generally acceptable, or that it is "full of mystery and paradox," applied only to the medium of exchange. He noted their partly pragmatic rationalization for including time deposits as money: (1) in addition to the medium of exchange function, money serves

---

[8] Culbertson had in mind specifically the hypotheses that the Great Depression was caused by the collapse of the stock market, exhaustion of investment opportunities with the end of the frontier, or declining birth rates.

as a "temporary abode of purchasing power", (2) the observed stability and regularity of the relationship between the broader aggregate and money income, and (3) separate data for demand and time deposits do not extend before 1914. He argued that this pragmatic compromise of theory is unjustifiable.[9] Choosing the aggregate that provides the best fit throws the medium of exchange function "out the window."

But what then of the identification problem and specification of the independent variable for statistical analysis? Is not identification of the independent variable or of the direction of causation precisely what is at issue in the major thesis of the book? Is not a methodology neglecting these problems essentially a return to naive empiricism, a hunting license for spurious correlations? (1964, pp. 371–72)

Culbertson considered three aspects of Friedman and Schwartz's concept and theory of velocity: their pragmatic definition of velocity corresponding to their pragmatic definition of money, their persistence in seeking a simple (few right-hand side variables) equilibrium theory of velocity, and the absence of the long and variable lag doctrine from their discussion of velocity.

Culbertson concluded his criticism with a methodological interpretation of their work that must surely have been the point that Friedman considered libelous. He characterized Friedman's methodological position as "narrow empiricism." This requires that theories be equilibrium theories and that they provide simple explanations of a limited data set. Thus, the money demand function is expected to have a small set of right-hand side variables, but it is also expected to account for the secular and cyclical behavior of velocity by allowing for shifts through time. Culbertson characterized the alternative mainstream methodology as "broad empiricism." This calls for taking care in identifying the model "on the basis of all known evidence." "It is aiming toward a more careful interpretation of the meaning of statistical tests and of findings of historical association, toward more explicit and careful identification of economic models" (1964, p. 375).

The potentially libelous remarks concern how Friedman used his methodology:

Then the theory must be characterized on the basis of neoclassical conceptions of methodology as a deliberate misrepresentation of the truth, one

---

[9] Culbertson judged that when the goals of using the most appropriate data and extending the time period covered by the historical survey come into conflict, the correct choice is to opt for the appropriate data. Otherwise the empirical conclusions for the entire period are jeopardized.

created by omitting some causal factors and contriving to find a spurious correlation in a limited body of data. In more modern terminology, the theory could be characterized as using a model that is deliberately misidentified to conform to a methodological prejudice (1964, p. 375).

Culbertson's concern with hidden motives was misplaced. There was nothing hidden about Friedman's methodology. The methods of the *Monetary History* were much the same as those of *A Theory of the Consumption Function*. The "narrow empiricism" that Culbertson objected to was endorsed by Friedman's Keynesian critic Tobin in his review. The methodology informing the methods was that which Friedman held since at least 1940 when he wrote his review of Triffin's *Monopolistic Competition and General Equilibrium Theory*. One might, as Culbertson did, accuse Friedman of foregoing the opportunity for a theoretical rationalization of the independence of money supply changes by opting for his pragmatic approach to the definition of money. But this need not lead to an accusation of deception.

Culbertson's charge also is surprising in that, as the review makes clear, he and Friedman were in agreement on the more important questions about economic policy and the historical record.[10] Their policy views placed them both outside the Keynesian mainstream. Perhaps this only caused their methodological differences to loom larger.[11] There was indeed an important difference between Friedman's Marshallian–National Bureau approach and the methodological mainstream. The methodological position that Culbertson labeled "broad empiricism" is the formalistic tradition that Friedman called Walrasian economics. Within this tradition, formal general-equilibrium theorizing is the better part of the game. It is considered preferable not to say anything unless you can say something with certainty. Thus Culbertson could conclude that, "If the crucial issue is identification of the independent variable, or determination of *what caused what* in the monetary equation, is it not pathetic to wind up with only a loose pronouncement about monetary change being sometimes a senior and sometimes an equal partner?" (1964, pp. 378–9, emphasis in original)

### Clower's review

Robert Clower's "Monetary History and Positive Economics" occupies a singular place among reviews of the *Monetary History*. Clower saw

[10] In his 1959 *Journal of Finance* article, Culbertson suggested that a rules-type policy would have been superior to the Fed's actual policy over the postwar period.
[11] One also thinks of the Chicago and Austrian traditions of economic liberalism as a similar case.

clearly that what was at stake between Friedman and his critics was not simply questions of whether money matters in the determination of income or what the transmission channel is for money's effects. He recognized that the issue was more fundamentally about methodology. Whereas Culbertson engaged Friedman in a methodological dispute, Clower took a position more distant from the issues. He understood clearly the nature of Friedman's distinctiveness. Clower saw Friedman as "the leading exponent of a radical research methodology which views much of formal economic analysis as 'disguised mathematics'; which regards theories as useful only if they 'fit as full and complete a set of related facts about the real world as it is possible to get'; which is contemptuous of any test of the validity of a hypothesis other than 'comparison of its predictions with experience'" (1964, p. 365). It is also an indication of Clower's insight into the methodological substratum of the *Monetary History* that the passages of Friedman's he quoted in his opening statement are not from the famous 1953 methodology essay but from "The Marshallian Demand Curve" (1949b). Clower recognized the Marshallian substance of Friedman's approach to monetary analysis.

Clower identified Friedman and Schwartz's analytical procedure, their method, in a passage from their summary chapter:

> The varied character of U.S. monetary history (from 1867 to 1960) renders this century of experience particularly valuable to the student of economic change. He cannot control the experiment, but he can observe monetary experience under sufficiently disparate conditions to sort out what is common from what is adventitious and to acquire considerable confidence that what is common can be counted on to hold under still other circumstances (Friedman and Schwartz, 1963b, p. 676; Clower, 1964, p. 367).

Clower interpreted this passage to mean that by viewing the economy as a dynamic system one can extract information from historical time series that allows distinction to be made between equilibrium and disequilibrium states. The information is contained in observed patterns of relations between the various variables. Stability of the relations indicates stability of the underlying system. Clower's interpretation contains an obvious reflection of one of the benchmark issues in Keynesian economics with which Clower himself was particularly concerned: the stability or instability of the economy (and stability and instability in economic theory). (See Clower, 1965.)

But there is much more in the review that is of particular significance for understanding causality issues. Clower saw Friedman and Schwartz's analytical framework as a way of identifying causes. "Moreover, we may attribute obvious deviations from 'normal' behavior to

various 'shocks,' some of which can be identified with specific historical events. In this manner, we may assign 'causal' significance to particular classes of events – 'monetary,' 'political,' 'technological,' etc. –
and perhaps even go so far as to assess the relative importance of each
as a source of economic change" (1964, p. 367). Though they had no
laboratory controls, Friedman and Schwartz were using the great experiment of monetary history to sort out and weigh the relative importance of causes and effects. Clower recognized the pedigree of
Friedman's methodology as few commentators have. He judged that
the methodology embodied in the *Monetary History* is "consistent with
what I know about the methodological views of the patron saint of
'positive economics,' Alfred Marshall" (1964, p. 367).

Clower noted that the starting point for Friedman and Schwartz,
once their data were in hand, was to establish patterns of empirical
regularities between variables such as the stock of money, income,
high-powered money, and velocity over the long run and through
business cycles. He approved of their heavy attention to the data and
judged that though the empirical relationships did not by themselves
make the underlying causal structure transparent, they did provide
patterns that any theory of the money economy should account for.
These regularities also lent credibility to any theory that could account for them. Thus Clower concluded that "the correlation consti-
tutes a promising point of departure for further research" (1964,
p. 369). The contrast with *post hoc* and "measurement without theory"
charges (see Chapters 5 and 7) could not be sharper.

Clower perceived the subtlety of the causality in Friedman and
Schwartz's analysis. On the surface, their seeking the simplest theory
that would account for the patterns in the data followed an "as if"
methodology that set aside questions of causality. "Their question
relates simply to the behavior of empirical data, not to the behavior of
people or markets. How the economic system *really* works is irrelevant; what Friedman and Schwartz want to know is whether the system works *as if* its object were to ensure the maintenance of some
'normal' relation between the stock of money and money income"
(1964, p. 369, emphasis in original). There is the universal question of
whether there is *any* way to distinguish causal relations from spurious
correlation. This posed for Clower as for formalist critics of Friedman and the National Bureau the question of whether "Friedman
and Schwartz's argument [is] directed toward the establishment of
causal rather than merely descriptive relations among economic phenomena" (1964, p. 370). In the end, contrary to surface appearances,
Clower saw Friedman and Schwartz making questions of causality

dominant in their analysis. He offered an explanation of how they made the transformation from "as if" use of theory to rationalize data patterns to an overriding concern for assigning causal responsibility.

Their first step was to show that the theoretical model can be used to summarize the facts represented by the data. Clower recognized that strictly within the *Monetary History*, Friedman and Schwartz did not adhere to Friedman's own methodological prescription to test models with data other than those from which the model is derived. However, he also recognized that their basic theoretical framework was the same as that in *A Theory of the Consumption Function*. Permanent income on the demand side and high-powered money on the supply were the key explanatory variables. So, when one's view of the theoretical model is extended beyond the *Monetary History*, there is a real sense in which the *Monetary History* provided a test of the model with data other than those from which the model was derived.

The second step in moving to causal analysis was identifying historical periods for which the model breaks down and giving a causal account of transitory factors responsible for the breakdown. In this step the causal role is filled by the transitory factors and their causes. Examples include the Federal Reserve's ineptitude during the 1930s and the changing expectations of economic stability after World War II.[12]

Their final step was to use the historical data to conduct "crucial" thought experiments to discriminate between alternative theoretical accounts of the correlations found in the data. This is the point at which they dealt with "reverse causation" accounts. This step also brought Friedman and Schwartz to their conclusion that the predominant channel of influence is from money to income rather than vice versa. And it reflects Friedman's methodological precept that ulti-

---

[12] This expectations variable originated in a comment by Reuben Kessel in Friedman's Workshop in Money and Banking. Friedman wrote to Schwartz in April 1960 and outlined the theoretical case for the variable and the results of some preliminary calculations. He said:

I must say I am very much encouraged by the results so far. If this works it will be the first real breakthrough we have had since we got the perm[anent] income measured income one. This is just the kind of variable we need. What has been puzzling me all along is that our predicted velocity and money stock fit the post war cyclical experience fine even though derived from a secular relation, yet they seem to be going haywire secularly. So we need a secular variable. Moreover, this secular variable makes real theoretical sense, doesn't conflict with anything else we have found, and offers the possibility of reconciling early deviations as well as recent ones. Hence my real interest (MF to AJS, April 16, 1960).

mately theories are tested by *confronting one another* in their relative ability to account for the data rather than in simply *confronting the data*.

Clower followed his reconstruction of Friedman and Schwartz's procedures with a comparison of them to the main tenets of the neo-Walrasian program. It was from this direction that persistent calls came for Friedman to identify the transmission mechanism for the effects of changes in the money supply. No account of the mechanism is given in the *Monetary History*.[13] The distinctive principle of the neo-Walrasian point of view is that market demand and supply relations be explicitly defined in terms of underlying microeconomic decision processes. For monetary theory the fundamental beliefs are that money matters little except in the long run, and legal-tender means of payment is the money that matters most. The short-run effects of money cannot be disentangled in data from effects of nonmonetary forces. The most important neo-Walrasian principle, according to Clower's account, is that most of the time, legal tender is only part of what people consider means-of-payment money, and the other part, debt money, is determined endogenously.

So Clower saw a key difference between Friedman and the neo-Walrasians concerning the matter of the independent causal role of money. But contrary to the belief that seemed to sustain Friedman's efforts throughout the course of his ongoing debate with the "money doesn't matter very much" neo-Walrasians, Clower argued that the differences would not be resolved by resorting to the facts. This was not because there were no facts, as some 1990s methodologists claim, but rather for two reasons. One, Friedman and the neo-Walrasians had different purposes for their models.[14] His was to explain historical experience, and theirs, to answer counterfactual questions regarding current policy options. The other reason was the scant chance for locating true causal relations in empirical data. According to Clower the question of how to distinguish causal from "merely descriptive" relations was not for economists but for philosophers, and the historical record of philosophy gave little basis for hope.

[13] Clower referred readers to "Money and Business Cycles" (Friedman and Schwartz, 1963a) for an "account of sorts."

[14] Clower did not actually say this as such. But he made the point that if two models are intended for different purposes, there is not a common objective standard for choosing between them. The reader is left with the implication that Friedman's and the neo-Walrasian's purposes are different.

In evaluating the fruits of the neo-Walrasian and Marshallian programs, Clower judged Friedman's approach superior in its record of producing empirical regularities that would stimulate further useful research. The successes included the consumption function, the accelerator, and the Phillips curve. These examples illustrate that for Clower the Walrasian–Marshallian duality superseded the more common Keynesian–monetarist duality for locating the distinctiveness of Friedman's work.[15] By contrast the neo-Walrasian program had, in Clower's view, yielded no novel and fruitful empirical results. For solving problems, developing and testing theoretical explanations of empirical relations, Clower saw no inherent advantage in the neo-Walrasian approach over the Marshallian. He judged the typical identification of econometric analysis with the neo-Walrasian approach, wherein Friedman's work did not qualify even to be called econometrics, as unjustified.

[15] Though Friedman was to become a critic of the Phillips curve, which was part of Keynesian doctrine, he admired the work of its creator, A. W. Phillips. In 1955 and again in 1960 Friedman tried to recruit Phillips to a faculty position at the University of Chicago.

# CHAPTER 7

# *Post hoc ergo propter hoc:* Part II

## Introduction

The most famous encounter of Friedman with another economist over the causal significance of his evidence on the lag of monetary policy was with James Tobin in the May 1970 *Quarterly Journal of Economics*. In some respects this was a replay of the exchanges ten years earlier with Culbertson and Clark. But no doubt because of Tobin's greater stature than Culbertson in the profession, because of the growth of Friedman's stature and notoriety in the dominant Keynesian milieu over the ensuing decade, and the widely held belief that money doesn't matter, the Tobin–Friedman exchange came to overshadow the earlier one between Culbertson and Friedman. Culbertson was no Keynesian; his methodological strictures against Keynesian consumption and money demand functions were just as severe as those against Friedman's lag doctrine. (See Culbertson, 1968, ch. 5.)

Culbertson had reacted to one report of Friedman's empirical evidence on the lag, his 1959 Joint Economic Committee testimony, and two of his policy proposals, "A Monetary and Fiscal Framework for Economic Stability" (1948b) and *A Program for Monetary Stability* (1960).[1] By 1970, when Tobin made his *post hoc* critique, Friedman had published three other statements of the fruits of his and Schwartz's empirical research that were receiving great attention. These were, with Schwartz as coauthor, "Money and Business Cycles" (1963a) and the *Monetary History* (1963b) and, with Friedman as sole author, "The Monetary Studies of the National Bureau" (1964a). He had also published, with David Meiselman, a direct empirical test of Keynesian and quantity theory hypotheses in "The Relative Stability of Monetary Velocity and the Investment Multiplier in the United States, 1897–1958" (1963). So when Tobin accused Friedman of com-

---

[1] Though not cited in the article, Friedman's 1959 article on money demand can also be seen as background for Culbertson's critique. See Culbertson (1968, ch. 5).

mitting the *post hoc ergo propter hoc* fallacy, there was a significant body
of Friedman's work on record, especially empirical work, and this
contained a substantial challenge to the dominant Federal Reserve
and Keynesian doctrine. Because of both the larger record of Friedman's work and Tobin's position in the Keynesian camp, he had ample
means and reason to mount a critique.

In between the Culbertson critique and Tobin's there were two
other *post hoc ergo propter hoc* charges from Keynesians. The first was
from John Kareken and Robert Solow in a paper that was published
in 1963 but circulated widely for a couple years before, making it
almost contemporaneous with Culbertson's. Then two years before
his famous *post hoc* article, Tobin joined William Brainard in such a
critique. In this chapter we examine these three *post hoc* critiques from
Friedman's Keynesian critics. The rejection of Friedman's work on
monetary lags became part of the context for demands that he reveal
the insides of the "black box" of monetarism and "write down his
model," which resulted in his publishing in 1970 "A Theoretical
Framework for Monetary Analysis" and in 1971 "A Monetary Theory
of Nominal Income," which the next chapter covers.[2]

### Kareken and Solow's critique
### and attempt to estimate lags

Evidence from the Keynesian side was presented by John Kareken
and Robert Solow in the Commission on Money and Credit's *Stabilization Policies* (1963). Friedman read the prepublication draft of
Kareken–Solow at about the same time that he was responding to
Culbertson and to Clark and made brief reference to it in his response
to Culbertson (1961). In a short *American Economic Review* comment
(1964b) he also gave attention to their empirical analysis, claiming
that their technique was incapable of discriminating between policy
lags and any other sources of serial correlation in the target variable.

[2] Paul Samuelson's comments in a *Journal of Money, Credit, and Banking* symposium typify critics' use of the "black box" trope:

My gravest objection to garden-variety monetarism is that it is a "black box" theory. Its
alleged empirical *post hoc* regularities stand on their own merits. . . . In the last fifteen
years I have again and again been chided by monetarists for insisting upon tracing out
all the channels of credit and fiscal operations. . . . Instead I have been urged to believe
in the philosophy of "as if," accepting the fact that changes in M are as inevitably
followed by changes in GNP as death follows the shooting of a gun. Out of considerable
experience, I have learned that it is inexpedient to trust in mechanical empirical regularities not spelled out by plausible economic theory (1970, pp. 43–4).

Kareken and Solow presented both a critique of Friedman's work on lags and some preliminary empirical results on lags derived from what they considered an appropriate theoretical model. They rejected Friedman's conclusions about policy lags as untenable, both logically and empirically. As was the case for Culbertson, their logical point was a rejection of the National Bureau method that amounted to the old "measurement without theory" charge.

Friedman has used the length and reliability of his lag as strong evidence that in the mutual interaction between the monetary sphere and the level of economic activity the causal thrust is primarily from the former to the latter. Stripped to bare essentials, the Friedman–Sprinkel method is simply to plot a time series of some measure of the rate of change of the seasonally corrected stock of money. If this series is compared with the National Bureau reference dates for general cyclical peaks and troughs, it is found that with great uniformity the peaks and troughs of the cycles in the monetary change series precede the business cycle peaks and troughs in the manner described. Since (to what degree of approximation?) the stock of money and its rate of change are what the monetary authorities wish them to be, we may identify the cause to be the peak or trough in monetary changes and the long-delayed effect to be the corresponding peak or trough in business activity (1963, pp. 15–16).[3]

They illustrated the futility of Friedman's causal inferences with a reductio ad absurdum. Kareken and Solow suggested supposing that monetary policy is used successfully to offset all disturbances that would otherwise buffet income. Then the data would reveal peaks and troughs of money growth accompanied by a steady income series, and one would conclude from this that money has no effect on income. This illustrated, according to Kareken and Solow, that "one cannot deduce conclusions about the effects of monetary policy or their timing without making some hypothesis, explicit or implicit, about what the course of events would have been had the monetary authorities acted differently" (1963, p. 16).

Kareken and Solow argued that only on rare occasions can one make causal claims on the basis of *ex post* data, for such claims require that all of the relevant *ceteris paribus* factors are accounted for. Thus, "there is no evading the necessity of beginning with some kind of model which permits one, for better or worse, to estimate the *ceteris paribus* effects of monetary policy" (1963, p. 16).[4]

After pointing out the mathematical reason for a rate of change series to lead a corresponding level series, Kareken and Solow cut through the issue of whether $\Delta M$ or $M$ is appropriate, arguing that

[3] The reference is to Sprinkel (1959).
[4] See Culbertson (1968, ch. 5) for comparison.

neither is. The monetary variable should instead be something that the Federal Reserve controls directly, that is, it should be a policy instrument. They pointed out that this has implications for the nature of the lag; it becomes the time between a policy action and the consequent effect on income. This was the same point Culbertson had made.

Kareken and Solow used Friedman and Schwartz's data to argue that $\Delta M$ and $\Delta Y$ move pretty much simultaneously.[5] They drew the following conclusion from lead-lag patterns and correlations:

> The most that we can squeeze out by way of a lead for the money supply is three months. The indubitable lead of the change in the money supply over the level of output follows arithmetically from this and has no causal significance at all. We must stress that it will not do to say, like a latter-day Galileo: "But nevertheless $\Delta M$ leads Q." True enough, it does. But so does $\Delta Q$ lead Q, as we have just shown. And it is no doubt equally true that $\Delta Q$ leads M. None of this can possibly offer any firm evidence about the web of cause and effect relationships connecting the real and monetary aspects of economic events, nor can it offer any *ex ante* guide to monetary policy (1963, p. 24).

However, unlike Clark, Culbertson, and Tobin, Kareken and Solow did not stop with their critique of Friedman's evidence. Rather, they made a long presentation of their own evidence on the influence of monetary policy on investment. They broke the total lag into its components and produced separate estimates via ordinary least squares (OLS) of an infinite distributed lag equation. For example, they regressed the Federal Reserve's monthly index of production of business equipment on the Department of Commerce index of new orders for nonelectrical machinery and lagged values of the production index. This was intended to give an estimate of the lag between the investment decision and production of capital goods. To explain new orders of nonelectrical machinery (a proxy for the investment decision), they experimented with several equations, including as explanatory variables combinations of industrial production, industrial capacity, net corporate profits, bond interest rates, and utilization of industrial capacity. They gave attention to identification problems, as one would expect in light of their criticism of Friedman for not having an adequate theoretical model, but in the end waved these problems off and used only OLS, presuming that their equation was an investment demand function.

In addition to fixed investment, Kareken and Solow estimated equations for inventory investment. They again encountered identi-

[5] Kareken and Solow used indexes of real economic activity, in contrast with the National Bureau's nominal index.

fication problems in the course of discovering a statistical regularity by way of what they admitted was statistical fishing.

As it happens, in the course of some statistical exploration of inventory investment, we did come upon one model in which a measurable interest rate effect on inventories does appear. The estimated interest elasticity, as will appear, is not large, but it has the right sign and is statistically significant (1963, pp. 39–40).

They warned readers about the hazards of spurious correlation made more dangerous by the ease with which investigators can experiment with equations on digital computers, and about the importance of being circumspect until empirical relationships can be properly identified with economic forces. But these identification pitfalls were not sufficient to restrain Kareken and Solow from presenting their discovery and investigating the implied lead–lag pattern over an eight-quarter period following the Fed's "engineering" of a change in short-term bank rates.

In trying to settle on a measure of the policy instrument, Kareken and Solow considered gross and net bank reserves.[6] They argued that over longer runs, the Fed exercises control over gross reserves; thus this is the appropriate instrument. Over shorter runs, the Fed controls net reserves. The problem once again was that of identifying demand and supply relations. To explore the relationship between changes in net and gross reserves, Kareken and Solow regressed the latter on the former. The estimated coefficient was 1.08, which implied that a $1 increase in net reserves by the Fed would create $1.08 in gross reserves. This was at odds with Kareken and Solow's a priori expectation that banks partially offset the Fed's open market operations by borrowing or paying back at the discount window. At first glance the problem with this equation seemed rooted in the fact that their estimate for the constant term was negative. But when they forced a zero intercept the coefficient remained greater than one for net reserves. They finally solved the problem by transforming both variables to first differences. Their justification for doing so was on two grounds, "statistical" and "economic." Statistically this eliminated the problem of a slope coefficient greater than one. "Economically the really pragmatic problem is how effectively the Federal Reserve can *change* the gross reserves of the member banks by *changing* their net reserves" (1963, p. 49, emphasis in original). But once again the estimates seemed perverse, for at 0.82, the slope coefficient suggested that over the long run the Fed could change gross reserves by only

---

[6] In current terminology these are total and unborrowed reserves.

$0.82 for any $1 injection or retraction of net reserves. So in the end Kareken and Solow decided to suppress the constant term in their regression equation.

The point of going through this in some detail is to show that when faced with the problems of actually estimating lead–lag patterns from historical data, Kareken and Solow found themselves experimenting with different sets of variables, various transformations of the variables, and various functional forms just as Friedman did. Their discussion of how they produced the estimates reveals an iterative juggling of the a priori theoretical framework they began with and the empirical estimates their computer produced. Though they recognized the importance of identification to assure that estimates correspond with theory and that the *ceteris paribus* conditions are met, in the end they backed away from identification. Discussing the market for bank loans, Kareken and Solow wrote:

We are faced, then, with one of the classical econometric problems: the simultaneous estimation of a supply function and a demand function. Methods for tackling this problem are known, and are the subject of much discussion and controversy. For our purposes, however, a direct attack along these lines has a number of disadvantages. The approved statistical methods are laborious. Also, they tend to enlarge the problem: it is easy to imagine starting from a model of the bank-loan market and little by little discovering that nothing can be attempted without a complete macroeconomic model of everything. Moreover, the newer methods have not been especially successful even in analyzing simple markets, and this is not a simple market (1963, pp. 52–3).

To ensure that their pragmatic methods did not obscure their methodological principles, they included a statement in a footnote that says: "This does not by any means imply that there is something wrong with modern simultaneous equation methods; to the contrary, it suggests that there may be something wrong with methods which ignore this problem" (1963, p. 53, n. 36).

In a joint summary with Albert Ando and E. Cary Brown, who wrote a companion study of fiscal policy lags, Kareken and Solow described their evidence as "fragmentary," "tentative," and "piecemeal."

When we began our work we expected that our main job would be to study very closely the detailed timing relations implicit in already established quantitative measures of the effectiveness of monetary and fiscal policy. We soon realized that no such foundation of established quantitative knowledge existed about (1) the working of the money and credit mechanism or (2) a large portion of the mechanism through which fiscal policy works (1963, p. 1).

They concluded that the (total) lag was neither so long as Friedman portrayed nor as short as the more optimistic proponents of monetary policy fine tuning at the Federal Reserve suggested. Yet their own evidence suggests a lag longer than Friedman's estimate of sixteen months for business cycle peaks and twelve months for troughs.[7] Their criticism of Friedman's methods notwithstanding, Kareken and Solow's attempt to estimate the monetary policy lag, the first attempt made from within the neo-Walrasian–Keynesian camp, reveals the formidable difficulties of trying to implement neo-Walrasian principles.

## Brainard and Tobin

The next Keynesian *post hoc* critique of Friedman's causality was the first of a pair by James Tobin, this one written with William Brainard for the 1967 AEA meeting (1968). They used simulations from a structural model of a "fictitious" economy to demonstrate that in a highly interdependent financial system, temporal priority will not necessarily correspond to causal priority. This exercise was right in line with Culbertson's critique in its strong antiempirical bent. Brainard and Tobin thought not only that Friedman's empirical technique was incapable of uncovering structural parameters; they expressed a general skepticism about the potential for recovering the parameters with econometric treatment of actual data.

The Brainard–Tobin article also resembles Culbertson's in that despite not producing any empirical evidence and despite their skepticism over the potential for producing meaningful evidence, they believed their model actually captured some essentials of the economic system. A disclaimer made at the beginning of the paper would seem to indicate otherwise: "We fully realize, of course, that this procedure cannot tell us anything about the real world" (1968, p. 99). This is followed closely by their statement that "we have tried to formulate a model we believe in qualitatively, though of course the numerical parameters are arbitrary" (1968, p. 99). Thus, Brainard and Tobin's position on the role of empirical analysis seems to be captured in the following three propositions:

(1)    The structure of the economy short of numerical values of the parameters can be known without empirical evidence;

(2)    The role of empirical evidence is for quantitative measurement of the qualitatively known parameters;

---

[7] See Mayer (1967). Mayer's article includes a survey of empirical studies of monetary policy lags and a critique of Friedman and Schwartz's estimate of the lag's variability.

(3)   The structural parameters are not recoverable via empirical
       evidence.

Propositions 1 and 2 are mutually consistent, as are 1 and 3, and
perhaps even 2 and 3. However the latter pair together delimit the job
for empirical analysis and at the same time indicate its futility.

The Brainard–Tobin model contains thirteen equations for determining equilibrium values of thirteen variables. There are also nine
exogenous variables. They explored the dynamics of adjustment to
changes in various policy and other exogenous variables. This whole
exercise was "inspired" by Friedman's analysis of policy lags, and in
particular by the authors' presumption that Friedman used his evidence to prove the direction of causation between money and economic activity. The lesson Brainard and Tobin wanted their readers to
learn is indicated in the following quotation:

In a highly interdependent dynamic system, the chronological order in which
variables reach cyclical peaks and troughs proves nothing whatever about
directions of causation. Although few people would seriously claim that cyclical lead–lag patterns are a reliable guide to direction of causal influence,
believers in the causal primacy of monetary variables have offered the timing
order of variables in business cycles as partial evidence for their position.
Simulation of cycles of known exogenous or causal source is a good way to
show that observed timing order can be very misleading. . . .
      Even though leads and lags do not provide information about causation, if
they could be depended on, they would be extremely useful in forecasting the
future course of the economy. Unfortunately, the tables provide numerous
examples of variables which lead another endogenous variable when the
economy is driven by one exogenous variable and lag it when driven by
another exogenous variable (1968, pp. 120–2).

This suggests that a well-specified model that yields empirical regularities may be out of reach. The economy's structure may be so
complex that there is no potential for exploiting lag patterns.


### Tobin's post hoc ergo propter hoc article

Tobin opened his 1970 article with an interpretation of Friedman's
claims about the causal relation between money and nominal income.
Interpretation would become an important part of the dispute, with
Tobin expressing frustration at Friedman's seeming tendency to
make bold statements and then, when challenged, to draw back. His
interpretation of Friedman's stand was: (1) "changes in the supply of
money M (defined to include time deposits) are the principal cause of
changes in money income Y," and (2) "in his less guarded and more

popular expositions, he comes close to asserting that they are the unique cause" (1970a, p. 301). The second point is exactly what Culbertson insisted Friedman *must* believe to give his estimates validity. Tobin placed the empirical evidence Friedman marshaled in support of these conclusions into three types: historical case studies, of which the *Monetary History* was the most important example; single equation time-series regressions, of which Friedman and Meiselman (1963) was the example;[8] and timing of leads and lags of cyclical turning points, which is found in Friedman's Joint Economic Committee testimony (1959a) and "Monetary Studies of the National Bureau" (1964a) and Friedman and Schwartz's "Money and Business Cycles" (1963a). The third type of evidence was Tobin's concern (as it had been Culbertson's) because, according to Tobin, production of this evidence constituted an important part of the National Bureau business-cycle program and because much of the modern quantity theory's appeal was based on this evidence.

In this interpretation of how the lead and lag evidence was used lies the significance of Tobin's title, "Money and Income: Post Hoc Ergo Propter Hoc?" His methodological point was not just that correlation does not prove causation. Friedman certainly would not take issue with that claim in principle. Tobin's charge was that by using the timing evidence without a theoretical foundation, Friedman made it the basis of belief in the causal efficacy of changes in the money supply. Friedman's practice was in conflict with the principle that correlation does not prove causation. His followers were being duped, and this accounted for the "popular and semiprofessional appeal" of the quantity theory. This is another variant of the charge against Mitchell, Burns, and the National Bureau, that their business-cycle work was "measurement without theory." As Koopmans did in the 1940s, Tobin portrayed National Bureau work as pseudoscience. But Tobin's charge depended crucially on the premise that the lead–lag evidence was the basis for Friedman's or others' belief in the quantity theory.

Tobin mentioned Friedman's own qualifications and warnings about drawing inferences solely from timing evidence but went on to state that the purpose of his paper was to spell out the lead–lag patterns of an ultra-Keynesian model and "one of Friedman's own" to illustrate "the dangers of accepting timing evidence as empirical proof of propositions about causation" (1970a, p. 303). Tobin re-

---

[8] Tobin cited Anderson and Jordan (1968) as another example of single equation time-series regression studies in support of Friedman's conclusions.

peated Kareken and Solow's point (and Culbertson's and Clark's) that Friedman would find the money stock growth rate leading the level of income even if the two levels series were perfectly coincident. He made no reference to either Culbertson or Clark and referred to Friedman's 1961 response to Culbertson as if it were a response to Kareken and Solow. This curious pattern of references can be accounted for by two facts. Kareken and Solow's paper circulated for some time in manuscript form before the Commission on Money and Credit volume came out. Secondly, Kareken and Solow were in the mainstream of the Keynesian macroeconomics community, and Culbertson was outside it.

Much of the article is Tobin's explanation of two models, one ultra-Keynesian and the other monetarist, and the implications that can be drawn from them about the timing of peaks and troughs of money and its growth rate and of income and its growth rate. In the Keynesian model the money supply is determined endogenously through the banking system's accommodation of the "needs of trade." The model is designed so that money has no causal role whatever in determining income. Yet it generates time series for money and income in which money's peaks and troughs lead income's. Tobin claimed that his "Friedman model" is implicit in "Money and Business Cycles." It features a money-demand function with permanent income as the only right-hand side variable, and an exogenous supply of money. A sine wave in the growth rate of the money supply generates the business cycle. So money supply changes cause the business cycle. However this model produces a time series in which the growth rate of money lags the growth rate of income, has a short lead over the level of income, and the level of money lags the level of income. Trend-corrected money also lags income.

Tobin compared these and other timing implications of the two models with the empirical evidence reported by Friedman and Schwartz (1963a) and Friedman (1961). He concluded that all of Friedman's evidence was consistent with the time series produced from the ultra-Keynesian model but not with those from the "Friedman model." He concluded the article with a complaint about the "two Friedmans," one of whom uses the permanent income hypothesis to explain procyclical movements of velocity but with the implication that changes in money have large and immediate effects on current income. The other Friedman explains the long and variable lag of money's effect on income as resulting from broad and diffuse channels for the transmission of money's effects.

### Friedman's response

Friedman developed three points in his reply (1970c) to Tobin. First, not surprisingly, was a reaction to the suggestion that the timing evidence was the basis for his belief in the quantity theory. The second, which is especially interesting, was that the concept of "principal cause" is fraught with difficulties. Recall Tobin's interpretation of Friedman as claiming that changes in the money supply are the principal cause of changes in income. Friedman's third point, which is less important than either of the first two for understanding his sensitivity to issues of causality or for understanding the important differences in Tobin's and Friedman's approaches, was that Tobin's models were not true to the theoretical premises they were intended to represent.

Friedman responded that Tobin's interpretation of his view, "that changes in the supply of money . . . are the principal cause of changes in money income" (Friedman, 1970c, p. 318), was not a statement that he had ever made, but it did capture the flavor of his views. Tobin's second interpretative statement, that "in his less guarded and more popular expositions, he comes close to asserting that they are the unique cause" (Friedman, 1970c, p. 318), was simply false. Friedman complained that what little textual evidence Tobin gave in support of these interpretations was taken selectively and used out of context to produce a caricature of his actual views.

The first statement of interpretation may have expressed the flavor of Friedman's views, but he nonetheless took issue with Tobin's use of the term "principal cause."

What impresses – or depresses – me about the statement is less its inaccuracy as a description of my views than its imprecision as a piece of scientific writing. What does "principal" cause mean? If there were an unambiguous way to count "causes," presumably it would mean, "accounts for more of the variance of money income than any other single cause" – which, if the causes were numerous enough, might be consistent with its accounting for only 1 per cent, say, of the variance of money income. Since there is no unambiguous way to count causes, the only way to assure that changes in the supply of money are *the* "principle cause," with no further qualification, would be for them to account for more than half of the variance of all changes in money income – from minute to minute, day to day, month to month, and so on – for periods of all durations (1970c, p. 319, emphasis in original).

In this retort Friedman took Tobin's causal interpretation of his views on money and produced two reductios ad absurdum. We see one of them in the passage quoted. The second is a suggestion by Friedman that by implication, if the money supply was frozen, changes in it could account for no part of the variance of nominal income. By this definition of cause, freezing the money supply *appears* to rob the money supply of causal power.[9] What Friedman left unsaid is that this does not square with the belief that the money supply can be used to exert control over income.

Friedman attempted to set the record straight regarding his views on the relationship between money and income with a long quotation from "Monetary Studies of the National Bureau." This merits reproducing because it suggests that Friedman's view of this relationship was considerably more circumspect than Tobin's characterization indicates. It shows clearly that as early as 1964, when he penned the following passage for the National Bureau's 44th annual report, Friedman was wary of potential snares in explicitly causal language.

Money does matter and matters very much. Changes in the quantity of money have important, and broadly predictable, economic effects. Long-period changes in the quantity of money relative to output determine the secular behavior of prices. Substantial expansions in the quantity of money over short periods have been a major proximate source of the accompanying inflation in prices. Substantial contractions in the quantity of money over short periods have been a major factor in producing severe economic contractions. And cyclical variations in the quantity of money may well be an important element in the ordinary mild business cycle (1964a, p. 277; 1970c, pp. 319–20).

Notice that he shaded away from identifying money as cause, replacing the loaded word with "determine" (as a verb), "proximate source," "major factor," and "important element" (as modified nouns). The shift is significant in the context of the critiques of Culbertson and Clark, though in isolation the language appears unremarkable. Few if any readers could believe that Friedman was not attributing a causal role to money.

Friedman referred readers to other statements of his views, including his 1958 testimony before the Joint Economic Committee. In this statement made one year before that which drew the first *post hoc* charge by Culbertson, Friedman's focus was more on money and prices than money and real or nominal income. The topic of the committee hearing was "The Relationship of Prices to Economic Stability and Growth." Friedman divided his remarks into three parts: "Relation of Stock of Money to Prices over Longer Periods," "Relation of Stock of Money to Prices over Shorter Periods," and "Changes in Prices and Changes in Output over Longer Periods."

This division is significant, for it reflects the distinctions Friedman made about the evidence on causality for short-term and long-term

[9] This is the mirror image of the reductio ad absurdum Kareken and Solow used on Friedman.

periods. He stated that "the direction of influence between the money stock and income and prices is less clear-cut and more complex for the business cycle than for the longer movements. . . . Thus changes in the money stock are a consequence as well as an independent cause of changes in income and prices [over the cycle], though once they occur they will in their turn produce still further effects on income and prices" (1958, p. 179).[10] Friedman made it clear that he believed "reverse causation" was more important over the short term than the long term but in neither case did this nullify an influence running from money to prices (and real income over the cycle). He used the timing evidence as one, but only one, of several types of evidence to convince members of the Joint Economic Committee that "the money stock plays a largely independent role." In the context of Friedman's remarks, his claim was that "forward causation" is more important than "reverse causation."

The longer statement quoted in the preceding paragraph and other parts of Friedman's 1958 testimony reveal that at that time, shortly before his exchanges with Culbertson and Clark, Friedman was not so hesitant to use explicitly causal language. In his discussion of the long-term relations, he used the robustness of the comovement of money and prices over different types of monetary institutions as evidence that "substantial changes in the stock of money are both a necessary and a sufficient condition for substantial changes in the general level of prices" (1958, p. 173). Necessity and sufficiency are commonly used in definitions of causality. Years later (1985) in correspondence Friedman would respond to an analysis of the causality implicit in his monetary theory that was based on a form of necessity and sufficiency by disavowing the particular formulation and the general notion of causality.[11] But at the conclusion of his 1958 testimony, Friedman repeated the necessity and sufficiency claim for money in slightly different language:

An essential requirement for the avoidance of either substantial inflation or substantial deflation over the coming decades is the avoidance of a substantially more rapid or a substantially less rapid increase in the stock of money than the 3 to 5 per cent per year required for price stability. A substantially

[10] The way Friedman and Schwartz put it in the *Monetary History* was: "Mutual interaction, but with money rather clearly the senior partner in longer-run movements and in major cyclical movements, and more nearly an equal partner with money income and prices in shorter-run and milder movements – this is the generalization suggested by our evidence" (Friedman and Schwartz, 1963b, p. 695; Friedman, 1970c, p. 321).

[11] See Introduction and Hammond (1992b, appendix).

more rapid rate of growth in the money supply will inevitably mean inflation; conversely, continued inflation of substantial magnitude cannot occur without such a large rate of growth in the money supply. A substantially slower rate of growth in the money supply, let alone an absolute decline, will inevitably mean deflation; conversely, continued deflation of substantial magnitude cannot occur without such a small or negative rate of growth in the money supply (1958, p. 185).

Saying that "a substantially more rapid rate of growth in the money supply will inevitably mean inflation" is the same as saying that in the circumstances, substantially more rapid growth of the money supply is sufficient for inflation. Saying that "inflation of substantial magnitude cannot occur without such a large rate of growth in the money supply" is likewise another way of making the claim that rapid growth of the money supply is necessary for inflation. What Friedman left ambiguous is the exact meaning of "substantial" and "large." His insertion of this hedge was deliberate, indicating that he did not believe he had discovered exact and immutable quantitative constants. The changes in language between 1958 and 1964 suggest that the challenges of Culbertson and Clark left their mark at least on the way Friedman presented his case for the macroeconomic power of money. The challenges also left him prepared to mount a counterattack on Tobin based on the conceptual and semantic snares of causality.

Friedman confessed that perhaps early in his career he had thought timing evidence was decisive for establishing an independent role for money (though he doubted this), but for at least a decade he had been aware of its limitations.[12] This evidence, however, remained crucial for other purposes. First, if money does influence income and the relationship is to be exploited for countercyclical policy, prediction of when effects will take place is crucial. Otherwise policy changes will be misaimed. Second, if there is a lag in money's effect and this is not taken into account in estimates of the relationship between money and income, the estimates will be biased. Friedman closed his answer to the *post hoc* charge by suggesting the difference between himself and Tobin was that he had long since accepted the idea of the power of money to influence income whereas Tobin still did not.

### Tobin's rejoinder

In a rejoinder (1970b) Tobin accepted Friedman's protest of awareness that timing evidence cannot prove causation and that the perma-

---

[12] A decade back from the exchange with Tobin would place him in the debate with Culbertson and Clark.

nent income hypothesis does not explain the timing sequences as if Friedman had made a confession. He claimed that Friedman had still failed to confront the problem of having two models (the permanent income hypothesis and the broad and diffuse transmission mechanism) to explain two types of phenomena (the power of monetary policy and the long and variable lag), neither of which was consistent with both phenomena. Tobin required a general theory that would explain all observed aspects of the business cycle. Although Friedman would no doubt have liked very much to have such a theory, with his Marshallian problem-solving approach to economics he was less uncomfortable than Tobin with using different hypotheses to explain different dimensions of the business cycle.[13]

## Conclusion

The articles reviewed in this chapter comprise some of the more important examples of what is generally thought of as Keynesian criticism of Friedman's monetary analysis over most of a decade up to 1970. But the critiques share another perspective – one that dominated economics at that time more thoroughly than did Keynesianism: This is neo-Walrasianism. Its principles included heavy emphasis on detailed theoretical specification in advance of and as guide for empirical analysis. Friedman's work was seen as open to the *post hoc ergo propter hoc* charge because he did not write out an explicit model of the cause–effect relations, a model required to be written out prior to measurement and estimation. Lacking such a model, the implication could be drawn that his belief in the causal power of money was based on nothing but statistical correlation. Under the best of circumstances, correlation could not prove causation.

But Friedman's critics thought his problems ran deeper. His inattention to modeling left him open to identification problems and to mistaking mathematically inevitable relations for causal relations. We have seen in this chapter and Chapter 5 that these themes were not exclusively Keynesian: They were first developed in print by Culbertson, who was not a Keynesian and who shared Friedman's belief in the macroeconomic power of money. We have also seen that Friedman's critics by and large did not try to replace his estimates of the lag with estimates of their own free of the flaws of his. In the one case where this attempt was made, Kareken and Solow met little success. Clower (1964) suggested that Friedman's critics were like runners who train

---

[13] For an illustration in his methodology essay see (1953a, p. 37).

but never run a race. We have seen this to be the case. But it may be that from the neo-Walrasian point of view, the theoretical modeling *was* the race. Several of Friedman's critics suggest this by the comment that there are *no data* that correspond to a properly specified theoretical model of money's role in the economy.

# CHAPTER 8

# Friedman and his critics
# on the theoretical framework

## Introduction

This chapter considers what has come to be known as the debate over Friedman's monetary framework, which took place initially in a September/October 1972 JPE symposium and continued in a 1974 Brown University symposium. The debate was the culmination of the theoretical criticism of Friedman and Schwartz's work on money and business cycles.

By the late 1960s they had published several major works from their National Bureau research project; Friedman had published a number of critiques of Keynesian analysis and of Keynesian inspired large-scale econometric models; he had challenged the efficacy of fiscal policy, which was a cornerstone of Keynesian "New Economics" in Washington; and he had sent forth a number of Chicago-trained monetary economists into leading academic institutions. There was a distinctive Chicago school of thought on money and monetary policy. Indeed, Friedman's interest and skill at communicating his views to the general public through forums such as his *Newsweek* column and debates such as with President Kennedy's chairman of the Council of Economic Advisors, Walter Heller, made the Chicago school famous outside as well as within academia. But within the community of economists, doubts remained about the theoretical underpinnings of the Chicago doctrine.

Because the prevailing orthodoxy in macroeconomics was Keynesianism, and therefore most of Friedman's critics identified themselves as Keynesians, Friedman and his critics alike tended to set the distinctive ideas emanating from Chicago in opposition to Keynesianism. Friedman's explanation of the Great Depression, his diagnosis of the cause and cure of inflation, his advocacy of monetary policy "rules" to replace "discretion," and his doubts about the efficacy of fiscal policy not accommodated by monetary policy were set in juxtaposition to Keynesian doctrine. From 1956 on, after publication of "The Quantity Theory of Money – A Restatement" in *Studies in the Quantity Theory of Money,* Friedman identified his monetary economics with the quantity theory of money.

In 1968 Karl Brunner coined the term "monetarism."[1] This new label for the Chicago-school monetary doctrine was taken up by Friedman's former student David Fand in his 1970 article, "Monetarism and Fiscalism," and by Brunner again in his 1970 "The 'Monetarist Revolution' in Monetary Theory." Friedman himself continued to identify his beliefs, or more precisely the theoretical engine of analysis for his monetary research, as the "quantity theory of money" but went along with use of the new term as it came into common parlance.[2] By the late 1960s any doubt that monetarism posed challenges for macroeconomic doctrine and practice of monetary policy had long since disappeared. Yet, notwithstanding the new label, friends and foes alike struggled to pin down the specifics of Friedman's challenges.

Taking one proposition that was in both Brunner's 1968 identification of monetarism and Fand's (number 2 in the following list), three additional propositions from Brunner (1, 3–4), and three more from Fand (7–9), Thomas Mayer (1978b) added five of his own to identify a twelve-point monetarist doctrine:

(1)  The quantity theory of money, in the sense of the predominance of the impact of monetary factors on nominal income.

(2)  The monetarist model of the transmission process.

(3)  A belief in the inherent stability of the private sector.

(4)  A belief in the irrelevance of allocative detail for the explanation of short-run changes in money income, and in a fluid capital market.

(5)  A focus on the price level as a whole rather than on individual prices.

(6)  A reliance on small rather than large econometric models.

(7)  A use of the reserve base or similar measure as the indicator of monetary policy.

(8)  A use of the money stock as the proper target of monetary policy.

(9)  An acceptance of a monetary growth rule.

---

[1] See Brunner (1968).

[2] Friedman adopted the label in his Wincott Lecture, at the University of London, September 16, 1970. "The counter-revolution also needs a name and perhaps the one most widely used in referring to it is 'the Chicago School'. More recently, however, it has been given a name which is less lovely but which has become so attached to it that I find it hard to avoid using it. The name is 'monetarism' because of the renewed emphasis on the role of the quantity of money" (1970a, pp. 7–8).

(10)   A rejection of an unemployment-inflation trade-off in favor of a real Phillips curve.
(11)   A relatively greater concern about inflation than about unemployment compared to other economists.
(12)   A dislike of government intervention.[3]

Some of these propositions appear to be theoretical, some empirical, and others express judgments about the proper approach for monetary analysis. Still others reflect what Friedman's critics were inclined to identify as the ideological component of his monetary doctrine.[4] But whether these propositions of monetarism are seen as matters of theory or evidence depends not so much on their substance as on the perceived basis for believing or rejecting them. Herein lies a very important difference between Friedman and his critics. Why, for example, would an economist accept or reject proposition 1, the quantity theory statement that the preponderance of the effect on nominal income is from monetary factors? Does theory or does empirical evidence provide warrant for the belief (or for its rejection)? Friedman claimed that his commitment to most of the propositions was grounded in empirical evidence as well as theory. He expected empirical evidence would be the marginal factor bringing the debates to resolution. For his critics, the questions were almost wholly matters of theory. This methodological breach was obscured by the Keynesian–monetarist duality with its emphasis on the propositions' content and the means of empirical testing (for example, reduced form versus structural models) and perhaps by Friedman's own faith that resolution would come from empirical evidence.

The charge that Friedman had not provided adequate theoretical support is reflected in the derogatory term, the "black box of monetarism," which relates directly to proposition 2 in Mayer's twelve monetarist propositions. It was widely believed in the late 1960s that Friedman had failed or simply neglected to provide an adequate theory of the transmission mechanism for monetary effects. Changes in the money supply were said to go into a black box and changes in income and prices to come out. One could not know for sure the

---

[3] Mayer (1978b, p. 2).
[4] An important empirically based proposition in Friedman's set of beliefs that we have examined in detail in Chapters 5 and 7 and that is conspicuously absent from the list is the long and variable lag in the effect of monetary policy. Mayer omitted this proposition because at the time he was writing, many Keynesians agreed with Friedman on the long lags.

direction of the cause–effect relationship or whether the relationship might even be entirely spurious.

After years of having his conclusions about the effects of monetary policy rebutted as theoretically ungrounded, Friedman gave in to the pressure and in 1970 published "A Theoretical Framework for Monetary Analysis," followed in the next year by "A Monetary Theory of Nominal Income."[5] Robert Gordon, editor of the JPE, solicited commentary on the articles and published four critical comments (by Karl Brunner and Allan Meltzer, James Tobin, Paul Davidson, and Don Patinkin) along with Friedman's response as a symposium, "Friedman's Monetary Theory," in 1972.[6] Friedman's two papers (or the combined paper that was published as National Bureau Occasional Paper 112) was an attempt to communicate with his critics on their own terms. He insisted that the important differences between his position and theirs were empirical, yet he tried to close the differences not by buttressing the empirical record bearing on the issues but by building a theoretical model of the type favored by his critics, a version of the neo-Walrasian–Keynesian, Hicksian IS–LM model. Friedman had insisted for a decade and a half that the quantity theory provided the framework for his analysis. The Keynesians used an income–expenditure theory. Friedman tried in the two papers to incorporate both into the IS–LM model. The attempt was seen at the time by the symposium's participants as a failure and has been considered a failure by subsequent commentators. None of the symposium's participants changed their mind on money's role in business cycles, and both the critics and Friedman came away from the exchanges bewildered about what the other side thought were the important issues.

Amidst this confusion Jerome Stein was sufficiently undaunted that he organized a continuation of the discussion at Brown University in 1974. He wrote in the introduction to the conference volume, *Monetarism:*

Neo-Keynesian theory is a highly developed method of analysis which is featured prominently in almost every textbook in macroeconomics. On the other hand, there is no monetarist theory *per se* which is taught and which can be contrasted with neo-Keynesian theory. In fact, there is a pervasive view that

[5] Friedman combined the two with revisions in NBER Occasional Paper 112 (1971a).

[6] Reprinted along with Friedman's article as a monograph in Gordon (1974), from which all subsequent citations of the symposium are taken.

the monetarists have a "black box" and have not explained the causal mechanism which could imply the propositions advanced by Friedman or the Federal Reserve Bank of St. Louis (1976a, p. 3).

He quoted commentary by Robert Rasche and by Tobin to indicate the task for participants in the Brown conference. Rasche wrote:

On the one hand, we are left without a clearly specified analytical framework for the monetarist approach which can be contrasted with the well developed static income determination model. On the other hand, and even more importantly, there is no general model which can produce the post-Keynesian model as a particular case, and the monetarist and classical models as alternative cases. Such a framework is useful in order to discriminate between alternative hypotheses and to construct empirical tests which have the potential to refute one, or both, positions (Rasche, 1973, p. 15; Stein, 1976a, p. 3).

Stein's quotation of Tobin is from his assessment of Friedman's framework articles in the JPE symposium:

If the monetarists and the neo-Keynesians could agree as to which values of which parameters in which behavior relations imply which policy conclusions, then they could concentrate on the evidence regarding the values of those parameters. I wish that these articles had brought us closer to this goal, but I am afraid they have not (Tobin, 1974, p. 77; Stein, 1976a, p. 3).

Thus after Friedman accepted the challenge to reveal his theory and did so in a fashion designed to facilitate communication, there remained the perception that he had no theory to justify his conclusions.

The task of producing a monetarist model that would satisfy the criteria of Stein, Rasche, and Tobin was taken up in separate efforts at the Brown conference by Brunner and Meltzer ("An Aggregative Theory for a Closed Economy" [1976]) and by Stein ("Inside the Monetarist Black Box" [1976b]). The two other major papers presented there were by Franco Modigliani and Albert Ando ("Impacts of Fiscal Actions on Aggregate Income and the Monetarist Controversy: Theory and Evidence" [1976]) and by Tobin and Willem Buiter ("Long-run Effects of Fiscal Policy and Monetary Policy on Aggregate Demand" [1976]). Friedman's role at Brown was as commentator on Tobin and Buiter. No less confusion remained about Friedman's theoretical framework at the close of the Brown conference, as indicated by the title of James Tobin's concluding comment, "Is Friedman a Monetarist?"

The JPE symposium discussion among Friedman, Brunner and Meltzer, Tobin, Davidson, and Patinkin concerning his attempt to "set out explicitly the general theoretical framework that underlies [his empirical studies with Schwartz]" became a hopeless tangle of thrusts and parries. Each commentator attacked from a different side, and at the end there was not only little agreement on which thrusts found flesh and which were successfully parried; there was also doubt about whether the attackers had engaged the real Friedman or a shadow.

There is little value in a highly detailed account of Friedman's framework articles and the commentaries. Rather I will sketch the outlines in sufficient detail to substantiate the thesis that an essential difference between Friedman and his critics was their methods and methodology. Friedman's methods for producing knowledge about money and the economy were National Bureau methods, and his methodology was Marshallianism. His critics were Walrasians.

After failing to satisfy the critics' demands, Friedman perceived the reason the dialogue was futile. In response to Tobin's critique in the JPE symposium he wrote:

The alternative [explanation for the failure of communication] that now appeals to me is that the difficulty is a different approach to the use of economic theory – the difference between what I termed a Marshallian approach and a Walrasian approach in an article I wrote many years ago (Friedman 1949b, reprinted in Friedman 1953c). From a Marshallian approach, theory is, in Marshall's words, "an engine for the discovery of concrete truth." . . .

From a Walrasian approach, "abstractness, generality, and mathematical elegance have in some measure become ends in themselves, criteria by which to judge economic theory" (1974b, pp. 145–6).

In response to Patinkin's critique in the JPE symposium he wrote:

A more fundamental reason for Patinkin's emphasis on long-run "neutrality," the interest rate, and the real balance effect, and for his slighting the short-run context of most of my framework is that Patinkin, even more than Tobin, is Walrasian, concerned with abstract completeness, rather than Marshallian, concerned with the construction of special tools for special problems (1974b, pp. 159–60).

Friedman turned again to this theme in his comments on Tobin and Buiter at the Brown conference. He distinguished two issues involved in the question of the effect of "pure" fiscal policy: (A) the theoretical conditions under which it would be "rigorously and precisely correct" to say that "pure fiscal policy does not matter for aggregate real demand, nominal income, and the price level" and (B) the empirical importance, or practical significance, of the conditions that would render fiscal policy impotent. Friedman suggested that his and Tobin's inability to reconcile their differences on the issue were due to "my Marshallian approach to theory, which leads me to regard issue (B) as fundamental, versus Tobin's Walrasian approach, which makes it difficult for him to recognize issue (B) as a meaningful issue at all" (1976, p. 311).

### Friedman's statement of his monetary framework

Friedman's article "A Theoretical Framework for Monetary Analysis" is in two parts (all citations are to the article in Gordon, ed., 1974, unless otherwise noted). In the first part Friedman discussed the quantity theory of money as the framework for his and Schwartz's analysis and gave an interpretation of the differences between his position and his critics' in quantity theory terms. In the second part he shifted from the quantity theory as framework to a "simplified aggregate model of an economy that encompasses both a simplified quantity theory and a simplified income–expenditure theory as special cases" (1974a, p. 29) (or a "simple common model").[7] This shift was crucial.

In the first place the quantity theory *was* the framework for his previous monetary analysis. At least as early as the mid-1950s he identified his research with the quantity theory, and in writing the JPE article he drew heavily from previous writings.[8] In keeping with his Marshallian belief that theory is an "engine for analysis" rather than a photographic picture of the economy, and his corresponding belief in the importance of empirical quantification, Friedman used the quantity theory as a framework to assess the differences between his and the Keynesian positions on matters of empirical relationships.

In the second place, by making the shift, Friedman gave in to critics' demands that he make an explicit statement of the theoretical framework lying behind the historical analysis in the *Monetary History*.[9] The gesture was a genuine attempt to foster communication by using an analytical framework that fit the type of theory his critics had in mind

---

[7] This division is different from that which we get if we simply divide the combined article as published by the National Bureau and in Gordon into the two original JPE articles. The first JPE article, "A Theoretical Framework for Monetary Analysis," includes the discussion using the quantity theory as framework and the "common model" under either a strict quantity theory assumption that real income is determined outside the system or a strict Keynesian assumption that the price level is fixed. The second JPE article, "A Monetary Theory of Nominal Income," bypasses this choice of restrictive assumptions by specifying the model in terms of nominal income. For our evaluation of this episode in Friedman's encounters with his critics, the division between quantity theory and "common model" is more useful.

[8] In particular, "Money: Quantity Theory," in the *International Encyclopedia of the Social Sciences* (1968a).

[9] See Friedman (1970b, n. 1), where he mentions this demand made in reviews of the *Monetary History* by Culbertson and Meltzer.

when they called for his theory and that would support mediation of the empirical issues on which his views differed from the Keynesians. But the attempt failed. In no small part it failed because in adopting (or proposing) a variant of the Hicksian IS–LM model, Friedman placed his entire monetary project right in the middle of the neo-Walrasian paradigm. On the surface it may appear that an equation is simply an equation, but in this case it was not. As Friedman must have known, a tremendous amount of methodological baggage came along with the IS–LM equations.

Friedman identified the quantity theory on the analytical level with the demand for money, recognizing the crucial significance of velocity of circulation (or the Cambridge k). "On an empirical level, it is the generalization that changes in desired real balances (in the demand for money) tend to proceed slowly and gradually or to be the result of events set in train by prior changes in supply, whereas, in contrast, substantial changes in the supply of nominal balances can and frequently do occur independently of any changes in demand. The conclusion is that substantial changes in prices or nominal income are almost invariably the result of changes in the nominal supply of money" (1974a, p. 3).

This analytical identification of the quantity theory complies with his Marshallian preference for simple models that facilitate empirical analysis. Friedman's empirical identification is consistent with his belief, stated at the outset of his article, that historically both acceptance and rejection of the quantity theory have been based on empirical judgments. But the form and content of his empirical identification of the theory, which is a summary statement of his and Schwartz's historical analysis, are incommensurate with Walrasian Keynesianism. In the first place, the statement is about genuine dynamics, adjustments that take place over real time. Secondly, Friedman used quantitative but imprecise terms such as "tend to," "slowly and gradually," "substantial," "frequently," and "almost invariably." In a Walrasian framework the language would be more precise but actually less quantitative. For example, the money supply would be either exogenous or endogenous, not something in between. Thirdly, Friedman's statement is thoroughly empirical. It is not about definitions or logical relationships but about contingent facts, and it reflects a judgment Friedman made as a result of detailed examination of empirical evidence.

Friedman provided a historical sketch of different versions of the quantity theory, tracing an evolution from transactions versions through income versions to cash-balance versions, including his own.

He related the choice of one version or another to questions of the nature of a money economy and the definition of money. His own option for a cash-balances version was related to his view of the essence of a money economy as the separation of the acts of purchase and sale, to the definition of money as a temporary abode of purchasing power, and to his choice of wealth as a constraint on money demand rather than income as a measure of the amount of work done by money. "Finally, with regard to analytical techniques, the cash-balances approach fits in much more readily with the general Marshallian demand–supply apparatus than does the transactions approach" (1974a, p. 10).

Friedman discussed Keynes's and the Keynesians' challenges to pre-Keynesian economics and to his monetary analysis in terms of the quantity theory, making distinctions between purely theoretical matters (such as Lange's contention that there may be no full-employment long-run equilibrium) and empirical matters (such as whether in the short run, prices are rigid). He classified Keynes as a Marshallian in methodology but said that an important change was his switch from Marshall's assumption that prices adjust quickly and quantities slowly to the reverse, quick quantity and slow price adjustment. He said Keynes had an empirical basis for making the switch, his observations of severe quantity disruptions during the Great Depression. In taking this new Keynesian assumption to its extreme, with the only adjustment in quantities, Keynes and the Keynesians parted company with quantity theorists. For if there is no price adjustment, or if monetary theory has nothing to say about price adjustment, there is no distinction between nominal and real magnitudes, and the "fundamental proposition of monetary economics" is pointless.[10] By Friedman's account, Keynesians treated prices as institutional data, determined outside the monetary system.[11] And "the National Bureau series of monetary studies illustrates the other side of the coin – the approach of those of us who do not regard ourselves as Keynesians. Many of the questions discussed in these [National Bureau] monographs would not have appeared to be open questions, and large parts of them would never have been written, had we, implicitly or explicitly, accepted

[10] This is the idea that individuals have control over the nominal amount of money they hold but no control over the purchasing power of money; in the aggregate through spending decisions, they determine the real quantity but not the nominal quantity. See Friedman (1974a, pp. 2–3; 1959a, p. 609).

[11] He mentioned several examples, including Hester and Tobin's Cowles Foundation monograph, *Financial Markets and Economic Activity* (1967).

Keynes's assumption that prices are an institutional datum" (1974a, p. 21). He thought the reason Keynesians such as Okun (1963) and Tobin (1965) attributed to him the extreme conclusion that money is all that matters was that they used extreme assumptions, namely that prices are institutionally determined and that velocity, or the Cambridge k, is completely elastic with regard to interest rates.

Friedman contended that the all or nothing conclusions were not appropriate characterizations of his and Schwartz's beliefs. Qualifications were essential to their conclusions. For one, "we have always tried to qualify our statements about the importance of changes in M by referring to their effect on *nominal* income" (1974a, p. 27, emphasis in original). Second, he and Schwartz were careful to distinguish time frames.

We have accepted the quantity-theory presumption, and have thought it supported by the evidence we examined, that changes in the quantity of money as such *in the long run* have a negligible effect on real income, so that nonmonetary forces are "all that matter" for changes in real income over the decades and money "does not matter." On the other hand, we have regarded the quantity of money, plus the other variables (including real income itself) that affect k as essentially "all that matter" for the long-run determination of nominal income. The price level is then a joint outcome of the monetary forces determining nominal income and the real forces determining real income. . . .

For shorter periods of time, we have argued that changes in M will be reflected in all three variables on the right-hand side of equation (6) [M = kPy]. . . . But we have argued that the effect on k is empirically not to absorb the change in M, as the Keynesian analysis implies, but often to reinforce it, changes in M and k frequently affecting income in the same rather than opposite directions. Hence we have emphasized that changes in M are a major factor, though even then not the only factor, accounting for short-run changes in both nominal income and the real level of activity (y). I regard the description of our position as "money is all that matters for changes in *nominal* income and for *short-run* changes in real income" as an exaggeration but one that gives the right flavor of our conclusions. I regard the statement that "money is all that matters," period, as a basic misrepresentation of our conclusions (1974a, p. 27, emphasis in original).

Friedman also attributed the difference between his and Schwartz's and Keynesian views of the transmission mechanism to the extreme Keynesian assumption of fixed prices. (Note that there is no question in Friedman's mind that he did have a view of the transmission mechanism.) The most extreme version of the Keynesian view puts the economy in the liquidity trap, and money has no effect on any price, including the interest rate. When Keynesians dropped the liquidity trap assumption but retained the assumption that prices are fixed, the transmission mechanism was forced into "an extremely narrow channel," *the* interest rate on financial assets. The quantity theory view was that money's effect on nominal income is transmitted through a wider channel that includes prices of capital goods and durable and semi-durable consumer goods, any and all goods that yield a flow of services over time. "Since we regarded prices as flexible, though not 'perfectly' flexible, it was natural for us to interpret the transmission mechanism in terms of relative price adjustments over a broad area rather than in terms of narrowly defined interest rates" (1974a, p. 29).

The second part of Friedman's article contains the "simple common model." This has six equations:

the consumption function, $C/P = f(Y/P,r)$
the investment function, $I/P = g(r)$
the income identity, $Y/P = C/P + I/P$
the money demand function, $Md = P \cdot l(Y/P,r)$
the money supply function, $Ms = h(r)$
the money market equilibrium, $Md = Ms$

There are seven unknowns: C, P, Y, I, r, Md, and Ms. Therefore one of the unknowns must be determined outside the model.[12] Friedman used the model to relate the quantity theory and Keynesian income–expenditure theory to one another by suggesting that a key difference is in which variable they treat as predetermined. For the "simple" quantity theory it is $Y/P$ (or y), real income, while for the simple Keynesian theory it is P.

Though Friedman presented this as a simple and common model, that is, a model that can produce both quantity theory and Keynesian results, he clearly did not think of the model as a satisfactory formalization of his beliefs about money. For one, he treated the two solutions to the missing equation as "simple" quantity theory and "simple" Keynesian solutions. This indicates that the model is not one that he, nor did he think his Keynesian critics, would lay serious claim to. Furthermore the model is missing something more than the "missing equation"; it is missing one of Friedman's most important theoretical contributions, the permanent income hypothesis. Also, in treating real income as determined by the Walrasian general equilibrium equations via the "classical dichotomy," the model violates what he

---

[12] Friedman's original title for a preliminary draft of the article was "The Missing Equation."

indicated was one of the cardinal rules of his and Schwartz's empirical analysis, stating conclusions in terms of nominal income.

Why would the choice of nominal income have been important to Friedman and Schwartz? Because the classical dichotomy and associated neo-Walrasian analysis, which was central to Patinkin's *Money, Interest, and Prices* (1965), was not considered by them to be a useful way of approaching macroeconomics and because the simple assumption that either prices or real income is independent of the money supply was not consistent with the patterns he and Schwartz had found in historical data.

His solution was to propose a third way to deal with the missing equation, by specifying the model in terms of nominal income and leaving the problem of explaining the division of changes in nominal income between prices and quantities on the "agenda for future research." This then was Friedman's "Monetary Theory of Nominal Income." Friedman said of this model:

I have not before this written down explicitly the particular simplification I have labelled the monetary theory of nominal income – though Meltzer has referred to the theory underlying our *Monetary History* as a "theory of nominal income" (Meltzer 1965, p. 414). But once written down, it rings the bell, and seems to me to correspond to the broadest framework implicit in much of the work that I and others have done in analyzing monetary experience (1974a, p. 46).

There is irony in the fact that it was a friendly critic, Allan Meltzer, who set Friedman off on what was to be a futile attempt to justify his empirical and historical conclusions via a neo-Walrasian model.

The model has four equations and four unknowns:

the money demand function, $Md = Y \cdot l(r)$
the money supply function, $Ms = h(r)$
the money market equilibrium, $Md = Ms$
the interest rate function, $r = k_0 + (1/Y \, dY/dt)*$.[13]

In addition to leaving the division of nominal income into prices and quantities as unfinished business, this model also does not provide separate determination of income's two components, consumption and investment. Friedman established a common quantity theory and Keynesian pedigree for the model by drawing elements from Irving Fisher and from Keynes regarding interest rates. From Fisher he took the distinction between nominal and real interest and from Keynes

[13] * indicates expected long-term value.

the notion that speculators keep the current interest rate equal to its expected future level.[14]

## Critiques of Friedman's framework

The four commentaries on Friedman's article illustrate clearly the futility of his attempt to accommodate critics' demands for an explicit statement of his theoretical framework. One commentary is by fellow monetarists Karl Brunner and Allan Meltzer. A second is by the foremost American Keynesian, James Tobin, who had the longest running record of published criticism of Friedman's empirical analysis. The third is by the post-Keynesian Paul Davidson, who, like Friedman, worked within a paradigm that was outside the neo-Walrasian mainstream. And the fourth is by Don Patinkin, who had one foot in the quantity theory (or classical) camp and the other in the Keynesian camp but who kept both planted firmly in the neo-Walrasian camp. Patinkin was also Friedman's chief adversary in disputes over the nature of the pre-1946 (or pre-1936) macroeconomic heritage at the University of Chicago.[15] The critics came to Friedman's article with different beliefs and pet concerns. Yet there is a common thread running through their commentaries: the priority of theory over empirical evidence. The different shapes and shades this thread takes in their evaluations bring into relief the unorthodox qualities of Friedman's approach to monetary analysis.

### Brunner and Meltzer

Brunner and Meltzer were, superficially at least, the friendliest of Friedman's critics. But the substance of their criticism cut as deep as any of the others. They were critical both of Friedman's attribution of his framework to the quantity theory and of specific features of his model. They accused him of contorting the quantity theory by making it into a theory of the demand for money, and elevating the importance of the stability of demand. "In the monetary theories of

[14] Other distinguishing features of the model are assumptions that demand for money is unit elastic with respect to real income, there is an exogenously fixed differential between the expected real interest rate and the secular rate of growth, and instantaneous equilibration in the market for money.

[15] The year of Friedman's appointment to the University of Chicago faculty, 1946, was the beginning of the "modern" Chicago School. The year 1936 marks the publication of Keynes's classic, *The General Theory,* and thus the beginning of the Keynesian revolution.

Keynes (1936) and Patinkin (1965) and in Metzler's classic article (1951), 'the quantity theory' is a proposition about the effects of a change in money in a fully employed economy where capital stock, real output, and employment remain unchanged" (1974, p. 67). Furthermore Friedman's concern over the independence of money supply was misplaced. "If Friedman's second argument means that the 'feedback' from current market interest rates, wealth, or income to money is small relative to the effect of interest rates and income or wealth on the demand for money, we concur. The part of his argument that we find misleading is the stress he places on the independence of monetary changes. Friedman's argument suggests that strict independence is a necessary condition for 'monetarism'" (1974, p. 72). Brunner and Meltzer argued that feedback from income or wealth and interest rates to the money stock does not vitiate the case for changes in money having effects on income and prices. Even if the central bank responded to income and interest rates in adjusting the monetary base, the effects would be the same.

This criticism exemplifies the difficulties of communication between Friedman and his critics. Friedman consistently maintained through the duration of his research on money that he did not believe the money stock was in fact totally independent, but neither did he believe that feedback would rob money of its causal power. For example, he testified to the Joint Economic Committee in 1958 that "the direction of influence between the money stock and income and prices is less clear-cut and more complex for the business cycle than for the longer movements. . . . Thus changes in the money stock are a consequence as well as an independent cause of changes in income and prices [over the cycle], though once they occur they will in their turn produce still further effects on income and prices" (1958, p. 179). In the *Monetary History* he and Schwartz wrote, "Mutual interaction, but with money rather clearly the senior partner in longer-run movements and in major cyclical movements, and more nearly an equal partner with money income and prices in shorter-run and milder movements – this is the generalization suggested by our evidence" (1963b, p. 695).[16]

How could "friendly" monetarist critics, who knew his work very well, have any doubt as to whether Friedman's belief was in the absolute or relative independence of changes in money? Perhaps because Brunner and Meltzer expected "descriptive accuracy" from his theo-

---

[16] He also quoted this passage in his response (1970c) to Tobin's *post hoc ergo propter hoc* article.

retical model, a "photographic reproduction" of the factual evidence amassed by Friedman and like-minded, empirically oriented researchers. In drawing implications from the formal theoretical model, Friedman assumed that the money supply was exogenous. He could have responded by quoting from his 1953 essay on methodology:

"The confusion between descriptive accuracy and analytical relevance has led not only to criticisms of economic theory on largely irrelevant grounds but also to misunderstanding of economic theory and misdirection of efforts to repair supposed defects. . . .

Marshall took the world as it is; he sought to construct an 'engine' to analyze it, not a photographic reproduction of it" (1953a, pp. 34–5).

For Friedman the theoretical model was not intended, nor could it be expected, to capture every nuance of the macroeconomy. The statements of beliefs that he would have his colleagues take seriously were the prose summaries of his evidence; the only statements of belief they took seriously were implications drawn from formal theoretical models.[17]

Meltzer had been one of the first critics to challenge Friedman to write down a formal model of the theory guiding his empirical research, in his 1965 review of the *Monetary History*. As a friendly critic, Meltzer took up the challenge himself along with Karl Brunner in "A Monetarist Framework for Aggregative Analysis" (1971) and "Money, Debt, and Economic Activity" (1972).[18] They thought it imperative that Friedman do the same.

For us, and perhaps for many others, the absence of an explicitly stated theory capable of generating the propositions that have been supported by empirical investigation has impeded the further development of monetary theory. The very success of Friedman's insightful comments and conjectures when tested against alternative conjectures increases the benefits that we expected to obtain from the development of an explicit theory capable of generating the empirical regularities that support "monetarism." . . .

Friedman's unpublished critiques of standard macroeconomic analysis developed over two decades with substantial benefit to monetary and economic

[17] Other examples of factors that Brunner and Meltzer argued should be accounted for in the model because there was empirical evidence of their significance included fiscal policy measures, taxes, and the outstanding stock of government debt. In total they suggested adding five variables and equations. They criticized Friedman for adopting the Keynesian transmission mechanism of the IS–LM model instead of giving relative prices a real role and for throwing in the towel on the key issue of the division of nominal income into prices and quantities.

[18] They continued the project with "An Aggregative Theory for a Closed Economy" (1976) at the Brown University "Monetarism" conference.

theory. Until recently, however, his many contributions did not include a detailed analytic statement of the framework guiding his research, connecting his empirical findings, or providing a foundation for the policies he advocated. Without such a statement, it was often impossible to separate valid implications of an empirically tested framework from less well supported conjectures (1974, pp. 63–4, 75).

Brunner and Meltzer may have been monetarists like Friedman, but they were closer to his Keynesian critics in their view of the role of theory.

### Tobin

The structure of Tobin's critique is the same as Brunner and Meltzer's, to show that Friedman's model, whether the "simple common model" or the "monetary theory of nominal income," is inconsistent both with empirical evidence, especially Friedman's summaries of his empirical evidence, and with other accepted theory. The simple common model treats either real income or the price level as predetermined. Tobin pointed out that neither Friedman nor the Keynesians really believed that the economy operates in this either/or manner. In particular he was critical of how Friedman used the model to depict the differences separating monetarists and Keynesians, on the grounds that the depiction (the solution to the missing equation) did not fit the facts. This was a critique of the representational quality of the model, just as Brunner and Meltzer's was. From Tobin's perspective Friedman tarred his Keynesian opponents with the extreme simplifications of the "simple" model but refused the tar for himself.

Tobin also, like Brunner and Meltzer, took issue with Friedman's identification of the quantity theory. He considered six different characteristic quantity-theory propositions from Friedman and rejected them all as not being the true quantity theory.

The true quantity theorem is a follows. Consider a system of supply and demand equations for goods and services and for stocks of assets and debts denominated in the monetary unit of account. Given tastes, technologies, and certain exogenous variables, these supplies and demands will be functions of nominal prices. Among the exogenous data will be some quantities defined in the monetary unit of account, including the monetary base of currency and bank reserves, and the outstanding stocks of government debts of other kinds and maturities. Now suppose that, with a given vector of these exogenous monetary quantities, the system is solved for equilibrium commodity prices $p_e$. If every exogenous monetary variable is then multiplied by the same positive scalar $\lambda$, then the price vector $\lambda p_e$ will solve the system, with every physical quantity unchanged and every endogenous variable measured in the unit of account scaled up or down by $\lambda$. This theorem, if it should be so dignified, is a simple consequence of the "homogeneity postulate" or the absence-of-money illusion (1974, pp. 86–7).

Tobin then pointed out that no real-world changes in the money supply meet the stringent conditions of this theorem, including exogeneity of the money stock. Thus it is rendered nugatory. The quantity theory, which is what Friedman *really* claimed as his theoretical framework, is reduced to a theorem with no counterpart in the real world!

### Davidson

Paul Davidson turned this objection to Friedman's framework on its head. As the critic representing post-Keynesianism, he did not echo the demand that Friedman adopt an acceptable Walrasian model; he *accused* Friedman of being a Walrasian! Keynes, on the other hand, was not a Walrasian, according to Davidson. He assumed sticky wage rates not to close a model but "to deal with a vital logical condition for a viable monetary system, as well as an obvious fact of life" (1974, p. 95). In adopting the Walrasian IS–LM model as his common framework for evaluating monetarism and Keynesianism, Friedman omitted three factors that by Davidson's interpretation were basic to Keynes's view: (1) Knightian uncertainty, (2) market institutions and constraints that arise because of uncertainty, and (3) money that serves as a medium of exchange and store of wealth. Davidson quoted from Keynes:

Money, it is well known, serves two principal purposes . . . it facilitates exchanges. . . . In the second place it is a store of wealth. So we are told, without a smile on the face. But in the world of the classical economy, what an insane use to which to put it! For it is a recognized characteristic of money as a store of wealth that it is barren. . . . Why should anyone outside a lunatic asylum wish to use money as a store of wealth? (Keynes, 1937, pp. 215–6; Davidson, 1974, p. 97).

So to Davidson, Friedman's framework was no better or worse than his "Keynesian" critics'. Neither a Keynesian world nor a monetary economy could be built on the Walrasian skeleton.

Friedman (p. 44) explicitly states that his quantity theory of money relies upon and is "summarized in the Walrasian equations of general equilibrium." He acknowledges that in long-run equilibrium in his view "all anticipations are realized . . . [and that he regards] long-run equilibrium as determined by the earlier quantity-theory model plus the Walrasian equations of general equilibrium" (p. 48). It is difficult to understand therefore, from a Keynesian point of view, why the resources of so many economists have been wasted on Walrasian models in general, and quantity theory models in particular, where the latter make a fetish about the importance of the rate of growth of the quantity of money. If the Walrasian equations – which describe a barter economy, an economy where "money can play no essential role" (Hahn 1971, p. 417) – are the logical norm or trend around which Friedman believes the actual world fluctuates, then the quantity of money is indeed nugatory (1974, p. 99).

## Patinkin

Patinkin was more concerned with the doctrinal history of the quantity theory and Keynesian economics than with the specifics of Friedman's "simple common model."[19] He struck a double blow against Friedman on doctrinal history. First, he charged Friedman with building a case from casual empiricism. This is an accusation that Friedman often made against Walrasian model builders about economic facts. Patinkin accused Friedman of the same thing in regard to historical facts. The second blow was accusing Friedman of actually having had a Keynesian theory all along rather than a true quantity theory. This was tied to the first charge, because Friedman's mistaking his theory as a version of the quantity theory when it was actually Keynesian was a result of his casual empiricism regarding the history of the two doctrines.

Patinkin hit early and hard on the importance of empirical evidence:

Clearly, questions about the history of economic doctrine are empirical questions which can be answered only on the basis of evidence cited from the relevant literature. Indeed, the "elementary canons of scholarship call for (such) documentation" (Friedman 1970c, p. 318). My criticism of Friedman is, accordingly, that on many occasions he has not provided such evidence; that, indeed, on some occasions he has ignored the detailed evidence which has been adduced against the views he expresses; and that on still other occasions he has indulged in casual empiricism in the attempt to support his doctrinal interpretations (1974, pp. 111–12).

Patinkin's quarrel was with Friedman's identification of the demand for money framework used in his analysis as part and parcel of the quantity theory. If he had simply presented the framework as it was, demand for money "as part of capital or wealth theory, concerned with the composition of the balance sheet or portfolio of assets" (Friedman, 1974a, p. 11; Patinkin, 1974, p. 112), there would be no problem. The problem came with the quantity theory label, and this was not a trivial matter according to Patinkin because there was a label

[19] He made several suggestions for the model. He urged that Friedman make it more general by introducing explicitly a production function, excess demand for labor function, and a real-balance variable in the consumption function. He also found fault with the *ad hoc* reduced-form nature of the dynamic adjustment equations.

that fits much better – Keynesian liquidity–preference theory. Friedman characterized Keynes as a quantity theorist before the *General Theory* and to a smaller extent in the *General Theory* but also saw a challenge to the quantity theory in the *General Theory*. Patinkin found two distinctively Keynesian features in Friedman's quantity theory that were not found in the "true" quantity theory: the emphasis on stocks of assets and portfolio balance, and the corresponding attention to the role of interest rates. He noted that in Friedman's 1956 "restatement" of the quantity theory, he took pains to set his work in the tradition of the University of Chicago faculty of Simons, Mints, Viner, and Knight, with no mention of Keynes. But in more recent discussion (1968a) he dropped the Chicago heritage and acknowledged his indebtedness to Keynesian liquidity–preference theory. Patinkin pushed Friedman to take the next step and face up

to the implications of the fact that whatever the similarities in policy proposals . . . the theoretical framework of the Chicago school of the 1930s and 1940s – a major center of the quantity theory at the time – differed fundamentally from his. In particular, the Chicago school – as exemplified especially by Henry Simons – was basically not interested in the demand function for money (Simons never even mentioned this concept!) and carried out its analysis instead in terms of Fisher's MV = PT equation. Furthermore (and in marked contrast with Friedman) the basic assumption of the Chicago school analysis was that the velocity of circulation is unstable. Correspondingly, it considered sharp changes in this velocity to be a major source of instability in the economy (1974, pp. 115–16).

Patinkin's argument on the nature of the quantity theory sharpens the picture of a triangle within which the symposium discussion moved. The three points of the triangle are Friedman's empirical and historical analysis (which is what created the calls for him to specify a theoretical structure), the formal structure(s) that he presents in the symposium articles, and economic theory defined broadly to include historical traditions such as the quantity theory and Keynesian theory. Brunner and Meltzer and Tobin were predominantly concerned with the side of the triangle running between the empirical evidence and the formal model, and this concern was the original impetus for Friedman's offering the model. Davidson and Patinkin were primarily concerned with the side connecting Friedman's model with the theoretical traditions.

## Friedman's comments on the critics

Friedman's comments on the critics reveal an emerging awareness that his effort to identify a common theoretical framework for resolving their differences was doomed. As Robert Clower suggested in his review of the *Monetary History*, Friedman and the critics were interested in different things. For Friedman, monetary theory, both its contemporary form and its history, was a means to empirical investigation of concrete facts of monetary relations. It was, in the terms of Marshall that Friedman made his own, an engine of analysis. For the critics, theories were nearly ends in themselves. This is not to say that the critics had no interest in acquiring knowledge of "money and the economy." Rather, they believed theory alone was the crucial means to this knowledge.

Friedman responded most briefly and most gently to Brunner and Meltzer. This may be because they were friendly monetarist critics. They were only marginally less insistent on the Walrasian principle of building a complete model than Tobin and Patinkin, but they made their critique in a manner intended as complementary with Friedman's empirical and historical analysis. Additionally, there was not the long history of highly charged criticism between Friedman and Brunner and Meltzer that there was with Tobin and with Patinkin.

But Friedman's response to Brunner and Meltzer makes clear that the Marshallian–Walrasian difference lay between them as well. "Apparently, I failed to make clear the purpose and scope of my article. It does not, as Brunner and Meltzer assume, present a fully developed theory that is intended to have as implications all of the empirical regularities that those of us working in this area have isolated. My aim was much less ambitious. It was to outline a general approach that could suggest what empirical issues required study, an approach that could then be elaborated in further detail in connection with such empirical studies" (1974b, pp. 134–5).

Davidson, like Patinkin, challenged Friedman's interpretation of Keynes's *General Theory*. Friedman devoted most of his response to Davidson to defense of his interpretation. He responded to Davidson's identification of his framework as Walrasian with a characteristically Marshallian argument for dealing with analytical problems sequentially. Recall that the object of Davidson's criticism was Friedman's invocation of a long-run equilibrium when all expectations are realized. This, according to Davidson, ruled out any genuine uncertainty, which Davidson argued was central to Keynes's conception of money's role. Friedman denied that his framework ruled out uncertainty and quoted Keynes to make the methodological point that an assumption of long-run equilibrium made at one point in an analysis is not the same as a commitment to the belief that the economy is always in long-run equilibrium. "After we have reached a provisional conclusion by isolating the complicating factors one by one, we then have to go back on ourselves and allow, as well as we can, for the probable interactions of the factors amongst themselves. This is the nature of economic thinking (Keynes, 1936, p. 297; Friedman, 1974b, p. 150).

In responding to Tobin, Friedman asked what could account for the difficulty of communication. He concluded that the problem was that he was a Marshallian and Tobin a Walrasian. Tobin persisted, in Friedman's view, in taking issues that to a Marshallian were quantitative (that is, greater than/less than), and making them qualitative (that is, either/or). Thus, the LM curve becomes either vertical or horizontal. Similarly, velocity either does or does not respond to interest rates. Furthermore, he insisted that Friedman write down *one* theoretical model as representative of the economy. These demands betrayed Tobin's Walrasian bent. From the Marshallian point of view "there is no such thing as 'the' theory, there are theories for different problems or purposes; there is nothing inconsistent or wrong about using a theory that treats the real interest rate as constant in analyzing fluctuations in nominal income but using a theory that treats the real interest rate as variable in analyzing fluctuations in real income; the one theory may be more useful for one purpose, the other theory for the other. We lose generality by this procedure but gain simplicity and precision" (1974b, pp. 145–6).

Friedman reserved the most force for his response to Patinkin. Patinkin disputed Friedman on the nature of the Chicago tradition, the nature of the historical quantity theory, and the nature of Friedman's monetary analysis. Friedman argued that the distinctive element of Chicago monetary analysis that influenced his work was the belief that monetary policy could and should be used to combat the Great Depression. He built his case with quotations from Jacob Viner's 1933 University of Minnesota talk and, for contrast, from Lionel Robbins's *The Great Depression* (1934). He used quotations from Keynes's *Tract on Monetary Reform* (1923) and *General Theory* (1936) to refute Patinkin's claim that Friedman's monetary analysis was really in the Keynesian, rather than the quantity theory, tradition.[20]

[20] Friedman's depiction of the Chicago tradition was chiefly in terms of the *policy views* of Chicago economists, but Patinkin's original critique (1969) of Friedman's original depiction of that tradition (1956b) centered on the *theory* the Chicago economists used in comparison with Keynes's and Friedman's. The rules of the JPE symposium gave Friedman the last word, but in reprinting his 1969 article, Patinkin added a rejoinder to Friedman's symposium response (1981,

According to Friedman, Patinkin's identification of the quantity theory with one condition, long-run neutrality of money, was a product of his Walrasian approach. The "fundamental reason for Patinkin's emphasis on long-run 'neutrality,' the interest rate, and the real balance effect, and for his slighting the short-run context of most of my framework is that Patinkin, even more than Tobin, is Walrasian, concerned with abstract completeness, rather than Marshallian, concerned with the construction of special tools for special problems" (1974b, pp. 159–60).

## The Brown conference on monetarism

That Friedman in his work with Schwartz was indeed working outside the Walrasian mainstream and that there could be no confluence of their work and the mainstream was made still clearer in the 1974 conference on monetarism at Brown University. Four major papers were given, with multiple discussants for each. After the symposium there was still the complaint that Friedman's monetarism did not have a theoretical foundation, whereas Keynesianism did. Friedman's statement that "I regard the description of our position as 'money is all that matters for changes in *nominal* income and for *short-run* changes in real income' as an exaggeration but one that gives the right flavor of our conclusions" (1974a, p. 27, emphasis in original) was still being quoted with puzzlement. He and Schwartz apparently did not have a theory, and others could not know what it was that they believed about the effects of money.

The purpose of the Brown conference was accordingly to "evaluate the existing empirical evidence . . . , resolve the theoretical problems . . . and agree on statistical tests which could help us determine which view of the world was correct, the neo-Keynesian or the monetarist" (Stein, 1976a, pp. 3–4). Two papers were given by monetarists and two by Keynesians. Brunner and Meltzer and Stein attempted to fill the monetarist lacuna with theoretical models that produce monetarist results. Franco Modigliani and Albert Ando used simulations from a large-scale econometric model, the MPS model, to evaluate the

---

pp. 264–5). There he pointed out that Friedman had yielded on the matter of the theoretical teachings of Henry Simons and Lloyd Mints and that there were not material differences between their renditions of Chicago policy views.

Other authors who have taken up the issues of prewar Chicago theory and policy views in relation to Friedman's and to prewar economists outside Chicago include Johnson (1971), Humphrey (1971), Laidler (1993), and Tavlas (1995).

short and medium-term effects of pure fiscal policy. They concluded "in the same vein in which we concluded our exchange with Friedman and Meiselman many years ago – there are no viable alternatives to the painstaking task of looking inside the black box. When this is done, one cannot fail to conclude that the effects of macro fiscal actions are certain to be long-lasting and likely to be substantial" (1976, p. 42). Tobin and Willem Buiter contributed "a theoretical exercise addressed to a rather esoteric and artificial question in the logic of aggregate demand. Does expansionary fiscal policy raise aggregate demand permanently or at best only temporarily?" (1976, p. 273) Remarkably, though evaluating the existing empirical evidence was at the top of Stein's list of tasks for the conference, there is no encounter with empirical evidence in any of the four papers! Three were exercises in pure theory and the fourth relied on simulations.

Friedman was a discussant for Tobin and Buiter's paper. His emphasis on the differences between his Marshallian and their Walrasian approaches is even more prominent in these remarks than in his response to Tobin in the JPE symposium, and he acknowledged that his attempt to use the Hicksian IS–LM model as a common framework was a mistake.

I continue to believe . . . that the fundamental differences among us are empirical, not theoretical. But this does not mean that we all use the same theory. It means that our differences do not arise from analytical mistakes in manipulating theory. No one can use in practice a fully comprehensive theory. We must all work with simplified theories. Different empirical presumptions make different simplifications appropriate and thereby make different theoretical structures (different analytical filing cases) most useful. I must plead guilty to having contributed to confusion on this score. In the attempt to communicate, I have tried for example to present monetarist analysis in IS–LM terms, even though recognizing that this was a cumbrous theoretical structure for this purpose, that the quantity theory structure was much more convenient (1976, pp. 315–16).

Friedman provided content to his judgment that the Marshallian–Walrasian difference was crucial to his long-running dispute with Tobin by distinguishing between two issues, one reflecting Tobin's concern and the other his. The Walrasian issue concerned "the theoretical conditions under which this assertion [that pure fiscal policy has no effects on income and prices] would be rigorously and precisely correct for both impact and long-run effects" (1976, p. 310). To a Marshallian the relevant issue was "the empirical importance of the effects of 'pure fiscal policy' arising from the failure of these conditions to be satisfied perfectly; i.e., whether, as a practical matter, sufficiently correct results will be obtained by treating them *as if* they were perfectly satisfied" (1976, p. 310, emphasis in original). He explained that to a Marshallian, "hedges" and "qualifying adjectives and adverbs," of which Tobin and Buiter complained, were essential, for they indicate the empirical quantitative nature of the problem.

Commenting on Ando and Modigliani's paper, Schwartz dealt with the endogenous–exogenous variables issue in a manner that fits neatly into Friedman's characterization of the Marshallian use of theory as one that determines the status of a variable in an analysis on the basis of the purpose of the analysis.[21] She argued that the problem of excluded exogenous variables cannot be solved by opting for structural rather than reduced-form models, because there necessarily are always omitted variables. Modeling should be approached with the notion of a recursive system. Income should be treated as endogenous and money as exogenous when the problem at hand is explanation of the income-determination process. When the problem is explanation of changes in the money supply, then it is appropriate to treat income as exogenous. The exercise performed by Modigliani and Ando, evaluating reduced-form estimates with those implied by the MPS model, had little potential for discovering knowledge of the real world, according to Schwartz. This was because the exercise assumed that all the information about the actual economy was contained in the MPS model. That model actually provided little of the knowledge available from the study of historical experience. The model builders had not designed their models to answer the types of questions that monetarists viewed as important.

### Conclusion

The JPE symposium and the Brown symposium together were the final big battle between Friedman and his Keynesian critics. Shortly afterward the rational expectations revolution swept both Keynesianism and monetarism from center stage. Though Friedman had a large influence on opinion within the economics community regarding the importance of money and the role of monetary policy, on technical issues of theory and evidence very little was settled. His neo-Walrasian opponents from the Keynesian side continued to be skeptical that he had a theory, and he had come to see that his research was incompatible with their approach.

It may be useful at this point to draw some speculative inferences from these failed attempts to reconcile differences between Friedman

[21] See Friedman (1953a, pp. 34–8).

and his critics. Patinkin hit hard with his argument that Friedman's work was not within either the quantity-theory or Chicago traditions, and Friedman defended with equal force. Why was the quantity-theory association so important to Friedman? If the object of the research program was to learn about money's role in business cycles, why be so concerned with theoretical labels? The answer may be in the gravity of the "measurement without theory" charge that had long been brought against the National Bureau. Economists think of science as theoretical and pride themselves on the fact that among the so-called social sciences, their discipline alone has a coherent and powerful body of theory. Were this self-image not widely held, there would have been no force in Tjalling Koopmans's charge against Burns and Mitchell. Economists argue about the role of evidence in developing and testing theory, and about the strengths and weaknesses of alternative theories, but no economist argues that theory is unnecessary. No economist wants to be on the receiving end of the "measurement without theory" charge.

Friedman took pride in his ability and reputation as an economic theorist.[22] From his experience in the 1930s as a student of Wesley Mitchell's and a staff member at the National Bureau, he concluded that he was a better theorist than Mitchell. He also concluded that some of the work being done at the National Bureau (but not that done by Mitchell) *was* void of theory.[23] Moreover, though Friedman dissented, much of the economics profession judged that Koopmans got the better of Rutledge Vining in their exchange over the Burns and Mitchell volume. In light of this backdrop for Friedman's National Bureau research project with Schwartz, it would be surprising if he did not regard it important to establish a theoretical pedigree for their work. Though Mitchell produced volumes of useful knowledge about business cycles, neither he nor anyone else produced a "National Bureau theory." So even if Friedman had wanted to make the National Bureau tradition paramount in the classification of their work, there was no "National Bureau theory" label for him to use.

The most obvious label for anyone to adopt in the late 1940s was "Keynesian." But here there were difficulties. The importance of money was diminished in much of the so-called Keynesian analysis, and Friedman and Schwartz's charge from the National Bureau was

[22] Among Friedman's contributions to economic theory that were published or in preparation as the monetary project took shape in the 1950s are Friedman and Savage (1948) and Friedman (1952d, 1957, 1962a).

[23] See Hammond (1992b).

to investigate monetary factors in business cycles. In addition, Friedman thought Keynesian policy prescriptions for fine tuning and for permanent public works programs derived from the instability and secular stagnation theses were misguided.

But the most enduring problem with the Keynesian label, as we have seen, did not concern the role of money or policy conclusions. It was that the economics of Keynes, who was a methodological Marshallian, was taken over by the Walrasians. Friedman put his concerns about this transformation on the record early.[24] The Walrasian approach of Cowles Commission (and later foundation) members such as Lange, Patinkin, Tobin, and Modigliani who became the leading Keynesians was a barrier to synthesis of Friedman's monetary research with Keynesian macroeconomics throughout the course of the Friedman–Schwartz project.

Finally, what was the appeal of the quantity theory as a label? Having considered the other options available to Friedman, the answer becomes obvious. Friedman and Schwartz's research project was on the role of money in business cycles, and the quantity theory was a monetary theory – historically the dominant monetary theory. The quantity theory provided a tradition to set their work within, and importantly, it was recognized as a theoretical tradition. It was also a tradition in which data collection and analysis had long been given large roles. The quantity theory was arguably the theoretical tradition with the longest record of historical and empirical analysis. For all these reasons it is not hard to see in hindsight why Friedman would be concerned over challenges to the pedigree of his work on money and business cycles as well as over challenges to the actual content of the conclusions he drew from the analysis.

[24] See, for example, Friedman (1946).

CHAPTER 9

# The great depression

## Introduction

In this chapter we review the debate set off by Chapter 7 of Friedman and Schwartz's *Monetary History*. "The Great Contraction" marked a watershed in thinking about the greatest economic calamity in modern times. Until Friedman and Schwartz provoked the interest of economists by rehabilitating monetary theory and history, neither economic theorists nor economic historians devoted as much attention to the Depression as historians.

Macroeconomists' time-series econometric methods do not allow them to attach importance to individual historical episodes. From their perspective the Depression appeared more an econometric problem to be circumvented than a puzzle to be understood. One of the key assumptions in time-series estimation of economic structure is that the structure remains unchanged through the period covered by the econometrician's data. Common sense suggested that the Depression, and the new government presence in economic and business affairs from President Roosevelt's New Deal and World War II, marked a point at which the structure of the U.S. economy was likely to have changed. This econometric problem, plus the greater urgency attached to understanding the contemporary economy in the heyday of the "New Economics" of the 1960s, suggested that the most appropriate data for econometricians was postwar quarterly data.

For the economic historians, the contraction of 1929–33 was too recent to hold much interest. Time would have to pass for the Depression to become history. The topics getting the most attention from economic historians in the 1950s were business, labor, and manufacturing history. Economic growth was also important, by one measure getting twice as much attention as business cycles and recessions/depressions together.[1] By the same measure, in the 1960s, economic growth doubled in popularity as a topic for economic historians, while

---

[1] See Whaples (1991, table 1). Also, the role of theory and causality in economic history was under question in the 1950s. See for example Meyer and Conrad (1957) and Kuznets (1957).

business cycles and recessions/depressions fell. Agriculture and international trade were also important.

Friedman and Schwartz's *Monetary History*, and especially the chapter on "The Great Contraction," accelerated the Depression's move from the category of contemporary experience to historical experience. Published on the heels of "Money and Business Cycles," it also gave the Depression contemporary relevance for issues of theory and policy, issues such as the relative power of monetary and fiscal policy and the Federal Reserve's capacity to fine tune away the business cycle.

For the reasons mentioned above, and because there was so much other provocative material in "Money and Business Cycles" and the *Monetary History*, it was several years before "The Great Contraction," Chapter 7 of the *Monetary History*, attracted serious critical attention of its own. This was despite the fact that it was reprinted as a separate book in 1965. The beginning of what eventually developed into a rich literature on the economics of the Great Depression, most of which was in one way or another in reaction to Friedman and Schwartz, was a book by the economic historian Peter Temin. Temin's *Did Monetary Forces Cause the Great Depression?* (1976) was published thirteen years after the *Monetary History*.

This book has arguably been as important as Friedman and Schwartz's Chapter 7 in shaping the subsequent literature; in the title as well as the text Temin defined the primary issue that subsequent authors have tackled — what caused the Great Depression? Because Temin wrote in reaction to Friedman and Schwartz, it has been easy to assume that this was the primary issue for them as well. But the reality is not quite this straightforward. Within in the context of their larger project on monetary factors in business cycles, the question of whether monetary forces caused the Depression was indeed important to Friedman and Schwartz. But the way they posed the question was different from the way Temin did. Friedman and Schwartz did not set out in the *Monetary History* to explain once and for all what caused the Great Depression. Their concern was more restricted and less ambitious. It was to investigate the role of money and the banking system in the Depression. That this was so easily transformed into the broader question of what caused the Depression, and at the same time narrowed to the either/or proposition of monetary forces or nonmonetary forces, is testimony to the skill with which Temin placed Friedman and Schwartz's history of money and banking in the context of contemporary macroeconomics and to the difficulty of framing questions of causation in a manner that yields straightforward interpretation and empirical testing without oversimplification.

A not insignificant portion of the critical heat generated by Friedman's writings on money has been the result of his seeming to his critics to make strong unicausal statements about the role of money and monetary policy and then back away from them when pressed by the critics. We have observed this dynamic of jockeying back and forth, not just about causes and effects of business cycles and inflations and deflations but also about what Friedman may have or may not have claimed, in his debates with Tobin. This is evident as well in the "monetarist" and "antimonetarist" literature that was spawned by "The Great Contraction."

However, unlike the episodes involving Friedman and critics that we have reviewed, Friedman stayed on the outside of the debate he and Schwartz, along with Temin, set off over the Depression. Friedman did not write a response to Temin's book and had no correspondence with Temin. In fact, Friedman has written very little about the Great Depression since 1963. Schwartz did take up the task of responding to Temin's book, in a 1981 volume edited by Karl Brunner, *The Great Depression Revisited.*

In this chapter we review the literature that has grown out of Friedman and Schwartz's Chapter 7 and Temin's book to see what Friedman and Schwartz and their critics have thought the primary issues were regarding money and the Great Depression. What were considered the most pressing and contentious questions about causes and effects in the Great Depression, and how were these questions framed and answered? How have Friedman and Schwartz, through "The Great Contraction," influenced economics, and how has the evolution of economics colored the way economists have treated this portion of their monetary project?

## "The Great Contraction" in the context of the *Monetary History*

The title of this section may seem to state the obvious – it goes without saying that a chapter in a book is written and usefully read in the context of the rest of the book. What context could be more natural? But Friedman and Schwartz's Chapter 7 provided the opening of an extended discussion of the economics of the Great Depression, and contexts in an ongoing discussion can shift in subtle but important ways. This is especially so when the author whose work initiates the discussion is in one way or another outside the mainstream. Such was the case for Friedman and Schwartz with "The Great Contraction."

Monetary history was not in fashion among economists in 1963, no more so than National Bureau business-cycle analysis. The 1960s were the heyday of hydraulic Keynesian theory, large-scale econometric models, and mathematical economics. In this setting Friedman and Schwartz were radical nonconformists. They were working on monetary economics in a framework that Friedman had identified as the pre-Keynesian or anti-Keynesian quantity theory, using National Bureau business-cycle techniques, with heavy reliance on the old-fashioned method of historical narrative. Furthermore, in other of his writings Friedman set his work up as a challenge to the prevailing Keynesian orthodoxy. Against this background it is not surprising that readers of Chapter 7 found more than is actually there.

The *Monetary History* is a history of money and monetary policy from 1867 to 1960, and Chapter 7 is a history of money and policy through the course of the Great Depression. Neither the book nor the chapter is a history of the U.S. economy, nor does either give a comprehensive explanation of business cycles over the periods covered.[2] Friedman and Schwartz's primary purposes were to explain how and why the stock of money changed as it did and what were the effects of those changes. The latter task is not the same as explaining the course of aggregate income and prices, unless the only cause of those changes is money and monetary policy. Friedman and Schwartz were clear that this was not their belief. Their introduction indicates plainly the book's subject: "This book is about the stock of money in the United States" (1963b, p. 3). And it carries a warning against reading too much into the organization of the narrative around National Bureau cycles:

Our extensive use of this [National Bureau] chronology perhaps justifies an explicit caveat that we do not present a comprehensive history of cyclical movements in economic activity in the United States. Monetary factors played a major role in these movements, and conversely, nonmonetary developments frequently had a major influence on monetary developments; yet even together the matters that concern the historian of money do not exhaust those that are relevant to the historian of cyclical movements (1963b, p. 6).

The importance of the fact that the *Monetary History* is a history of money cannot be overstated, because some of the controversy that surrounded the book on matters of separating causes and effects is the result of this fact being misplaced. In trying to determine the causal role of money in business cycles, Friedman and Schwartz ap-

---

[2] For example, Friedman and Schwartz did not give any treatment of the severe 1913–14 recession as there was no evidence that money played a role in it.

peared to be ignoring or diminishing the causal role of other non-monetary factors. And indeed they were. If they did not, the book would not be a monetary history; it would be a comprehensive history of business cycles.

To illustrate this point, consider the attention that would be given to the influence of U.S. foreign policy on world affairs in a history of American foreign policy, in comparison with the attention it would get in a history of the world. Next to the history of the world, the history of American foreign policy would look like a narrow unicausal account. The author of the history of the world would appear to have a sophisticated view of a complex web of forces shaping world history, in which the various forces act and react to one another and no one cause drives the whole. By contrast, the historian of U.S. foreign policy would appear as a provincial apologist for the U.S. perspective on world affairs, with an overblown sense of the importance of what happens in Washington, D.C. Much of this apparent difference in causal presumptions of the two authors would simply be a difference in their aim.

Friedman and Schwartz made no claim to have laid bare the entire chain of causes and effects that produced the Great Depression. Their concern was with the role of money and financial institutions, in particular with the role of monetary policy. They came to the provocative conclusion that the Federal Reserve could have cut short the economic decline by severing the link between banking crises and monetary deflation. This would have required only that the Fed follow principles that were readily available in Walter Bagehot's *Lombard Street* (1873) and Congressional documents from the hearings that led to creation of the Federal Reserve. Their second guessing of the Federal Reserve was a point that drew fire from critics and lent support to the presumption that Friedman and Schwartz had a narrow and unidirectional conception of the Depression's causes.

In writing *Did Monetary Forces Cause the Great Depression?*, Peter Temin presumed that the primary issue for Friedman and Schwartz was to discover the cause of the Great Depression. He noted pointedly that they made few direct statements about the causes of changes in income but many about the causes of changes in the money stock. This created the impression that they were being coy, making an argument that the Federal Reserve caused the Depression but leaving themselves an escape.

If Friedman and Schwartz were arguing that the Federal Reserve caused the Depression, their explanation of changes in the money stock, which Temin noted is replete with direct statements of causation, would be an important step. This is because one of the primary rules of thumb that economists use in separating causes from effects is that factors identified as causes should be independent of those that are effects, that is, they should be exogenous. To argue that the Federal Reserve caused the Depression, it would be important to establish a degree of independence for the money stock from income and prices. If there were none, if changes in income and prices fully accounted for changes in money, that would be *prima facia* evidence that the Federal Reserve did not play a causal role in the Depression. If the Fed exercised no control over money, they would exercise no control over income and prices through the vehicle of money. On the other hand, if Friedman and Schwartz's concern was less with explaining the Great Depression than explaining the course of money and monetary policy during the Depression, then the fact that they made many causal statements about money but few about income would not suggest a hedged argument but would be consistent with the purpose of their analysis.

The method that Friedman and Schwartz used in Chapter 7 was a combination of historical narrative and counterfactual analysis. Their analytical skeleton was an identity with which they broke the money stock up into its components.[3] From this identity they moved to an explanatory relationship from which they drew inferences about whether changes in money were attributable to the monetary base (high-powered money), to the currency/deposit ratio, or to the reserve/deposit ratio. In the shift from identity to explanatory relationship, they relied on historical documents for information on the Federal Reserve's policy aims and actions, on economic theory of expectations and the behavior of the nonbank public and commercial banks, and on judgments about what the Federal Reserve was chartered to do. No less important were their presumptions of what effects on income and prices would follow if the Federal Reserve did control the money stock.

Friedman and Schwartz's primary use of the money stock identity was to sort the facts, in much the same way that a historian of diplomacy would begin with a political map of the world. Diplomatic events of the world are the sum of diplomatic events in the individual countries, as the countries are defined in relation to one another by a map.

---

[3] High-powered money, the ratio of bank deposits to reserves, and the ratio of bank deposits to currency. See (1963b, p. 51, n. 60).

The historian who wants to explain world diplomacy over a period of time would quite naturally begin with this framework and collect facts about what diplomats in the various countries were doing. Aggregation across countries and through time would produce the full set of facts of world diplomacy.

This first step of collecting facts with guidance from a map, which itself is a tautological framework, is such a natural part of the historical enterprise that its importance can easily be overlooked. No historian would think to challenge another's historical account with an argument that this first step, using a political map to sort the facts, is illegitimate. Yet economists do challenge each other over what amounts to the same procedure. One of the regular critiques of the quantity theory is that economists using it mistake the equation of exchange identity for a causal relation.

The next step for the historian is to add explanation of the facts that goes beyond the facts themselves. For the diplomatic historian this would involve explaining why diplomatic initiatives were taken and what their effects were on life outside the halls of government. At this stage the factual material assembled with the tautology is combined or treated with theoretical hypotheses of one sort or another, and the arithmetical account is transformed into a causal account.[4]

In making a causal account of diplomatic history the historian would use hypotheses about singular events, such as that statements made by diplomats explain their actions, to reveal some of the true causes of their actions. Thus if the president said he supported and signed a trade treaty because he thought it would promote growth of jobs for American workers, this would potentially be counted among the causes of that treaty coming to fruition. The historian would also use more general historical theories, such as, for example, Marxist historical determinism.

The quantity theory of money, loosely defined as the idea that changes in the money supply affect both prices and output, is the most important general theory that Friedman and Schwartz used. However, not all of their hypotheses were derived from it. They came to the conclusion that the ultimate cause of the financial collapse in the 1930s was a financial structure that made heros necessary. This gave the death in 1928 of Benjamin Strong, governor of the New York Federal Reserve, a pivotal place in Friedman and Schwartz's narra-

---

[4] See Friedman and Schwartz (1963b, ch. 7, sect. 2, pp. 332–50) for an example of their use of these two steps.

tive.[5] Friedman and Schwartz argued that the structural instability of the financial system let Strong's death and the shift of power from the New York Fed to the other Federal Reserve banks, small and apparently insignificant events in relation to the economic dislocations of the Great Depression, have large effects. Thus they concluded the chapter with a paradox.

The foregoing explanation of the financial collapse as resulting so largely from the shift of power from New York to the other Federal Reserve Banks and from personal backgrounds and characteristics of the men nominally in power may seem farfetched. It is a sound general principle that great events have great origins, and hence that something more than the characteristics of the specific persons or official agencies that happened to be in power is required to explain such a major event as the financial catastrophe in the United States from 1929 to 1933.

Yet it is also true that small events at times have large consequences, that there are such things as chain reactions and cumulative forces. It happens that a liquidity crisis in a unit fractional reserve banking system is precisely the kind of event that can trigger – and often has triggered – a chain reaction. And economic collapse often has the character of a cumulative process. Let it go beyond a certain point, and it will tend for a time to gain strength from its own development as its effects spread and return to intensify the process of collapse. Because no great strength would be required to hold back the rock that starts a landslide, it does not follow that the landslide will not be of major proportions (1963b, p. 419).

### Temin's critique

Temin attempted to set up a test of Friedman and Schwartz's hypothesis against an alternative. To do so he had to determine what their hypothesis actually was. Temin recognized that they were more concerned with potential cures for the Depression than with causes. But in his judgment there was insufficient information to reach a conclusion on the counterfactual question of what the Fed might have done to reduce the Depression's severity and end it sooner. He thought prospects were better for treating the question of what caused the Depression in the first place. This question was not only more likely to yield an empirically verified conclusion, Temin thought, but it was also more fundamental, being logically prior to the question of what could have been done about the Depression. If you want to find an

---

[5] Concern with the stabilizing or destabilizing tendencies of the financial structure is in evidence in Friedman's work in the field of money and banking from his very earliest publications. See Friedman (1948b).

efficacious cure, first find the cause. Thus Temin inferred from Friedman and Schwartz's conclusion that the Federal Reserve could have ameliorated the Depression, an antecedent judgment that the Fed caused the Depression.

Temin criticized the way Friedman and Schwartz moved from the identity they used to break the money stock into its components to the theoretical explanation of changes in the monetary aggregate. He charged them with failing to identify the function that shifted. It is standard practice for economists to move from an identity, such as that sales equal purchases, to theoretical or hypothetical supply and demand equations. But in making this move, with the aim of empirical verification, the most vexing problem encountered is the identification problem. Prices and quantities are jointly determined by supply and demand. Whether observed changes in prices and quantities are the result of shifts in supply along a stationary demand function, or shifts in demand along a supply function, or shifts in both is very difficult to determine with precision and certainty.

Yet such identification is essential for making causal judgments about historical facts, given the common convention of assigning causal responsibility to the factor that is in motion rather than to that which is at rest.[6] Temin argued that Friedman and Schwartz's explanation of the Great Depression was circular inasmuch as they assumed the very condition their conclusion depended on, the independence of money supply. In other words, they assumed without a demonstration that the money supply function, and not the demand function, shifted.

Friedman and Schwartz were not the only subjects of Temin's criticism. He was also critical of conventional macroeconomic analysts for relying on econometric modeling to the exclusion of historical events. Among econometricians' strongest urges, Temin thought, was the urge to endogenize, to make each variable in an econometric model a function of each of the others. He reasoned that this all but ruled out any chance of finding the causes of the Great Depression by econometric techniques, for causes are by their nature exogenous. If, for example, the money stock is completely explained by changes in prices and income, that is, is fully endogenous, but prices and income are not fully accounted for by the money stock, the money stock is the effect rather than the cause. If a complete explanation of income requires that the money stock be considered, and likewise a complete explanation of the money stock requires consideration of income, by

[6] See Hammond (1986).

Temin's thinking, one cannot conclude that either of the variables is the cause and the other the effect. When econometricians make all the variables in a model functions of the others, they rob them all of any right to designation as causes.[7]

Temin concluded from data from the Depression that there was no rise in short-term interest rates or fall in real money balances between the stock market crash in October 1929 and Britain's departure from the gold standard in September 1931. Thus there was no evidence that shifts in the money supply function contributed causally to the Great Depression during this period.[8] He found more evidence in favor of a Keynesian explanation of a shift in consumption expenditures that resulted in part from a drop in income and wealth produced by the stock market crash and a poor agricultural harvest in 1929. Yet, by his account these two factors were responsible for only a small portion of the observed drop in consumption expenditures, leaving most of the purported cause of the Depression itself without explanation.[9]

The poor harvest fit Temin's definition of a cause quite well. Weather is the classic case of an exogenous factor that contributes to economic fluctuations. This was the core of William Stanley Jevons's famous sunspot theory of business cycles (1884). But this definition of cause as exogenous factor that brings about the effect, and Temin's conclusion that the two key events he could identify to explain the drop in consumption left most of the drop unexplained, put Temin in what he recognized as an uncomfortable position. His hypothesis was that the drop in consumption expenditures was the key proximate cause of the Depression. But most of that drop was exogenous, not just in the sense that its cause remained outside the economic model, but in the deeper sense that its cause remained a complete mystery. On the one hand, the purported cause had the requisite quality of exogeneity, but on the other hand, it appeared to be a deus ex machina. Can a cause that itself remains a mystery resolve the mystery of the Depression?

[7] For philosophical accounts of causality in general equilibrium systems, see Hausman (1983, 1990).

[8] He found that there was evidence for the monetary hypothesis before and after this period.

[9] Thomas Mayer (1978a) argued that Temin's data suggested a drop in the consumption function because he compared 1930 with 1921 and 1938. Mayer compared 1930 with the entire interwar period and found no evidence of a shift in the function.

It is somewhat unsatisfactory to say that the Depression was started by an unexplained event, but this alternative is preferable to statements that are inconsistent with the data. The spending hypothesis is consistent with the data if we accept the autonomous nature of a large part of the fall in consumption in 1930. It is not, however, a complete story (Temin, 1976, p. 83).

Temin's rebuttal of what he interpreted as the Friedman and Schwartz hypothesis, that monetary forces caused the Depression, was less than fully convincing without an equally complete explanation to put in its place.

## The great depression revisited

As we noted, Schwartz answered Temin's challenge at a 1978 conference sponsored by the Center for Research in Government Policy and Business at the University of Rochester. Schwartz's article in the conference volume, *The Great Depression Revisited* (1981), opens with a reaffirmation that she and Friedman never aimed to demonstrate that the money supply affected income without reverse causation, that it was exogenous. They recognized that the money stock was influenced by developments in the economy. Schwartz said, in effect, that their definition of cause did not require complete exogeneity. The definition of cause as an exogenous variable, which had been attributed to them, made the task of countering their explanation all the easier. She quoted Temin to show how the attribution was made: "Either changes in the stock of money caused income to change, or vice versa. The resolution was equally simple. The stock of money was determined by a variety of forces independent of the level of income . . . and the direction of causation therefore must be from money to income, not the other way" (Temin, 1976, p. 14; Schwartz, 1981, p. 9).

Schwartz quoted a lengthy p‍‍age from "Money and Business Cycles" to show that this was not their view:

The key question at issue is not whether the direction of influence is wholly from money to business or wholly from business to money; it is whether the influence running from money to business is significant, in the sense that it can account for a substantial fraction of the fluctuations in economic activity. If the answer is affirmative, then one can speak of a monetary theory of business cycles or − more precisely − of the need to assign money an important role in a full theory of business cycles. The reflex influence of business on money, the existence of which is not in doubt in light of the factual evidence summarized above, would then become part of the partly self-generating mechanism whereby monetary disturbances are transmitted. . . . As noted above, Cagan shows that the public's decisions about the proportions in which it divides its money balances between currency and deposits is an important link in the feedback mechanism whereby changes in business affect the stock of money (Friedman and Schwartz, 1963a, pp. 49–50; Schwartz, 1981, p. 10).[10]

Schwartz's retrospective on her earlier work with Friedman was that the *Monetary History* primarily contributed to showing how the money stock shrank during the Great Depression. They showed that whatever confluence of forces caused the Depression, its severity was magnified by deflationary pressures operating through the money supply and originating in the banking crises. Having made this clarification, Schwartz proceeded through the greater portion of her chapter to answer Temin's critique and deal with his alternative hypotheses in the unicausal terms in which he had cast them. That is, she challenged his evidence and offered new evidence of her own to try to bring to a resolution the question of whether monetary forces *or* real forces caused the Depression.

Thus Schwartz went along with Temin's preference for considering the question of what caused the Depression rather than what could have been done to shorten it and reduce its severity, and with his transformation of the question of the causes to simple one-way causality. This is why, in another paper in the Rochester symposium, Gordon and Wilcox (1981) labeled the Friedman–Schwartz position of the *Monetary History* "soft-line monetarism," Temin's book "hard-line nonmonetarism," and Schwartz's position in the symposium "hard-line monetarism."

Schwartz's defense of the hard-line monetarist position and critique of Temin were based on new evidence and reevaluation of old evidence. Her primary new evidence was a set of Granger causality tests. Granger tests are designed to settle, or to see if one can settle, the question of whether in a specified sense of statistical exogeneity, variable A causes variable B or vice versa. Thus the test is the natural statistical complement for a unicausal conception of causality. Schwartz's evidence indicated that for 1919 to 1939, M2 was exogenous and a proxy for income was endogenous (indicating that money was the cause and income the effect), and for 1929 to 1939, neither was endogenous with respect to the other.

She introduced a new variable, the reciprocal of the price level, as an alternative to Temin's short-term interest rate as the price of money. Temin had showed that short-term rates fell when they should have risen if their movement reflected a decline in the money supply.

[10] Schwartz's reference to Cagan's work is to *Determinants and Effects of Changes in the Stock of Money, 1875–1960* (1965).

Along the same lines, Schwartz argued that if observed changes in the nominal money stock in 1930 and the first three-quarters of 1931 were produced by the banking system's accommodation of a decline in money demand, the expected changes in income and the price level would have been increases, just the opposite of what occurred. Schwartz cited evidence from other studies to call into question Temin's estimate of the consumption function and to lend support to her contention that the money demand function was stable throughout the Depression.

Schwartz turned a familiar charge around by suggesting that Temin and other critics of her work with Friedman who offered nonmonetarist explanations of the Great Depression committed the *post hoc ergo propter hoc* fallacy. "The authors of the various versions [of the spending hypothesis] write as if the cycle is necessarily propagated by the component of GNP that first reaches a peak or that is most volatile. Is this more than the most vulgar post hoc–propter hoc reasoning? If not, where is the evidence?" (1981, p. 20)

In concluding her article, Schwartz returned to the question that was uppermost for her and Friedman, not what caused the Depression, but what could have been done about it. Though Temin had drawn her into debating the question he preferred, she noted that he had refused to consider the question they were most interested in, what better policy options were open to the Fed. We have seen that his objection to dealing with this question was that it was counterfactual and that he thought there was insufficient evidence for its adjudication. Taking issue with this, Schwartz cited the apparent power of expansionary open market operations the Fed conducted in 1932. She asked:

Can he really mean that the Federal Reserve undertook the open-market purchases in 1932 as a passive response to an increased demand for money that was a result of rising output and prices that lagged the change in monetary policy? There is evidence also on what alternative policies would have accomplished if we turn to the system's open-market purchases in 1924 and 1927. The omission of discussion of these policy measures in Temin's book reflects his assumption that money is passive. Supply simply adjusts to the demand. This is a real-bills vision with a vengeance (1981, pp. 41–2).

So in the end, Schwartz rejected unidirectional causality by interpreting Temin's hypothesis as this sort of account and suggesting that there are instances in which it is clear that the Federal Reserve exercised control over the money stock. Thus she concluded that Temin's critique failed under his own critical standard by requiring too heavy a burden for the evidence to support – total endogeneity of the money stock. Schwartz had returned to the "soft monetarism" position she occupied with Friedman in 1963, where there is no presumption that causation is in one direction only. In rejecting total dependence of the money stock on the business cycle, she reestablished the central importance of the question of whether there was *a degree* of independence of the money supply. Could the Fed have offset declines in the money stock originating elsewhere?

Most of the other authors in the 1981 symposium shared the opinion of Gordon and Wilcox that Temin and Schwartz were on a dead end in debating whether monetary *or* real forces caused the Depression, viewing this particular question as a throwback to the era of hard-line Keynesianism prior to the *Monetary History*. Gordon and Wilcox remarked that there is no longer much doubt that money matters (and that it mattered during the Depression) and that unicausal explanations are inherently weak, because they are excessively easy to contradict.[11] "From this orientation, a modern monetarist would not be required to devote excessive attention to showing that money played a major causal role in the Great Depression, because the potency of money is no longer a matter for debate" (1981, p. 51). Or, as Peter Lindert (1981) put it in a piece that was on the whole critical of Schwartz, it is "totally untenable" to argue that more expansionary policy by the Fed would not have reduced the severity of the Depression.

Much of the evidence cited by the several authors in favor of this, at least partial, resolution of the debate was in the form of international comparisons, such as international patterns in the behavior of velocity. The general sense of the commentary in the symposium was that the nature of the task that remained was not to pit sweeping hypotheses against one another but to fill in the gaps in knowledge of how the Great Depression originated and unfolded. This indeed is the spirit of most of the literature on the Depression since the 1981 Rochester symposium.

The next item in the literature on the Great Depression that we consider is Temin's 1989 book, *Lessons from the Great Depression*. That book is written mostly in this spirit of filling in the gaps. But Temin's opposition to Friedman and Schwartz is still evident, even though his

[11] Gordon and Wilcox also noted that the difference in the questions of interest to Friedman and Schwartz and to Temin (and Schwartz in her symposium piece) is reflected in their attention to different time periods. Friedman and Schwartz's primary concern was with the period after the first wave of bank failures in October 1930, whereas Temin's was on the first two years of the Depression.

new view of the causes of the Depression is quite different from that in *Did Monetary Forces Cause the Great Depression?* and much closer to a monetarist view.

## Temin's revised hypothesis

In the later book, *Lessons from the Great Depression,* Temin was still looking for the causes of the Depression. Finding evidence for a number of purported causal factors in the literature, none of which seemed adequate as the cause of the Depression, Temin drew a distinction between causes, impulses, and propagation factors. He placed most of the purported causes into the impulse and propagation factor categories, and assessed the relative strength of the evidence in their favor. This led to his building a case for the one factor that he considered a strong candidate for the role of "cause." It was still Temin's view that identification of the cause was the large gap to be filled in knowledge of the economics of the Great Depression. "In fact one of the problems with modern views of the Depression has been the absence of causes. Rejecting Friedman and Schwartz's rather special view has seemed to leave a void. . . . Putative propagating mechanisms have proliferated, but eligible causes have not" (1989, p. 35). The factor Temin identified as the cause of the Depression is the international gold standard.

Temin in fact had come a long way around to Friedman and Schwartz's position, since the international gold standard is a monetary factor. But he crafted his exposition so that he made this move without acknowledging doing so and without abandoning his stance in opposition to their evaluation of the Depression. His shift toward their view was to abandon the argument that an exogenous drop in consumption expenditures was the cause of the Depression, and adopt a monetary, if not monetarist, explanation.

Temin's dropping the consumption explanation is not surprising, because the largest part of the drop in consumption expenditures remained unexplained. As we have seen, this left Temin in an awkward position in his 1976 book. No cause was discovered subsequently for the unexplained portion of the drop in expenditures. But additional evidence was produced in support of a deflationary contraction of the money supply by the Federal Reserve in 1928 and 1929 (Hamilton, 1987), and for an increase in money demand (Field, 1984a,b). Together, these new studies lent support to an affirmative answer to the question Temin used to frame the issue in his 1976 book, "Did monetary forces cause the Great Depression?"

An example of how Temin kept his distance from Friedman and Schwartz and other monetarists can be seen early in the book, where he informs his readers that "I follow Keynes here and assign a primary role to tight monetary policy in the late 1920s" (1989, p. 7). He was following Keynes, not Friedman and Schwartz, and not the early Keynesians who argued that money did not matter! Temin explained that, although it played a primary role, tight monetary policy was not the cause of the Depression. It was the propagation mechanism, and World War I was the impulse. The international gold standard was the cause.

So, though Temin yielded on important particulars about monetary forces and the Depression, he did not conclude that the Federal Reserve caused the Depression. With the distinction between impulses, propagation mechanisms, and causes, he kept to his pursuit of a unicausal explanation, to the pursuit of a "final cause." This cause was a structural characteristic of the turn of the century international economy.

His explanation was that the international gold standard imparted a deflationary bias to fiscal and monetary policy after World War I and upset the equilibrium that had prevailed with prewar exchange rate parities. The factor that systematically brought about deflationary policy throughout the world, and thus the cause of the Great Depression, was the governments' commitment to the gold standard. World War I was the impulse that made that commitment inconsistent with growing income and stable price levels. The New York stock market crash, the agricultural crisis, the Smoot–Hawley Tariff, and the U.S. banking crises, to which Friedman and Schwartz assigned a key role, were all reduced to subordinate roles as propagation mechanisms. Restrictive policy actions arose inexorably from the structural deflationary bias of the postwar gold standard.

Temin thought that his account corrected a weakness in Friedman and Schwartz's. Recall that they attributed a large effect (the deepening of the Depression) to a small cause (the death of Benjamin Strong and liquidity crises). Temin's cause matched the effect in scope and size. The Depression was international in scope as well as unmatched in severity; the gold standard was also international and had a powerful and broad influence on policy decisions.

Though Temin took care to differentiate his explanation of the Depression from Friedman and Schwartz's, there are marked similarities. Foremost is the important role he assigned to restrictive monetary policy, whether this factor is called a cause or a propagation mechanism. Deflationary monetary policy is the most important propagation mechanism in his account. Second, his distinction between action and regime, though it was meant to separate propagation mechanisms from the more important causes, actually is in harmony with Friedman and Schwartz's account. Recall that they concluded that the ultimate explanation of the Great Depression was a financial system that made heros such as Benjamin Strong necessary for its proper functioning. "It was a defect of the financial system that it was susceptible to crises resolvable only with such leadership. The existence of such a financial system is, of course, the ultimate explanation for the financial collapse, rather than the shift of power from New York to the other Federal Reserve Banks and the weakness of the Reserve Board, since it permitted those circumstances to have such far-reaching consequences" (1963b, p. 418). Both Friedman and Schwartz and Temin identified ultimate causes and primary responsibility for the Depression in institutional structures. Thirdly, in both his books, Temin the economic historian treated the Great Depression as an historical event to be understood historically. This was a departure from standard macroeconometric analysis, as Friedman and Schwartz's account was.

### Current understanding of the depression

Two articles from a 1993 *Journal of Economic Perspectives* symposium on the Great Depression provide an overview of the current state of thinking about the causes of the Great Depression. Christina Romer surveyed the evidence to produce a sketch of what is known about the causes of the Depression in "The Nation in Depression" (1993), and Charles Calomiris summarized current thinking on "Financial Factors in the Great Depression" (1993).

Romer departed from a tendency, due in part to Temin's second book, to identify international causes of the Depression. The appeal of international explanations is that they match scopes of cause and effect, avoiding the imbalance that weakened the appeal of Friedman and Schwartz's account. With an international cause, explanations of the Depression need not bear the burden of explaining how the Depression spread across countries.

Romer's thesis runs against this tide. She argued that the center of the Depression was in the United States, a conclusion she drew from evidence on the timing of the downturn in the United States and elsewhere and from evidence matching domestic causal factors with the more significant phases of the Depression in the United States. Most of the purported causes in the earlier literature, which Temin labeled propagating factors, are given some role in her explanation of the downturn and recovery in the United States, with none standing out in a special position relative to the others. Romer's account does not assign a special "final cause" role to any factor.

Romer contended that we now largely understand how the Depression and recovery came about in the United States. The start of the recession, from July 1929 through October, was the result of the Fed's tightening monetary policy in 1928. This tight policy could well have had international roots, such as the Fed's concern to prevent a gold outflow to France in face of the undervaluation of the franc. The onset of the Great Depression, from October 1929 through 1930, was caused by a collapse in consumer spending that resulted from the stock market crash. The connection between the crash and consumer spending was the uncertainty created by the crash and the consequent decline in demand for irreversible consumer goods, as well as wealth and liquidity effects. Romer followed E. N. White (1990) in attributing the stock market crash to the preceding boom's being a bubble. As such, this brings the identification of causes of the onset of the Depression to a close, for bubbles are virtually inexplicable, by definition.

The Depression worsened from April 1931 to July 1932, for which Romer blamed the series of banking panics that were the focus of Friedman and Schwartz's account. The deposit/currency ratio rose, pushing up real interest rates; pessimistic expectations were heightened; and there was financial disintermediation. Romer concurred with Friedman and Schwartz's view that, at least up through October 1930, the Federal Reserve could have stepped in with expansionary open market operations and staved off the cumulative contractionary effects of the first wave of panics.

Whatever one's view of the pressure that the gold standard ultimately put on the Federal Reserve's ability to respond to the financial panics in 1931, there is little doubt that the Federal Reserve could have done something to stop the first wave of panics in late 1930. If one believes that the panics built on one another through the effect on income and the effect on expectations, then a different decision by the Federal Reserve in the fall of 1930 might have prevented the later panics that so decimated the U.S. financial system. In this case, one would have to say that American policy mistakes in 1930 played a crucial role in determining the course of output not just in 1930, but in later years as well (1993, pp. 33–4).

Romer attributed the U.S. recovery from the Depression, beginning in 1933, to a shift to expansionary monetary policy. Under pressure from Congress, the Fed adopted expansionary policy in the spring of

1932 but reverted to more cautious policy in midsummer. A more substantial and permanent shift occurred in 1933, after President Roosevelt devalued the dollar. She attributed the large increase in M1 that followed, forty-nine percent from April 1933 to April 1937, to a money supply shift (that is, more expansionary policy) rather than to the "reverse causation" that figured in most of the accounts that deny the power of monetary policy. The evidence for this is that growth of the monetary base virtually matched the growth of M1. Reverse causation would show up in changes in the reserve/deposit and currency/ deposit ratios.

Calomiris (1993) argued that the theory of imperfect capital markets is an important tool for explaining the links between financial and real factors in the Depression. He saw this literature as a shift away from the emphasis on interest rate elasticities, wealth effects, and uncertainty that played major roles in the 1960s and 1970s debate over the role of monetary factors in causing the Great Depression.

A paradigmatic study in this new literature is Ben S. Bernanke's 1983 article, "Nonmonetary Effects of the Financial Crisis in the Propagation of the Great Depression." Bernanke argued that financial crises such as banking panics disrupted the financial sector's ability to provide market-making and information-gathering services. They thereby increased the real cost of financial intermediation. To Bernanke, this was the key to money's extended nonneutrality during the Great Depression.

Bernanke portrayed his work as a supplement to Friedman and Schwartz's account, as did Calomiris. Calomiris wrote:

The "new view" of Bernanke and others was not a rejection of Friedman and Schwartz's argument that monetary shocks were important. Its main contribution was to show that monetary shocks, and other disturbances during the early phase of the Depression, had long-run effects largely because they affected the institutional structure of credit markets and the balance sheets of borrowers (1993, p. 72).

One of the appealing features of this theory is that it identifies a theoretically and empirically appropriate transmission mechanism. It is consistent both with rational expectations theory, which flourished after the *Monetary History,* and with the empirical evidence on the Depression presented by Friedman and Schwartz and others. In the contemporary context of rational expectations, the focus in Bernanke's theoretical model is unanticipated money, rather than the measured money stock. As we saw in Chapter 5, Friedman and

Schwartz's preference for using the growth rate of the money stock rather than its level in their cycle analysis was partly on this basis.

Calomiris drew three implications from what he called the non-monetary propagation hypothesis, with its emphasis on real consequences of financial crises. The first is that a money supply shock has larger effects if it occurs at a time of high leverage or in an economy with undiversified and geographically fragmented banks. This is another way of resolving the causality problem faced by Friedman and Schwartz of disproportionality between the sizes of cause and effect. The second implication is that if there is "path dependence" in financial markets, effects are nonreversible. Calomiris argued that the Federal Reserve could not have undone the real effects of financial crises by restoring the money supply. "Thus, according to the new view, even if Friedman and Schwartz and their supporters were entirely correct about the importance of monetary shocks in precipitating the Depression, it does not follow that open market operations to restore the money supply would have had offsetting effects in promoting recovery from the Depression" (1993, p. 74). The third implication Calomiris drew from the new literature on credit market imperfections is that it matters how the Fed controls the money supply. Depending on the circumstances, for example, changes in the discount rate could have different effects from open market operations. Thus, to whatever extent the Fed was able to reverse the harmful effects of crises, this ability could be enhanced or not, depending on the policy instrument chosen.

## Conclusion

Much has changed since the *Monetary History* appeared in 1963. Monetary theory and history were not then in fashion, hydraulic Keynesianism and macroeconometrics were. Economists had little analytical interest in the Great Depression. They had great confidence that they could not only prevent future depressions but keep the economy continuously at full employment. Thanks largely to Friedman and Schwartz and to Temin, the Great Depression became an analytical issue for economists, with recognition of the benefits of taking an explicitly historical approach. The role of money is prominent in all contemporary accounts of the Depression, including Temin's. The literature that has poured forth has filled many of the gaps in knowledge of the causes and cures for the Depression and contributed to the understanding of business cycles in general.

From the perspective of macroeconometric modeling, exogeneity was the primary quality associated with causality. A cause was part of the explanation of the effect, but the effect was not part of the explanation of the cause. Friedman and Schwartz went part way with this definition, but not so far as Temin interpreted them as going. In their view it was sufficient that the Federal Reserve had power to influence the money stock for money to stand as a cause. The money stock need not have been totally independent of income and prices. It was more important to find that the empirically observed relationship between money and income held up under disparate circumstances.

Temin, and to some extent Friedman and Schwartz, was interested in a "final cause" of the Depression. In his 1976 book, this led him to put two unicausal accounts into competition against each other. In his later book, he found the final cause by making the distinction between cause (final cause), impulse, and propagation factor. He located the final cause in the structure of the international monetary system. This provided the comfort of a match between the scope of the cause and scope of the effect. Friedman and Schwartz were mostly concerned with the course of events through the Depression, including especially Federal Reserve policy decisions, but they too looked to the structure of the U.S. monetary system for a more fundamental cause.

In the recent literature on the Depression, authors are less inclined to take a unicausal approach than either Temin or Schwartz in her Rochester symposium paper. Monetary forces are not viewed as the only cause of the Depression, but they are given an important role in accounts of its causes. Though Temin's *Did Monetary Forces Cause the Great Depression?* portrayed Friedman and Schwartz's account as unicausal, the *Monetary History* ultimately contributed to richer, more historically grounded use of causality than the precise but austere endogeneity–exogeneity duality of econometrics.

# CHAPTER 10

# Measurement without measurement:
# Hendry and Ericsson's critique

## Introduction

Friedman and Schwartz's original 1949 plan for their project envisioned three years' work to measure and analyze the cyclical behavior of monetary and banking phenomena, their relations to cycles in other important variables, and the causal role of monetary and banking phenomena in business cycles for the United States. They expected to have a final report by the end of 1951. As it turned out they worked throughout the first half of the 1950s building their data set. By 1955, with much of the data collection and production done, they were negotiating with Geoffrey Moore, director of research at the National Bureau, over the structure of their report. Friedman envisioned two volumes, one that would be primarily for data presentation and the other for the National Bureau–style analysis of trends and cycles. The data presentation volume would be similar to Burns and Mitchell's *Measuring Business Cycles,* with heavy emphasis on exposition of their measurements. This volume was eventually published in 1970 as *Monetary Statistics of the United States.*

Their work on the analytical volume started in earnest in the mid-1950s and continued into the 1960s. The core of what was to be the cycles portion of the volume was published in 1963 as "Money and Business Cycles." An analytical narrative of the history of money grew from a chapter into the *Monetary History* (1963b). But the analytical volume was still conceived as a single work on both trends and cycles in 1963. Soon thereafter Friedman and Schwartz changed their plans and split the analytical volume into two: one for analysis of cycles, another for analysis of trends. It turned out that *Monetary Cycles* was never completed. *Monetary Trends* was finished in draft and submitted to a National Bureau reading committee in 1966.[1] Following the committee's suggestion, Friedman and Schwartz delayed publication in order to expand coverage to include data for the United Kingdom. In

[1] The committee members were Soloman Fabricant (committee chair), Phillip Cagan, and Jack Guttentag.

doing so they got more delay than they bargained for. *Monetary Trends* was published sixteen years later, in 1982. This long gestation time for *Monetary Trends* is important for understanding the critical treatments of the book that are the focus of this chapter.

## The JEL reviews

Three monetary economists from different backgrounds and perspectives reviewed the book in 1982 for the *Journal of Economic Literature* (JEL). Thomas Mayer's review was the broadest in scope, and he was a long-time participant in the controversy over monetarism.[2] Charles Goodhart wrote from the British and the Bank of England perspective.[3] Robert Hall considered *Monetary Trends* in light of free banking theory, or what was called the new monetary economics. This was a literature that had grown up in the interval between Friedman and Schwartz's 1966 draft submitted to the National Bureau committee and the 1982 published volume.

All three reviewers judged that in setting up their book around the theme of the quantity theory (or monetarism) versus Keynesianism, Friedman and Schwartz fought a war that they had already largely won. This was no doubt due to the very long time that the book was in the making. *Monetary Trends* was rooted in the postwar issues of macroeconomics: the stability of money demand, the power of money supply changes to affect income and prices, and the relationship between prices and interest rates. Hall wrote:

Friedman and Schwartz argue against what might neutrally be called the early post-war view of the macroeconomic role of money: Velocity will move easily to reconcile any level of nominal income to any money stock. The demand for money in this view is a "will-o'-the-wisp," as the authors put it. Monetary policy has little influence over real activity; stabilization policy necessarily relies on fiscal instruments. The volume is completely convincing in disposing of this idea; today's reader is likely to be puzzled why so much space is devoted to a view that has no serious adherents among professional economists. Friedman and Schwartz are generals fighting an earlier war, a situation accentuated by the long lags in putting this volume into print (1982, p. 1552).

From England, Goodhart also noted that much of what was challenging and original in Friedman and Schwartz's work in 1966, when their U.S. version went to the National Bureau reading committee, had become part of the mainstream of monetary economics.

[2] See Mayer's *Monetarism and Macroeconomic Policy* (1990).
[3] Goodhart served as one of the most senior advisers in monetary economics to the Bank of England.

The three reviewers were unanimous in their praise for the care and detail with which Friedman and Schwartz laid out both their data and the adjustments and tests they made on them. According to Mayer, "such tender loving care of the data is foreign to modern economics with its great emphasis on application of advanced techniques to any set of numbers almost regardless of their meaning" (1982, p. 1529). Mayer added that Friedman and Schwartz eschewed elaborate econometric techniques and that this was one of the weaknesses of the book. Goodhart echoed Mayer's praise for the contribution Friedman and Schwartz made in developing much of the data, as well as for their careful treatment of it. He noted likewise that their analytical techniques were out of step with modern econometrics. Their approach was to work intensively on small sets of variables, adding to the set sequentially to build up to an explanation. This was in contrast to the standard approach of deriving a money demand equation from a utility function (a "parade ground drill," according to Mayer) and using all variables simultaneously in a multiple regression. Goodhart expressed his own inclination toward Friedman and Schwartz's practice.

Friedman and Schwartz's approach was unorthodox in other respects, especially their National Bureau time-series analysis. Recall that the book is the trends portion of a study of trends and cycles. Beginning with time series on annual data, Friedman and Schwartz computed reference-cycle phase averages, which they used as their unit of measurement for levels of variables. This reduced each full cycle of expansion and contraction in a series to a single observation. For rates of change, they used slopes of linear functions fitted to logarithms of three successive phase averages. This technique of using cycle averages to separate longer-term from short-term variations was developed by Burns and Mitchell (1946) and became a standard feature of National Bureau analysis. But it was never widely popular outside the National Bureau. By the 1980s macroeconomic econometricians had relegated it to the statistical dustbin. Mayer predicted that many of the book's readers would be especially interested in intracycle movements in the original series, which the National Bureau technique eliminated. Goodhart also expressed reservations about their approach. He feared that: (1) it could not, and probably should not, eliminate *all* of the variation resulting from cycles, (2) it introduced serial correlation into the data, and (3) it effectively ruled out Granger–Sims-type causality tests.

This brings us to another theme in the reviews, the reviewers' regrets that Friedman and Schwartz did not push further to resolve the issue of causality between money and income. Does money cause income, or does income cause money? Hall asserted that the battle over monetarism was won, and Mayer wrote that even post-Keynesians would now accept the quantity theory over very long periods. Goodhart judged that virtually all economists would accept that over medium- and long-term periods, movements in the money stock and nominal income are closely related. But each of the three raised questions about the strength of the case presented in *Monetary Trends* for the predominance of forward causation.

Mayer remarked more than once that he was disappointed that they did not follow up on their earlier work on the direction of causation.[4] The transmission mechanism for monetary impulses was central to causality, and Mayer noted that the discussion in *Monetary Trends* was less detailed than that in their early paper, "Money and Business Cycles" (1963a). He pointed out that some of the empirical results in *Monetary Trends,* in particular the closer relationship between nominal income and current money than between nominal income and current and lagged money, could be interpreted as evidence of reverse causation. "Hence, even to someone like myself who agrees with F–S [Friedman–Schwartz] that causation runs mainly from money to income, it seems unfortunate that F–S discuss the direction of causation so little. Although every reader will be bound to respect the excellence of this book's empirical work, I suspect that a considerable number whose priors are anti–quantity theory will reject its quantity theory 'message' because of the causation problem" (1982, p. 1535).

Goodhart thought the causality issue was still very much alive. Thus his concern that Friedman and Schwartz's phase-average observations ruled out Granger–Sims tests. There may have been broad consensus on the medium- and long-term correlation between money and nominal income, but correlation is not causation. Goodhart sent a preliminary draft of his review to Friedman, in which he interpreted Friedman and Schwartz as making a priori assumptions about the direction of causation. Friedman objected to the term "a priori assumptions." He responded:

The only statement in the review to which I have a strong negative reaction and which I believe is factually incorrect is the statement . . . that the direction of causality is assumed a priori. That is not correct. What you mean to say is that the direction of causality is not examined in this book, but certainly we have not assumed it a priori; we have regarded it as an empirical proposition

---

[4] Friedman and Schwartz (1963a,b) and Cagan (1965).

established by other work that we and others have done (MF to CAEG, May 10, 1982).

Friedman referred Goodhart to sections of the *Monetary History* (1963b) and to "The Monetary Studies of the National Bureau" (1964a), where he and Schwartz dealt with the issue. He also explained his doubts about the worth of Granger–Sims tests.

I may also note that personally I have no great confidence in Granger–Sims tests of causality. They are interesting but highly inconclusive in particular because the way in which they tend to be used very often throws out the baby with the bath. People tend to combine them with the Box–Jenkins method of analyzing time series, take residuals from the ARIMA processes, and try to relate those to one another to see directions of causality. That is very likely to be a case of correlating noise. The relationships one is really interested in in the main are those between the ARIMA processes themselves. Let me recall your attention to the comments in our book on the rational expectations approach and the problems with many of the more extreme interpretations of it. Those comments are equally relevant to the Granger–Sims causality approach (MF to CAEG, May 10, 1982).

Goodhart removed the references to a priori assumptions about causation, replacing them with a statement that Friedman and Schwartz relied on their previous work to establish direction of causation. But he did not think the causality issue closed, and he thought that by not dealing with it, Friedman and Schwartz had foregone the opportunity to make converts. He asked if "anyone not already convinced that nominal incomes are held in a monetarist strait-jacket" (1982, p. 1541) would have adjusted the data for price controls and the OPEC oil embargo as Friedman and Schwartz did.[5]

Goodhart replicated some of the United Kingdom regressions from Friedman and Schwartz's Chapter 9 with unadjusted annual data and found that on the whole they were consistent with the phase average results, which were consistent with the monetarist view. His tests showed direct relations between inflation and contemporaneous money growth, lagged values of inflation, and interest rates. Yet, Goodhart suggested, these results could also be interpreted as evidence of reverse causation. The Bank of England might "lean against the wind" when inflation rises, which could account for the positive correlation between inflation and interest rates. But they might not lean heavily enough to prevent inflation from causing more rapid money growth.

---

[5] They made adjustments on the presumptions that price controls caused the data to understate the price level and that the drop in real income from the OPEC embargo was matched by an increase in the price level.

The lesson he drew from this exercise in interpretation of the empirical results was that more attention should be given to the issue of exogeneity and simultaneity. "Only if one starts with the prior belief that current money growth (and current changes in interest rates?) are determined exogenously of current inflation, do my own results appear clearly and strongly monetarist" (1982, p. 1547).

Writing from the perspective of the new monetary economics, Hall suggested that the quantity-theory results could be a vestige of government regulations. With the institutional and regulatory frameworks in place in the United States and United Kingdom over the period covered by *Monetary Trends* (1867–1975), money (government monetary liabilities and bank deposits) was a causal factor in the determination of nominal income. But with different institutions – prices not quoted in terms of the government liabilities and banks were not required to hold deposit reserves in these liabilities – this set of assets would have no causal power. So Hall concluded that Friedman and Schwartz's results stand but that their standing was less permanent and fundamental than it might seem. The empirical relationships were contingent on continued regulatory stability. With Mayer and Goodhart, he thought the issue of the source and evidence of money's causal efficacy was not closed.

### Hendry and Ericsson: Bank of England paper

Shortly after *Monetary Trends* was published, the Bank of England Panel of Academic Consultants made the book the subject of one of their meetings. This was a time when Milton Friedman and monetarism were highly visible and contentious topics in the United Kingdom.[6] Friedman had long been interested in British economic affairs,

---

[6] Monetarism was a more politically charged issue in the United Kingdom than the United States. In comparing British and American monetarism, David Laidler (1978) concluded that different ethical judgments about the importance of high employment or price level stability were *not* what separated British monetarists and Keynesians. Rather, they disagreed over whether micro- or macropolicies were better suited to the task of promoting high employment. Nonetheless British opponents of monetarism often portrayed the differences in ethical or class-interest terms. For example, in concluding an extensive *technical* critique of monetarism, Meghnad Desai wrote:

But a monetarist policy can only work if a government can stay immune from popular pressure, as nineteenth century governments could. It requires a long period of high

and his engagement was deepened by his work on British data for *Monetary Trends*. He made regular contributions to scholarly and public debate on economic policy in England through the 1970s.[7]

The 1970s were a decade of high inflation and unemployment in the United Kingdom. They were also a decade of financial liberalization and increased attention to monetary policy. In 1976 the Bank of England adopted monetary-aggregate intermediate targets for monetary policy. This was a move toward the monetarist approach to business-cycle policy. Increasingly there was discussion of taking the next step, replacing interest rates with the monetary base as the short-run target. Margaret Thatcher was elected Prime Minister in 1979 and made reducing inflation through control of the money supply a major plank in the Conservative Government's policies. In 1980 the Conservative Government announced a plan to lower the growth rate of £M3 over several years that was called the medium-term financial strategy. The Thatcher government's overt use of Friedman's ideas to justify their policies created additional interest in his and Schwartz's book.

Friedman was notified of the planned October 28th meeting of the Bank's Panel of Academic Consultants in a September 9, 1983, letter from a Bank official, J. C. R. Dow. Dow told Friedman that two panel members had been commissioned to write papers for the meeting. Arthur J. Brown, of Leeds University, performed the first statistical estimates of demand for money in the 1930s.[8] David F. Hendry, of Nuffield College, Oxford, was a leading British econometrician. Dow extended an invitation to Friedman or Schwartz to attend the meeting. He mentioned that the Bank already had a preliminary draft of

---

and increasing unemployment to achieve its true goal of altering the balance of power between labour and capital in post-Keynesian societies (1981, p. 225).

[7] In the 1970s, Friedman published two letters to the editor in *The Times*: "Monetary Policy and the Inflation Rate," May 2, 1977c, and "Relying on the Free Market," August 15, 1978b. He frequently wrote articles and gave lectures that were published in London by the Institute of Economic Affairs: *The Counter-Revolution in Monetary Theory* (1970a), *Monetary Correction* (1974c), "Inflation, Taxation, Indexation" (1974d), *Unemployment versus Inflation? An Evaluation of the Phillips Curve* (1975), "Nobel Lecture: Inflation and Unemployment" (1977b), *From Galbraith to Economic Freedom* (1977a). In addition, during the decade, he published in England: "Has the Tide Turned?" *The Listener*, April 27, 1978a, "Correspondence with Milton Friedman: A Debate on Britain's Policy," *Director*, December 1979, and "Monetarism: A Reply to the Critics," *The Times*, March 3, 1980.

[8] See Brown (1939).

Hendry's paper, and it "subjects your statistical methods to considerable criticism and does so on a scale which is considerably more massive and thorough than we originally envisioned" (JCRD to MF, September 9, 1983). Neither Friedman nor Schwartz attended the meeting.

Both of the papers, by Brown and by Hendry and Neil R. Ericsson, were critical of Friedman and Schwartz's analysis of the relationships between money, income, and prices in the United Kingdom.[9] There were common themes in the two papers, including the suggestion that Friedman and Schwartz's National Bureau processing of the data series to produce phase averages eliminated most of what was of interest in them. The review by Hendry and Ericsson covered less of the material in *Monetary Trends* than Brown's but was a very critical dissection of their money demand estimates for Britain. It proved to be the source of great controversy.

Unlike the three JEL reviewers, who were monetary economists, Hendry was an econometrician. He was leader of a movement often referred to as "British econometrics." The standards and practices that comprise Hendry's British econometrics were developed as an alternative to standard "North American econometrics." From this perspective of British econometrics, Hendry and Ericsson wrote their critique of *Monetary Trends*. We have seen that through the course of Friedman and Schwartz's National Bureau monetary project, critics renewed the Cowles Commission "measurement without theory" charge against their work. Hendry and Ericsson trumped this older charge. They attempted to undermine the metrics of National Bureau methods, converting the "measurement without theory" indictment into "measurement without measurement." It is salient to understanding the controversy their paper provoked that Friedman and Schwartz's National Bureau methods were outside *both* the traditional North American approach and the newer British approach to econometrics.

Hendry's primary concern in econometrics was with model specification and validation. C. L. Gilbert (1986) has summarized the important principles of Hendry's approach. Like all new schools of thought and practice, Hendry's British econometrics grew out of dissatisfaction with standard practice. Gilbert calls standard practice of North American econometrics the "average economic regression." Economists following this approach go through three steps: (1) specify an

---

[9] Ericsson, who became Hendry's coauthor, was an economist at the Board of Governors of the Federal Reserve.

empirical model that is derived from theory known to be correct; (2) check for estimation problems, such as serial correlation, heteroscedasticity, and "wrong" signs; and (3) correct the estimation problems. According to Hendry, the weakness of this approach is its emphasis on estimation rather than testing. In most instances the economic theory is never put to any real test. Rather, the estimates are tested for econometric problems and for congruity with the theory. They are then corrected to eliminate serial correlation and other econometric problems and to make them conform with the economic theory. One outcome of such practices, lamented by practicing econometricians in and outside the British school, is that theories are seldom falsified. Economists with quite different, and seemingly irreconcilable theories, often use a common data set but conclude that the evidence supports their irreconcilable theoretical priors. As Gilbert put it, econometricians use their empirical model to *illustrate* theory that they believe independently. This was the concern that prompted Goodhart to suggest that Friedman and Schwartz made a priori assumptions about the direction of causation.

Hendry's ambition was to develop standards for testing empirical models. He thought testing was the paramount characteristic of science. He considered standard "North American" econometric procedures "inherently non-scientific." Hendry's approach was intended to make econometrics scientific along the line of his conception of science by finding a middle ground between classical statistical methods and atheoretic time-series methods such as vector autoregression, the choice of another group of dissenters from the standard approach.[10] To follow Hendry's methods, an economist begins with a very general model, one that is only loosely based on economic theory. He or she submits the model to specification tests to simplify it and make it more specific; thus the "general to specific" label that is often applied to the approach. The imperative is to rigorously test empirical models, discarding those that do not pass econometric muster. As Hendry explained, this puts econometrics in a destructive role. "Thus, I advocate an approach which combines constructivist aspects in a basically destructive methodology: crudely put, by eliminating the worst models, we are left with the less bad ones" (1985, p. 74).

The constructivist aspect of his program that Hendry refers to in this statement is "encompassing." This is the requirement that for one

---

[10] Work in atheoretical vector autoregressions, by Sims and others, also developed out of dissatisfaction with too much a priori theory imposed on empirical models. See Darnell and Evans (1990, ch. 7).

model to be judged superior to another, it must explain the other's successes and some of its failures. Encompassing is one of a number of requirements that acceptable models must meet. The other requirements are that (1) the residual is unsystematic; (2) the variables are such that agents could act contingently upon, that is, could react to; (3) there is constancy in parameters; (4) the model is consistent with economic theory; (5) the model is admissible, that is, logically possible, given properties of the measurement system; and (6) the regressors are at least weakly exogenous.[11] All seven of these conditions are considered necessary but not sufficient for sustaining empirical inferences.

Hendry and Ericsson's Bank of England paper (1983) concentrated on the U.K. money demand model in *Monetary Trends*. They chose this part of the book because they viewed it as central to the analysis of money's effects on prices and income, and to Friedman's monetarist claims, and because it was one of the few parts of the book that could be subjected to their econometric tests. They tested Friedman and Schwartz's money demand model to see if it met the necessary conditions for valid empirical inference, and derived an alternative model from Friedman and Schwartz's raw data to encompass the phase-average model in *Monetary Trends*.

This exercise served several purposes. First and foremost, it provided a demonstration of Hendry's approach to econometrics. In particular, it produced evidence of how badly empirical modeling can go astray when testing is not vigorously pursued via appropriate methods. The conclusions about Friedman and Schwartz's empirical money demand model are summarized in the opening section of their paper:

(I) Exogeneity is nowhere defined and despite assertions as to its existence or otherwise for certain variables, such claims are not tested.
(II) "Stability" – in the sense of parameter constancy – is asserted for several relationships but again is not tested.
(III) Coefficients are divided by standard errors in static equations estimated by least squares from the phase-average data, and inferences based on Student's 't'-distribution are conducted. The statistical model justifying this procedure for analyzing contemporaneous aggregates is not stated, and no evidence is offered concerning the satisfaction of the many necessary conditions needed to validate such inferences (which include homoscedastic, white-noise residuals).
(IV) There are several legitimate conditional factorisations of joint densities over money, income, prices, and interest rates. The set of equations reported by FS [Friedman and Schwartz] does not correspond to any of these factorisa-

---

[11] See Hendry (1987) and Gilbert (1986).

tions, and is more analogous to an interdependent model. Yet if the latter is postulated, least squares does not yield valid inferences.

(V) In what sense is a relationship "stable" if shift dummy variables constructed after prior analysis of the data must be included in the model to avoid parameter non-constancy?

(VI) The analysis of phase-average data loses a great deal of information about dynamic (short-run) responses, thereby reducing the efficiency of the statistical analysis and potentially distorting the conclusions. A comparative analysis of the annual data is essential to investigate this issue (1983, p. 48).

Submitting Friedman and Schwartz's work to the tests that revealed these econometric flaws was part of Hendry's challenge to traditional North American econometrics. But this is problematical, for *Monetary Trends* was not a representative example of traditional North American econometrics. As Mayer noted in his review of *Trends*, Friedman and Schwartz eschewed standard econometric methods. For example, they did not even report Durbin–Watson statistics. So, if Hendry and Ericsson's paper was meant to expose weaknesses of the "average economic regression," they picked an example that was not average.

Thus it appears that Hendry and Ericsson had another purpose, to discredit monetarism. To be sure, they denied this. After stating that "our primary concern here is to demonstrate that one cannot take at face value many of the inferences conducted by FS, leaving their conclusions stranded as assertions devoid of empirical support" (1983, pp. 47–8), they included the disclaimer: "This paper, however, is not an 'anti-monetarist' polemic; rather, it is a pro-econometrics tract which highlights the practical dangers of seeking to analyze complex stochastic processes while eschewing modern econometric methods" (1983, p. 48).

Notwithstanding the disclaimer, the appearance remains that their paper was meant to discredit Friedman and Schwartz's monetarism as much as it was their statistical methods. The timing and setting circumstantially support the hypothesis that the review served the interests of the Bank of England in the Bank's struggle with the Thatcher Government's Treasury over monetary policy. This interpretation is also supported by the fact that Friedman and Schwartz's work did not fit into standard econometric practice. Most econometricians would have been critical of time-series analysis with no Durbin–Watson statistics and no adjustment for serial correlation. The purpose of exposing the weaknesses of standard econometric practices is hardly served by an evaluation of nonstandard analysis.

The derisive tone of the criticism is a third factor suggesting that the disclaimer was less than genuine. The paper opens with a pair of quotations, one from Friedman's 1953 methodology essay on the role of prediction and another from Charles Dyke (1981) asserting that in the social sciences there are no refutations, only embarrassments. These epigrams are a prelude to an embarrassment of Friedman and Schwartz. In references to Friedman and Schwartz's analysis they put the word "explanation" in quotation marks, not only denying their model the status of best explanation but insinuating that it fails even to meet minimal standards to qualify as explanation.[12]

A fourth factor suggesting multiple motives is evidence from Hendry's writings and actions following the Bank of England meeting. In a 1985 paper, "Monetary Economic Myth and Econometric Reality," Hendry wrote:

A supposed corner-stone of the monetarist viewpoint is the recent book by Friedman and Schwartz (1982). . . . A remarkable feature of their book is that none of the claims was actually subjected to *test* (cf. Hendry and Ericsson (1983)). Rather, equations were reported which did not manifestly contradict their theories and this non-contradiction was taken for "corroboration." On close examination, quite a number of their claims were not econometrically testable, but the "stability of the demand for money as a function of a small number of arguments" could be tested. . . . Testing may be destructive, but since Friedman and Schwartz immediately drew major policy implications from their study, it may prove less destructive of economic well-being to highlight unsubstantiated claims and poor models prior to their policy implementation (1985, pp. 76–7).

This passage belies Hendry and Ericsson's claim that their paper was not an antimonetarist polemic. It also suggests a misinterpretation of *Monetary Trends,* for as other reviewers noted, Friedman and Schwartz drew no policy implications in the book. At another point in the article, Hendry made fun of Friedman by borrowing one of his favorite figures of speech: "Since the proof of these puddings is in their eating, some dumplings were sampled" (1985, p. 82).

Finally, an account follows in the next section of the controversy that broke over a highly distorted report of Hendry and Ericsson's paper in *The Guardian* (Manchester). There is no doubt that the journalist used their econometric critique to discredit the Thatcher Government's preference for monetarist-oriented policy and to impugn

[12] See p. 49. A few pages later they express bewilderment that Friedman and Schwartz could venture a judgment on the relative strengths of competing hypotheses. "Now, FS appear to claim (in some sense) a 'better explanation of economic behaviour' than 'Keynesian' theory. It is unclear to us in what sense this claim could possibly hold, but it certainly does not hold in the encompassing sense" (1983, p. 52).

Friedman and Schwartz's honesty. Hendry rebuffed Friedman's request that he make a public statement to distance his and Ericsson's critique from the account in *The Guardian*. He wrote to Friedman:

How newspapers have chosen to interpret the findings of your book with Anna Schwartz is an issue between yourselves and them. I am sure you are more than able to defend yourselves from illegitimate interpretations of your book by others. Indeed, if your assertion is true that newspapers have produced "a spate of libellous and slanderous" articles "impugning Anna Schwartz's and (your) honesty and integrity", then you must have ready recourse to a legal solution (DH to MF, July 13, 1984).

This exchange was set off by a pair of articles written by Christopher Huhne in the December 15, 1983, *Guardian* reporting on the Hendry and Ericsson paper. Huhne's main theme was that Friedman and Schwartz manipulated their data in order to obtain monetarist results.[13] *The Guardian*'s headlines for the articles were "Monetarism's guru 'distorts his evidence'" and "Why Milton's monetarism is bunk." By Huhne's account, *Monetary Trends* was "to be the definitive statement of his [Friedman's] theories and supporting evidence" (*Guardian*, December 15, 1983a). The lead article reported Hendry as saying that Friedman "resorts to 'simply incredible' manipulation of official data and that 'almost every assertion in the book is false'." It also quoted an unnamed Bank of England economist as saying that the critique "blows Friedman out of the water." In the second of the pair of articles, Huhne made the charge of data manipulation: "Hendry describes [the manipulations] as 'simply incredible' and which less academic souls would call jiggery-pokery." Friedman's (the articles made no mention of Schwartz) adjustment of price level data for periods of price controls was "very circular, and very naughty."

Friedman was outraged at this newspaper account of the Hendry and Ericsson critique. But he turned away requests from the British press for a response to either the *Guardian* article or Hendry and Ericsson's paper. He thought it a mistake to try to respond to every criticism of one's work and considered the newspaper account such a distortion that it deserved no response. As for the Hendry and Ericsson paper, Friedman found their econometric discussion impenetrable but thought their charges against him and Schwartz were without force. To satisfy Hendry and Ericsson's standards, he thought he and Schwartz would have had to use econometric methods that were not even invented when they did the work on their book.

---

[13] Nicholas Kaldor (1985, p. xix) also accused Friedman and Schwartz of intellectual dishonesty.

The message in their Bank of England paper does seem to be that Friedman and Schwartz should have used "British econometrics." For example, "even if FS had tested and not rejected the necessary conditions for valid inference entailed in (A), (B) and (C), as discussed in Hendry (1983) these criteria are minimal in that they often can be satisfied simply by *designing* empirical models appropriately" (1983, p. 52, emphasis in original). Also, consider once more the disclaimer that their article is not antimonetarist, but proeconometrics – promodern econometrics. The time frame for modern econometrics is revealed in Hendry and Ericsson's references to econometrics literature. Many of the references are from the 1980s.[14] Their bibliography includes one econometrics entry from the 1920s, four from the 1960s, nine from the 1970s, and twenty-six from the 1980s. The earliest article by Hendry in the list was published in 1978 (two entries). There is one other article of his from 1979, and the remaining four are from the 1980s. It would have been nearly impossible for Friedman and Schwartz to use Hendry's methods even had they been so inclined. Most of Friedman and Schwartz's work that went into the book was completed well before the 1980s; *Monetary Trends* was three decades in the making.

### The AER articles

A briefer version of Hendry and Ericsson's Bank of England paper was published in the *American Economic Review* in 1991, with a response from Friedman and Schwartz. The path from the Bank of England Panel of Academic Consultants' meeting in October 1983 to this published exchange over seven years later was as torturous as it was long. This was the only published response by Friedman and Schwartz. The Bank of England commissioned Hendry and Ericsson's paper knowing they would be critical of *Monetary Trends* and knowing that this criticism would support their opposition to monetary-base targeting. They did not know *The Guardian* would turn a technical

---

[14] For example, "It seems natural that a poorly fitting equation cannot account for why a well fitting equation fits well. For a comprehensive account of testing for encompassing, see Grayham Mizon and Richard (1983)" (1983, p. 52). Or, "A prior question is whether there *exists* any 'long-run', or equilibrium, relationship between money, prices and incomes. If a relationship is defined across *evolutionary* variables (ie ones which need differencing to be stationary), then one characterisation of its existence or otherwise is whether or not deviations from the relationship are unbounded over time (see eg Clive Granger and Andrew Weiss, 1983)" (1983, p. 52, emphasis in original).

econometric critique into a wholesale assault on monetarism and Friedman. Bank officials could not have wished for the type of article Huhne wrote in *The Guardian* Samuel Brittan suggested shortly afterwards in the *Financial Times* (January 19, 1984) that the Hendry critique was part of a plan by the Bank, but things got out of hand. "The net result has been to draw public discussion back from sensible precepts of economic navigation into a fundamentalist dispute between flat-earthers and round-earthers." The Bank subsequently distanced themselves from the controversy by making no statement about it. This drew criticism from both sides. Friedman's friends wanted a clarification from the Bank about the nature of the criticism in their official paper by Hendry and Ericsson. His and the Government's foes at *The Guardian* chastised the Bank ("Wet Blankets . . . ," January 4, 1984) for downplaying the significance of Hendry and Ericsson's critique.

This confluence of the technical policy issue of targeting with the deep undercurrent of British intellectuals' disdain for free-market liberalism, represented as it was in the political sphere by Margaret Thatcher and in the world of ideas by Friedman, proved a bitter experience for all involved in the dispute over *Monetary Trends*. Friedman was on the verge of agreeing to be interviewed for a television program on the controversy until he learned that Huhne was to be the moderator. Hendry wrote privately that he and Ericsson in no way implied trickery, deception, or cheating by Friedman and Schwartz, but refused to make a public statement to disassociate himself from *The Guardian's* report. Friedman told friends that the experience reinforced his longstanding belief that once a book is published, it is best not to answer critics but to let the book stand on its own.

Hendry and Ericsson submitted a revision of their paper to the *American Economic Review* in July 1987. Friedman and Schwartz were among the referees, and John Taylor, who was coeditor of the AER, offered them a chance to respond in the event that the paper was accepted for publication. At that point Friedman reconsidered his judgment that it was best not to respond. He decided that he and Schwartz had perhaps been ill served by not making any response to the critique, and he saw the AER as an appropriate forum for doing so. But, even though it would mean that they would not get to respond, he advised Taylor not to accept Hendry and Ericsson's paper.

Friedman was forthright in stating in the referee report that he did not have the technical knowledge to evaluate the paper on econometric grounds. But he had no qualms about judging it on methodological grounds. In Friedman's view Hendry and Ericsson's approach placed "excessive emphasis on mining statistical data to conform to formal tests at the expense of economic content" (MF to JBT, September 1, 1987). He continued: "I have long had relatively little faith in judging statistical results by formal tests of statistical significance, in part because of the bias introduced by the kind of mining of data HE [Hendry and Ericsson] engage in. I believe that it is much more important to base conclusions on a wide range of evidence coming from different sources over a long period of time" (MF to JBT, September 1, 1987).

He also thought that the paper was unacceptable as a critique of their book. He rejected the notion that an econometric evaluation of one of their money demand functions for the United Kingdom provided sufficient basis for rejecting the whole of the evidence in the book. This put entirely too much emphasis on a single money demand function and on regression analysis. He also thought their particular econometric interpretation of the contents of *Monetary Trends* created distortions. For example, Hendry and Ericsson attributed to them the claim that money is exogenous. Friedman's referee report reveals the gulf between his Marshallian approach and econometric conceptions of exogeneity:

Our actual statement is: "We shall for the most part take it for granted that the nominal quantity of money available to be held is largely independent of the variables entering into the demand function – that, in the jargon of econometrics, it can be treated as an exogenous variable entering into the determination of such endogenous variables as nominal income, prices, interest rates, and real income." To that we attach a footnote in which we say: "Of course, that does not mean that the nominal quantity of money is not an endogenous variable from a different point of view" (1987, p. 1).

This footnote provides a key to their differences. In his Marshallian approach, as opposed to Hendry's econometric approach, exogeneity is not a characteristic of the data that can be tested once and for all. In this sense it is like the assumption of perfect competition. Though unrealistic in a strict sense, the assumption can be a useful component of an explanatory theory. On the other hand, Friedman did not regard the assumption of exogenous money as something that one simply makes up at will, for the explanatory success of a theory depends on the economic relations underlying the data. Friedman thought that one could know something about the usefulness of the assumption apart from checking the econometric success of the theory. Thus he called attention to the discussion in *Monetary Trends* concerning whether money should be treated as endogenous and prices exogenous during the gold standard era. So there was a crucial difference between Hendry and Ericsson and Friedman in how they judged whether it is better to treat money as endogenous or exogenous. For Hendry and Ericsson the decision depended on formal econometric tests; for Friedman it depended on the problem at hand (the "point of view") and knowledge of economic institutions and policy frameworks. For Hendry and Ericsson all relevant information for making the judgment is in the data being analyzed; for Friedman much of the relevant information, both in facts and theory, is outside the data.[15]

Despite Friedman's recommendation, John Taylor decided to publish Hendry and Ericsson's paper if certain changes were made. When a revision was completed and resubmitted in December 1989, just before Taylor stepped down as coeditor of the AER, he sent it to Friedman for a second review. So Friedman prepared this referee report for the new coeditor, Bennett McCallum. Once again, he recommended against publication on the grounds that the paper had "essentially zero economic content" (MF to BTM, January 10, 1989). However, he acknowledged that the tone of the criticism was less personal, and stated that he and Schwartz would welcome its being published along with their response.

In their paper for the AER (1991) Friedman and Schwartz gave an explanation of how their approach to empirical work differed from Hendry's econometrics. They described theirs as an eclectic approach, drawing on a wide array of quantitative and qualitative evidence, building up to broad hypotheses from investigations of small sets of factors, and testing informally, but with data other than those used to derive the hypotheses. They developed further the argument about exogeneity that Friedman made in his referee report. The following passage exhibits the Marshallian use of theoretical concepts familiar from Friedman's writings on methodology in the 1940s and 1950s:

In our view, exogeneity is not an invariant statistical characteristic of variables. Everything depends on the purpose. In economic analysis, it may be appropriate to regard a variable as exogenous for some purposes and as endogenous for others. A simple example is the quantity of money. For the United States after World War I, we believe it is appropriate to regard the money stock as exogenous (i.e., determined by the monetary authorities) in an economic analysis of long-run money demand. We do not believe it would be equally appropriate to do so for week-to-week or month-to-month movements for which, in HE's words, "the money stock appears to be endogenously determined by the decisions of the private sector" (HE [1991], p. 27). For the period before World War I, as we repeatedly state in both *Monetary*

---

[15] Thomas Mayer (1995, ch. 8) interprets this difference in scientific standards as econometric fit versus economic meaning. From this perspective, Mayer argues, Hendry and Ericsson's method was measurement without economic theory.

*History* and *Monetary Trends,* it is not appropriate to regard the money stock as exogenous even for money-demand analysis, particularly for phase averages. For that period, the money stock is best regarded as endogenous, because the United States and much of the rest of the world was on a gold standard. Even for the post–World War I period, it would not be appropriate to regard the money stock as exogenous in a broader study of the Federal Reserve as a political institution, created by Congress, subject to its ultimate control, with members of the Board appointed by the President. For such studies, of which there are a good number, the money stock is best regarded as endogenous (1991, pp. 41–2).

The approach revealed in this passage is a long way from statistical tests of exogeneity, which Friedman never used in his monetary analysis.[16] There is a pragmatic character of their approach, which is derived from Friedman's Marshallian approach, to the use of theoretical concepts. He and Schwartz say that exogeneity is not an invariant characteristic of the data. For a given data set, whether exogeneity or endogeneity is the appropriate assumption depends on the purpose of the analysis. An assumption of exogeneity would not be appropriate if the purpose was to explain the behavior of a central bank. If the purpose is to understand behavior of the quantity of money, either exogeneity or endogeneity may be appropriate, depending on the circumstances. So factual circumstances, in addition to the economist's purpose in the study, have bearing on what is the proper assumption. Pragmatism does not leave one free to make just any assumption, willy-nilly.

Economists often define endogeneity and exogeneity by whether a variable is determined inside or outside *a model.* At one extreme it becomes merely a matter of choice whether a variable is treated as exogenous or endogenous. Friedman and Schwartz's approach shares with Hendry's the view that this is not a matter of mere assumption. The facts make a difference. For Friedman and Schwartz the facts are not recovered from data via formal statistical tests but rather from knowledge of institutional arrangements and mechanisms. The underlying institutions and mechanisms are what Hendry calls the "data generating process." Does the central bank or do households and businesses have more power to determine the quantity of money? Friedman and Schwartz believed that to understand this reality underlying the data, one must take account of institutions, such as a gold standard mechanism or independent central banks with fiat moneys, and the time frame of analysis. Over shorter periods the money stock

[16] Schwartz did on one occasion in a paper on money's role in the Great Depression that she wrote without Friedman as coauthor. See Schwartz (1981).

is determined to a greater extent by the private sector and to a lesser extent by the public sector. Over longer periods this is reversed.

To an econometrician such as Hendry, this approach lacked rigor and definite standards. By contrast, his approach was to determine exogeneity or endogeneity formally on a statistical basis for a given data set. One may then rationalize the test results with information on policy procedures and institutions, as he and Ericsson did in the AER article:

The constancy of [equation](10) reinforces our interpretation, which is also consistent with the institutional structure of U.K. money markets in which the money stock appears to be endogenously determined by the decisions of the private sector since the Bank of England in effect acts as a lender of the first resort by standing ready to rediscount first-class bills at the going Bank Rate or Minimum Lending Rate (see e.g., R. Hawtrey, 1938; Congdon, 1983; Goodhart, 1984) (1991, p. 27).

Notice how in this passage Hendry and Ericsson made rhetorical use of their readers' knowledge of Bank policy procedures and of references to literature in monetary economics to lend intuitive appeal to their test results. The problem with a formal testing procedure is that test results by themselves have little rhetorical value. But "British econometrics" standards strictly speaking do not allow a role for this sort of institutional information. The authors to whom Hendry and Ericsson refer for authority on the endogeneity of the British money supply – Hawtrey, Congdon, and Goodhart – did not base their conclusions on Hendry's econometric methods. Thus Hendry and Ericsson let ad hockery slip in through the back door.

A second theme Friedman and Schwartz developed in their article to distinguish their approach from Hendry and Ericsson's is closely related to exogeneity. This is the "regression effect," or the "errors in variables" approach. Recall that Hendry and Ericsson argued that formal tests of exogeneity should be used to determine which variables are legitimately placed on the right-hand side of an equation. Friedman and Schwartz explained why they found it useful to run pairs of regressions with variables switched from one side to the other. Their explanation recalled the statistics Friedman learned as a graduate student at Columbia University from Harold Hotelling.[17]

The argument is that if there are errors in measurement of the right-hand side (independent) variables, estimates of their coefficients will be biased. Error may come into the measurement in two ways. First, variables that are used are often proxies for, and thus

---

[17] See Friedman (1992).

imperfect measurements of, the factors that theory calls for. Second, the data often measure the proxies themselves imperfectly. Friedman and Schwartz judged that measurement errors of this sort were often a more serious problem than sampling error, which was Hendry and Ericsson's main concern. One way to estimate the degree of bias introduced into the estimates is to switch the positions of the dependent and independent variables. Estimates of Y on X and X on Y provide outer bounds of the true coefficient.

This provides an added illustration of how Friedman and Schwartz relied more heavily on theory and knowledge drawn from outside the data set to determine causes and effects. They used statistical analysis primarily to find statistical association, not to draw conclusions about what was the cause and what the effect. Regression equations were not defined strictly in terms of cause–effect relations with effects on the left-hand side and causes on the right. Nor were causal roles assigned strictly on the basis of regression estimates.

A third methodological principle that Friedman had long held to be important, and which he and Schwartz contended that Hendry and Ericsson's approach lacked, was testing hypotheses on data other than those used to derive them. This concern was what led to the long delay in completing *Monetary Trends*. The National Bureau reading committee thought, and Friedman and Schwartz agreed, that extending coverage to the United Kingdom would provide a check on the results derived from U.S. data. Despite a suggestion from McCallum that he consider dropping it, Friedman insisted on keeping an addendum in their AER paper that recounted a story from his experience with the Columbia University Statistical Research Group during World War II. He had a regression run to determine the best formula for an alloy that was to be used in aircraft. He used data from actual experiments to estimate the relationship between the composition of the alloy and its ability to withstand heat. His formula failed the test when the alloy ruptured very quickly. Friedman told McCallum that he thought this example was significant because it gave a graphic illustration of the importance of testing hypotheses with data outside the sample.

## Conclusion

The critical reaction to *Monetary Trends* typifies the reaction of Friedman and Schwartz's fellow economists throughout their collaboration on the National Bureau monetary factors in business cycles project. In the JEL reviews, Mayer, Goodhart, and Hall paid tribute to their skill and care in developing and presenting data on money, prices, and income, and in documenting their adjustments and analysis of the data so that others could follow in their path. These reviewers acknowledged that the weight of evidence and argument built up over three decades substantiated many of the monetarist claims that were so contentious in the beginning. Yet, in admiring *Monetary Trends* and the record of research that preceded that volume, they noted the lack of modern econometrics and expressed regret that Friedman and Schwartz did not press harder to resolve questions of causation.

Hendry and Ericsson, on the other hand, were not admirers of any sort. Ironically, they used Friedman and Schwartz's statistical estimation techniques as a whipping boy in order to discredit the North American econometric practice (in Gilbert's terms, the "average economic regression"), which had grown out of the very Cowles Commission program that was the origin of the measurement without theory charge against National Bureau methods. Cowles Commission methods, having been on the cutting edge of scientific standards for economics in the postwar period, were passing into disrepute to be replaced by another contender, Hendry's British econometrics. The constant in this historical transition was that National Bureau methods remained in place as the foil for revolutionaries.

Another constant was that though economists in the 1980s conceded much to Friedman and Schwartz on substantive issues of money's macroeconomic importance and the role of monetary policy, these issues remained intensely controversial and ideologically laden in some quarters. Among some members of the press and academic circles in Britain, Milton Friedman embodied the intellectual force of Margaret Thatcher's public policy revolution and thereby was fair game for misrepresentation and condemnation. Hendry and Huhne did not have to invent the way they undermined Friedman's ideas; they could follow the pattern set long before in the American press and intellectual community.[18]

[18] See, for example, Baltimore and Luria (1976), Wald and Pauling (1976), and Friedman (1977d).

# Conclusion

In carrying on the distinctive National Bureau business-cycle work begun by their mentors Arthur Burns and Wesley Mitchell, Milton Friedman and Anna Schwartz revived interest in monetary economics and built a consensus on the macroeconomic power of changes in the money supply. Economists and public officials have a much better understanding of what central banks can and cannot do with regard to income and prices than they had forty years ago, an understanding for which Friedman and Schwartz deserve and are given much credit. To this extent, the court of public and professional opinion has treated their work favorably. Yet their methods and results were intensely controversial every step of the way. What has been called the "black box of monetarism," or an inadequate theoretical framework, was a persistent theme in reactions to their work, even from critics who shared their views on the significance of money and the role of monetary policy.

When they began their collaboration in the late 1940s, Friedman thought that Marshallian value theory provided a good explanation of relative prices and the quantity theory, of price level statics. But he thought little was known about the dynamic problem of business cycles. Friedman and Schwartz believed that empirical investigations were the surest route to this undiscovered knowledge.

At the time, there were two traditions to call upon for empirical work, the National Bureau approach and the Cowles Commission econometric program. The National Bureau approach emphasized observation and measurement, and the Cowles Commission approach, formal integration of economic and statistical theory. Though Friedman had the requisite background in mathematical economics and statistical theory to pursue econometrics if he had so desired, he did not make that choice. He believed that National Bureau methods offered better prospects for learning the secrets of business cycles. This was the less popular choice, for most economists had greater confidence in the exciting new econometrics that was being created at Cowles.

It soon turned out that for an economist with a commitment to empirical research, Friedman's choice was really the only one. The Cowles researchers virtually gave up on the empirical side of their project by the early 1950s, turning their efforts to mathematical economics. Meanwhile, Friedman and Schwartz continued to work in the National Bureau tradition of collection, development, and analysis of data. They and their associates worked from 1948 through the first half of the next decade to develop banking and monetary data, the raw material for their empirical analysis. In 1963 they finally began publishing results from their analysis of the data.

The controversy generated by Friedman and Schwartz's work is usually viewed in light of the Keynesian–monetarist debate. The great drama played out in journals, textbooks, and the popular press during the greater part of the time they worked together was the struggle between Friedman and his monetarist followers at Chicago and a few other outposts and Keynesians most everywhere else. Keynesians believed that money does not matter and were optimistic about prospects for eliminating the business cycle through fiscal fine tuning, both ideas that the monetarists thought were wrong. Friedman, Schwartz, and the other monetarists began as a clear minority but with the help of fifteen years of inflation during the 1960s and 1970s gradually won the day.

There were real and substantial differences in Keynesian and monetarist doctrine. Keynesian ideas that money does not matter, that the economy is inherently unstable, and that policymakers can have the knowledge and insulation from political interference to fine tune the economy were matters of consensus in the late 1940s and 1950s. Monetarists were considered as rather quaint but dangerous flat-earthers. The Keynesian consensus was a formidable obstacle for Friedman and Schwartz to overcome. But there were two reasons deeper than this doctrinal rift that made Friedman and Schwartz's work controversial – their National Bureau methods and Marshallian methodology. Both were radically unorthodox in the 1940s and became increasingly so as neo-Walrasian formalism's hold on economics was tightened. Regardless of what Friedman and Schwartz's views on money might have been, National Bureau methods and Marshallian methodology would have attracted the label "measurement without theory."

Wariness by economists of National Bureau methods predated their use by Friedman and Schwartz. Before the birth of Cowles Commission econometrics, neoclassical economists looked askance at analysis coming out of the National Bureau because of Mitchell's association with institutionalism and his occasional antineoclassical polemics.

Since the 1940s there was additional reason for neoclassical economists to lack confidence in National Bureau methods as neoclassical
economic theory and statistical theory were increasingly formalized.

Closely linked to the mathematization of economics and economic
statistics was the emergence and dominance of the neo-Walrasian
program. The emphasis there, in Friedman's words, was "abstractness, generality, and mathematical elegance," in contrast to the Marshallian concern for theory as "an engine for the discovery of concrete
truth." Like his preference for National Bureau methods over Cowles
Commission econometrics, Friedman's Marshallian inclinations were
deep seated, having been formed long before he and Schwartz began
their project. The Marshallian apologia in his 1953 essay on methodology was the product of years of effort to work out the foundations and implications of this methodology, work that began in a
manifest way with his review of Robert Triffin's *Monopolistic Competition and General Equilibrium Theory* (1941).

The question posed in the Introduction about Friedman's sensitivity to causality can now be addressed. Causality and the problem of
induction were at the heart of critics' challenges to Friedman. Economics is a search for causal connections, but the problem of induction as worked out logically by philosophers and understood viscerally
by economists denies sure access to causal connections via statistical
association. Correlation does not prove causation. What does?
To most economists in the period covered by this book, the answer
has been empirical evidence accompanied by the appropriate neo-
Walrasian theory. But when push came to shove, the theory is what
they counted on and required.

Friedman seems to have become aware of the possible futility of
giving empirical evidence a primary role in demonstrating causation
to his fellow economists soon after he and Schwartz began presenting
their results. His initial reaction in the 1960s was on the level of
rhetoric. He ceased using explicitly causal language. This did not
make his economics any less dependent on causality, and he and his
critics continued arguing about money as cause and effect, albeit on
his side without the word "cause." Only later, in the 1970s debate over
his theoretical framework, did he identify the deeper methodological
obstacle to acceptance of his conclusions.

Friedman and Schwartz's critics, Keynesian and monetarist alike,
have objected to their work on the grounds of inadequate or insufficient economic theory. David Hendry and Neil Ericsson, for example,
their most recent critics, objected to the lack of statistical theory
to undergird their money demand estimates. Friedman believed

throughout most of the period that he and Schwartz worked together that the key issues concerning money and business cycles were empirical and that disputes with critics would be resolved with empirical evidence.

But their opponents seldom based their critiques on superior or additional evidence. Among the critiques we have considered, there have been hard rejections of his evidence on the basis of its incompatibility with received theory (such as Culbertson, 1960) as well as rejections of his conclusions on the basis of a Keynesian model consistent with Friedman's evidence (such as Tobin, 1970a) and on the basis of simulations from a structural model of an admittedly fictitious economy (such as Brainard and Tobin, 1968). There have also been soft rejections from fellow monetarists who considered Friedman and Schwartz's theoretical framework insufficient to account for their evidence and who attempted to make the necessary repairs (such as Brunner and Meltzer, 1971, 1972, 1974, 1976). Though the divergence between the emphases of the Marshallian and Walrasian approaches to economics was a constant theme in Friedman's writings on methodology since the 1940s, only near the end of the monetary project did he recognize that the methodological breach made any hope for reconciliation between himself and Schwartz and their critics futile.

The challenges to Friedman and Schwartz's evidence and conclusions about money and income typically took the form of questioning their identification of causes and effects. They were charged with treating money as the cause when it was in fact the effect and of treating it as the sole cause when it was at most one of many causes. They were accused of omitting important causes that did not fit with monetarist doctrine. The distance between Friedman and Schwartz's methods and methodology and those of the mainstream made it doubly difficult for themselves and their critics to either resolve their differences over money's roles as cause and effect or to put the questions aside as unresolvable.

Friedman's sensitivity to causality developed in response to accusations by J. M. Clark and John Culbertson that he ignored reverse causation and treated money as the sole cause. He began to use the qualified language seen for example in the 1964 annual report, "The Monetary Studies of the National Bureau," and indicated in his 1985 letter to me where he wrote:

I have always regarded "cause" as a very tricky concept. In my technical scientific writings I have to the best of my ability tried to avoid using the word. In the quotation with which you start the paper I do not say at all that money stock is a cause. I believe that you will not be able to find a statement in the *Monetary History* or in other scientific writings of mine in which I make such an assertion (MF to JDH, June 13, 1985).

In the 1985 letter Friedman also mentioned the care he took to insert what he called "weasel words" such as "substantial," "rapid," and "roughly correspondingly" when describing money's role in determining income and prices. The foregoing history of Friedman and Schwartz's project suggests that these weasel words are more than verbal hedges designed to deflect the blows of criticism but are in fact a natural component of the description of economic reality perceived through the lens of Marshallian methodology and National Bureau methods.

Today, half a century after the Cowles Commission–National Bureau dispute occupied center stage in business-cycle economics and Friedman campaigned to keep Marshallian methodology from being pushed offstage, neo-Walrasianism seems to have prevailed. New-classical economists, some of whom are heirs to Friedman's conclusions about money, follow the Walrasian approach. New-Keynesians, though heirs to some of the Keynesians' conclusions about market coordination failure, also follow the Walrasian approach.

However, there are signs that in the long run Friedman and Schwartz's approach may not pass completely out of favor and may indeed prove to be the only effective way to discover the cause–effect answers that are the quarry of business-cycle economists. On the thirtieth anniversary of the publication of the *Monetary History,* the *Journal of Monetary Economics* published three retrospective review essays. Two of the essays are by younger economists, Jeffrey A. Miron and Bruce D. Smith, who took their training at the Massachusetts Institute of Technology in the early 1980s. Their institution and their time in graduate school were thick with neo-Walrasianism. Robert E. Lucas, Jr., author of the third review, was not only a founder of new-classical economics, but the person most responsible for moving "Chicago economics" away from Friedman's style and into the Walrasian mainstream. Each of these authors, in his own way and in one case perhaps unwittingly, provide signs of the long-run staying power of Friedman and Schwartz's approach to the study of business cycles.

Miron's (1994) theme is that the "narrative approach" of the *Monetary History* may be the only way to discover cause–effect relations in business cycles. He tells a story of his professor, Stanley Fischer, asking a class of students, whose exposure was mostly to pure theory of monetary economics and for whom empirical economics meant techniques for estimating "fully articulated, general equilibrium models," what evidence there was that money played a causal role in the Great Depression. To the students' surprise Fischer told them the best evidence was in the *Monetary History*. Miron uses this story to open his argument that the key to Friedman and Schwartz's approach was their use of natural experiments thrown up by history to obtain identification of demand and supply functions. Ironically, Tjalling Koopmans's "measurement without theory" criticism of the National Bureau approach in 1947 was that it could not provide identification. Miron observes that no amount of economic and statistical theory can substitute for empirical facts in identification.

Lucas (1994) points out that the method of the *Monetary History* has proven more durable than the empirical program of Keynesian economics, which was large-scale macroeconometric modeling. But the more telling tribute that Lucas pays to Friedman and Schwartz is his suggestion that if he were ever to go to Washington as a policy advisor, the most crucial item to take with him from his library would be the *Monetary History*. If this is so, presumably Lucas would leave behind in Chicago not just Keynesian books and articles from the 1960s but much of the new-classical and new-Keynesian work that has been done since then.

The third article in the set of retrospective reviews takes issue with a key conclusion drawn by Friedman and Schwartz. Smith (1994) surveys empirical evidence that is favorable to James Tobin's "real bills" thesis that the manner in which money is created determines its effect. Tobin argued from theory that money created by commercial banks would generally have different effects from money created by central banks, and money created to finance the purchase of goods would have different effects from money created to finance the purchase of bonds. But Tobin provided no empirical evidence to support his view and to refute Friedman and Schwartz's empirically based conclusion that the quantity of money matters, regardless of how it is created.

More recently, in fact beginning in 1982, the year Friedman and Schwartz published *Monetary Trends*, economists began to assemble empirical evidence favorable to Tobin's view. Smith's article covers studies of the American colonial period, of the Second Bank of the United States, of the ends of severe European inflations, of China and President Franklin D. Roosevelt's silver purchase policy, and of Taiwan in the 1970s and 1980s. The interpretation of these episodes in monetary history is still under contention, but Smith argues that on the whole the evidence tends to shift the balance back toward Tobin's hypothesis. Whether or not that is the case, the evidence itself is vindication for Friedman and Schwartz, for in refuting their hypothesis, the authors of these studies use the method of the *Monetary History*.

# The major data required

A. Aggregate supply and rate of use of generally acceptable means of payment.
  1. Currency, by type (including separately gold stock) and, perhaps, by denomination.
  2. Deposits subject to check less duplications (for earlier periods may not be possible to separate time deposits or to correct fully for duplications). For both 1 and 2, kept separately in hands of (a) public, (b) banks, (c) Treasury. Want also total, per capita, and per capita in constant dollars.
  3. Minor forms of circulating media: special bringing together of data on volume of substitutes for ordinary forms of currency in panic periods, as well as of such minor forms of circulating media as postal money orders, traveler's checks, etc. Purpose here is not to get any comprehensive series by months or years over a long period of time, but rather to get some rough indications of the importance of those items, which in general, it will be necessary to neglect.
  4. Bank clearings, and bank debits, and derived velocity figures of deposits.
  5. National income figures, and derived "income velocity" figures.
B. Aggregate supply of assets easily marketable at virtually fixed nominal prices.
  1. Circulating medium (currency plus demand deposits, A 1 & 2).
  2. Time deposits.
  3. Federal obligations other than those included in B 1. Want separately in hands of (a) public, (b) banks, (c) Federal government; and short term vs. long term.
  4. Cash surrender value, life insurance policies.
  5. Deposits of public with brokers.
    Special importance will probably attach to total of 1 plus 2,

and 1 plus 2 plus 3 in hands of public. May want this per capita and per capita in constant dollars.

6. Short term state and municipal bonds.
7. Other short term debt.
8. Net obligations of Federal government, treating Federal Reserve system as governmental agency.

C. Lending and investing activities of banking system.

1. Loans — For recent years a breakdown by type is available and perhaps should be used. For earlier years may be possible to get some data at least on call vs. the other loans, and on security vs. other loans.
2. Investments, if possible, classified at least as government bonds vs. other investments.
3. Loans to other banks.
4. Balances due from banks other than Federal Reserve Banks.
5. Deposits in Federal Reserve Banks.
6. Vault cash.
7. Balances due to banks (identical with 4 except for "float" for aggregate but not for different classes of banks).
8. Borrowings from banks other than Federal Reserve Banks.
9. Borrowings at Federal Reserve Banks.
10. Capital and surplus.
11. Ratios of loans, investments, and loans and investments to deposits.
12. Owned reserved (relevant definition not obvious. At minimum, items 5 plus 6 minus 9. Possibly account should also be taken of some or all of items 4, 7 and 8).
13. Ratio of reserves held to reserves required (further work needs to be done to determine most meaningful series of reserves held, particularly inclusion or exclusion of balances — or perhaps reserve balances — with other banks).
14. Ratio of owned reserves to reserves required.
15. Analysis of factors accounting for changes in reserves — this heading is intended to be suggestive. Is it possible to carry kind of analysis Reserve Board has popularized in recent years back to earlier periods?
16. Loans on securities by other than banks.
17. Other data on lending activity of nonbanks. This heading is intended to be suggestive.
18. Bank failures, number and liabilities.

19. Interest rates: no explicit discussion of these series is included here, though they are obviously pertinent, because the behavior of interest rates is being handled in another of the Studies in Cyclical Behavior. We should therefore be able to get the relevant data from that study.

*Source:* Friedman (1948a)

# Bibliography

Anderson, L., and Jordon, J. "Monetary and Fiscal Actions: A Test of Their Relative Importance in Economic Stabilization." *Federal Reserve Bank of St. Louis Review* (November 1968): 11–24.

Bagehot, W. *Lombard Street*. London: H. S. King, 1873.

Baltimore, D., and Luria, S. E. "The Laureate." Letter to the Editor, *The New York Times* (October 24, 1976).

Behrens, C. F. *Commercial Bank Activities in Urban Mortgage Financing*. New York: National Bureau of Economic Research, 1952.

Bernanke, B. S."Nonmonetary Effects of the Financial Crisis in the Propagation of the Great Depression." *American Economic Review* 73 (June 1983): 257–76.

Brainard, W. C., and Tobin, J. "Pitfalls in Financial Model Building." *American Economic Review* 58 (May 1968): 99–122.

Brittain, S. "The Debate that Refuses to Die." *Financial Times,* London (January 19, 1984).

Brown, A. J. "Interest, Prices, and the Demand Schedule for Idle Money." *Oxford Economic Papers* 1 (May 1939): 46–69.

Brown, A. J. "Friedman and Schwartz on the United Kingdom." In Bank of England Panel of Academic Consultants, *Monetary Trends in the United Kingdom,* pp. 9–43, Panel Paper No. 22, October 1983.

Brunner, K. "The Role of Money and Monetary Policy." *Federal Reserve Bank of St. Louis Review* 50 (July 1968): 8–24.

Brunner, K. "The 'Monetarist Revolution' in Monetary Theory." *Weltwirtschaftliches Archiv* 105 (1970): 1–30.

Brunner, K., ed. *The Great Depression Revisited*. Boston: Martinus Nijhoff, 1981.

Brunner, K., and Meltzer, A. H. "A Monetarist Framework for Aggregative Analysis." *Kanstanzer Symposium on Monetary Theory and Monetary Policy* 1 (1971).

Brunner, K., and Meltzer, A. H. "Money, Debt, and Economic Activity." *Journal of Political Economy* 80 (September–October 1972): 951–77.

Brunner, K., and Meltzer, A. H. "Friedman's Monetary Theory." In *Milton Friedman's Monetary Framework,* ed. R. J. Gordon, pp. 63–76. Chicago: University of Chicago Press, 1974.

Brunner, K., and Meltzer, A. H. "An Aggregative Theory for a Closed Economy." In *Monetarism,* ed. J. L. Stein, pp. 69–103. Amsterdam: North-Holland, 1976.

219

Buchanan, J. M. "Frank H. Knight." In *International Encyclopedia of the Social Sciences,* ed. David Sills, vol. 8, pp. 424–8. New York: Macmillan, 1968.

Buckley, W. F. "The Friedman View." *National Review* 44 (February 17, 1992): 62–3.

Burns, A. F. "Introduction." *What Happens During Business Cycles: A Progress Report,* W. C. Mitchell. New York: National Bureau of Economic Research, 1951a.

Burns, A. F. "Reply to Jacob Marschak." In *Conference on Business Cycles,* pp. 25–33. New York: National Bureau of Economic Research, 1951b.

Burns, A. F., and Mitchell, W. C. *Measuring Business Cycles.* New York: National Bureau of Economic Research, 1946.

Bye, R. T. *Critiques of Research in the Social Sciences: II, An Appraisal of Frederick C. Mills' "The Behavior of Prices."* New York: Social Science Research Council, 1940.

Cagan, P. "The Monetary Dynamics of Hyperinflation." In *Studies in the Quantity Theory of Money,* ed. M. Friedman, pp. 25–117. Chicago: University of Chicago Press, 1956.

Cagan, P. "The Demand for Currency Relative to Total Money Supply." NBER Occasional Paper no. 62. New York: National Bureau of Economic Research, 1958.

Cagan, P. *Determinants and Effects of Changes in the Stock of Money, 1875–1960.* New York: Columbia University Press for the National Bureau of Economic Research, 1965.

Calomiris, C. W. "Financial Factors in the Great Depression." *Journal of Economic Perspectives* 7 (Spring 1993): 61–86.

Chamberlin, E. H. *The Theory of Monopolistic Competition.* Cambridge: Harvard University Press, 1933.

Chamberlin, E. H. *The Theory of Monopolistic Competition: A Re-Orientation of the Theory of Value.* 5th ed. Cambridge: Harvard University Press, 1946.

Clark, J. M. "Wesley C. Mitchell's Contribution to the Theory of Business Cycles." In *Methods in Social Science: A Case Book,* ed. S. A. Rice, pp. 662–80. Chicago: University of Chicago Press, 1931.

Clark, J. M. *The Wage-Price Problem.* [New York?]: American Bankers Association, 1960.

Clower, R. W. "Monetary History and Positive Economics." *Journal of Economic History* 24 (September 1964): 364–80.

Clower, R. W. "The Keynesian Counter-Revolution: A Theoretical Appraisal." In *The Theory of Interest Rates,* ed. F. H. Hahn and F. Brechling, pp. 103–25. London: Macmillan, 1965.

Congdon, T. "Has Friedman Got it Wrong?" *The Banker* (July 1983): 117–25.

Culbertson, J. M. "Timing Changes in Monetary Policy." *Journal of Finance* 14 (May 1959): 145–60.

Culbertson, J. M. "Friedman on the Lag in Effect of Monetary Policy." *Journal of Political Economy* 68 (December 1960): 617–21.

Culbertson, J. M. "The Lag in Effect of Monetary Policy: Reply." *Journal of Political Economy* 69 (October 1961): 467–77.

Culbertson, J. M. "United States Monetary History: Its Implications for Monetary Theory." *National Banking Review* 1 (March 1964): 359–79.

Culbertson, J. M. *Macroeconomic Theory and Stabilization Policy.* New York: McGraw Hill, 1968.

Darnell, A. C., and Evans, J. L. *The Limits of Econometrics.* Aldershot, England: Edward Elgar, 1990.

Davidson, P. "A Keynesian View of Friedman's Theoretical Framework for Monetary Analysis." In *Milton Friedman's Monetary Framework,* ed. R. J. Gordon, pp. 90–110. Chicago: University of Chicago Press, 1974.

Desai, M. *Testing Monetarism.* London: Frances Pinter, 1981.

Dyke, C. *Philosophy of Economics.* New York: Prentice Hall, 1981.

Eisner, R. "Divergences of Measurement and Theory and Some Implications for Economic Policy." *American Economic Review* 79 (March 1989): 1–13.

Epstein, R. J. *A History of Econometrics.* Amsterdam: North-Holland, 1987.

Fand, D. "Monetarism and Fiscalism." Banca Nazionale del Lavoro *Quarterly Review* (September 1970): 3–34.

Field, A. "Asset Exchanges and the Transactions Demand for Money, 1919–29." *American Economic Review* 74 (March 1984a): 43–59.

Field, A. "A New Interpretation of the Onset of the Great Depression." *Journal of Economic History* 44 (June 1984b): 489–98.

Friedman, M. "Review of *Business Cycles in the United States of America, 1919–32* by J. Tinbergen." *American Economic Review* 30 (September 1940a): 657–60.

Friedman, M. "Economics 176, Business Cycles: Lecture Notes, and Examination Questions." Mimeo, Box 75, Milton Friedman Papers, Hoover Institution, Stanford University, 1940b.

Friedman, M. "Review of *Monopolistic Competition and General Equilibrium Theory* by R. Triffin." *Journal of Farm Economics* 23 (February 1941): 389–90.

Friedman, M. "Lange on Price Flexibility and Employment: A Methodological Criticism." *American Economic Review* 36 (September 1946): 613–31. Reprinted in *Essays in Positive Economics,* M. Friedman, pp. 277–300. Chicago: University of Chicago Press, 1953.

Friedman, M. "Lerner on the Economics of Control." *Journal of Political Economy* 55 (October 1947): 405–16. Reprinted in *Essays in Positive Economics,* M. Friedman, pp. 301–19. Chicago: University of Chicago Press, 1953.

Friedman, M. "Lecture Notes 'Price Theory.'" Mimeo, Box 76, Milton Friedman Papers, Hoover Institution, Stanford University, undated.

Friedman, M. "Brief Statement of Plan for Study of Monetary Factors in Business Cycles." Mimeo, Box 94, Milton Friedman Papers, Hoover Institution, Stanford University, undated.

Friedman, M. "Organization, Scope, Present Status, and Budgetary Requirements of Study on 'Monetary Factors in Business Cycles.'" Mimeo, Box 94, Milton Friedman Papers, Hoover Institution, Stanford University, undated.

Friedman, M. "Preliminary Plan for Compilation of Data for Study of Monetary Factors in Business Cycles." Mimeo, Box 94, Milton Friedman Papers, Hoover Institution, Stanford University, September 10, 1948a.

Friedman, M. "A Monetary and Fiscal Framework for Economic Stability." *American Economic Review* 38 (June 1948b): 245–64. Reprinted in *Essays in Positive Economics*, M. Friedman, pp. 133–56. Chicago: University of Chicago Press, 1953.

Friedman, M. "Outline of Work in First Phase of Banking Study: Cyclical Behavior of the Quantity and Rate of Use of Circulating Media." Mimeo, Box 94, Milton Friedman Papers, Hoover Institution, Stanford University, January 28, 1949a.

Friedman, M. "The Marshallian Demand Curve." *Journal of Political Economy* 57 (December 1949b): 463–95. Reprinted in *Essays in Positive Economics*, M. Friedman, pp. 47–99. Chicago: University of Chicago Press, 1953.

Friedman, M. "Wesley C. Mitchell as an Economic Theorist." *Journal of Political Economy* 58 (December 1950): 465–93.

Friedman, M. "Commodity-Reserve Currency." *Journal of Political Economy* 59 (June 1951a): 203–32. Reprinted in *Essays in Positive Economics*, M. Friedman, pp. 204–50. Chicago: University of Chicago Press.

Friedman, M. "Comment on 'A Test of an Econometric Model for the United States, 1921–1947,' by C. Christ." In *Conference on Business Cycles*, pp. 107–14. New York: National Bureau of Economic Research, 1951b.

Friedman, M. "Comments on Monetary Policy." *Review of Economics and Statistics* 33 (August 1951c): 186–91. Reprinted in *Essays in Positive Economics*, M. Friedman, pp. 263–73. Chicago: University of Chicago Press, 1953.

Friedman, M. "Price, Income, and Monetary Changes in Three Wartime Periods." *American Economic Review* 42 (May 1952a): 612–25. Reprinted in *The Optimum Quantity of Money*, M. Friedman, pp. 157–70. Chicago: Aldine, 1969.

Friedman, M. "Economics 432: Monetary Dynamics." Mimeo [syllabus], Box 78, Milton Friedman Papers, Hoover Institution, Stanford University, Spring Quarter 1952b.

Friedman, M. "The Relevance of Economic Analysis to Prediction and Policy." Mimeo, Box 43, Milton Friedman Papers, Hoover Institution, Stanford University, undated (1952c).

Friedman, M. "The 'Welfare' Effects of an Income Tax and an Excise Tax." *Journal of Political Economy* 60 (February 1952d): 25–33. Reprinted in *Essays in Positive Economics*, M. Friedman, pp. 100–13. Chicago: University of Chicago, 1953.

Friedman, M. "The Methodology of Positive Economics." In *Essays in Positive Economics*, M. Friedman, pp. 3–43. Chicago: University of Chicago Press, 1953a.

Friedman, M. "The Effects of a Full-Employment Policy on Economic Stability: A Formal Analysis." In *Essays in Positive Economics*, M. Friedman, pp. 117–32. Chicago: University of Chicago Press, 1953b.

Friedman, M. *Essays in Positive Economics*. Chicago: University of Chicago Press, 1953c.

Friedman, M. "Leon Walras and His Economic System." *American Economic Review* 45 (December 1955): 900–09.

Friedman, M., ed. *Studies in the Quantity Theory of Money*. Chicago: University of Chicago Press, 1956a.

Friedman, M. "The Quantity Theory of Money – A Restatement." In *Studies in the Quantity Theory of Money*, ed. M. Friedman, pp. 3–21. Chicago: University of Chicago Press, 1956b.

Friedman, M. *A Theory of the Consumption Function*. Princeton: Princeton University Press for the National Bureau of Economic Research, 1957.

Friedman, M. "The Supply of Money and Changes in Prices and Output." In *The Relationship of Prices to Economic Stability and Growth*, pp. 241–56. 85th Cong., 2nd sess., Joint Economic Committee Print, 1958. Reprinted in *The Optimum Quantity of Money*, M. Friedman, pp.171–87. Chicago: Aldine, 1969.

Friedman, M. Testimony (on May 25, 1959) and "The Quantity Theory of Money – A Restatement." In *Hearings on Employment, Growth, and Price Levels*, pp. 605–69. 86th Cong., 1st sess. pursuant to S. Con. Res. 13, part 4, Joint Economic Committee, 1959a.

Friedman, M. "The Demand for Money: Some Theoretical and Empirical Results." *Journal of Political Economy* 67 (August 1959b): 327–51. Reprinted in *The Optimum Quantity of Money*, M. Friedman, pp. 111–39. Chicago: Aldine, 1969.

Friedman, M. *A Program for Monetary Stability*. New York: Fordham University Press, 1960.

Friedman, M. "The Lag in Effect of Monetary Policy." *Journal of Political Economy* 69 (October 1961): 447–66. Reprinted in *The Optimum Quantity of Money*, M. Friedman, pp. 237–60. Chicago: Aldine, 1969.

Friedman, M. *Price Theory: A Provisional Text*. Chicago: Aldine, 1962a.

Friedman, M. "The Interpolation of Time Series by Related Series." *Journal of the American Statistical Association* 57 (December 1962b): 729–57.

Friedman, M. "The Monetary Studies of the National Bureau." *The National Bureau Enters its 45th Year*. 44th Annual Report. New York: National Bureau of Economic Research, 1964a. Reprinted in *The Optimum Quantity of Money*, M. Friedman, pp. 261–84. Chicago: Aldine, 1969.

Friedman, M. "Note on Lag in Effect of Monetary Policy." *American Economic Review* 54 (September 1964b): 759–61.

Friedman, M. "Reply to James Tobin." Mimeo, Box 47, Milton Friedman Papers, Hoover Institution, Stanford University, 1964c.

Friedman, M. "Interest Rates and the Demand for Money." *Journal of Law and Economics* 9 (October 1966): 71–85. Reprinted in *The Optimum Quantity of Money*, M. Friedman, pp. 141–55. Chicago: Aldine, 1969.

Friedman, M. "Money: Quantity Theory." In *International Encyclopedia of the Social Sciences*, pp. 432–47. New York: Macmillan, 1968a.

Friedman, M. "The Role of Monetary Policy." *American Economic Review* 58 (March 1968b): 1–17. Reprinted in *The Optimum Quantity of Money*, M. Friedman, pp. 95–110. Chicago: Aldine, 1969.

Friedman, M. *The Optimum Quantity of Money and Other Essays.* Chicago: Aldine, 1969.

Friedman, M. *The Counter-Revolution in Monetary Theory.* IEA Occasional Paper no. 33. London: Institute of Economic Affairs, 1970a.

Friedman, M. "A Theoretical Framework for Monetary Analysis." *Journal of Political Economy* 78 (March–April 1970b): 193–238.

Friedman, M. "Comment on Tobin." *Quarterly Journal of Economics* 84 (May 1970c): 318–27.

Friedman, M. *A Theoretical Framework for Monetary Analysis.* NBER Occasional Paper no. 112. New York: National Bureau of Economic Research, 1971a.

Friedman, M. "A Monetary Theory of Nominal Income." *Journal of Political Economy* 79 (March–April 1971b): 323–37.

Friedman, M. "A Theoretical Framework for Monetary Analysis." In *Milton Friedman's Monetary Framework,* ed. R. J. Gordon, pp. 1–62. Chicago: University of Chicago Press, 1974a.

Friedman, M. "Comments on the Critics." In *Milton Friedman's Monetary Framework,* ed. R. J. Gordon, pp. 132–77. Chicago: University of Chicago Press, 1974b.

Friedman, M. *Monetary Correction.* IEA Occasional Paper no. 41. London: Institute of Economic Affairs, 1974c.

Friedman, M. "Inflation, Taxation, Indexation." In *Inflation: Causes, Consequences, Cures,* pp. 71–88. IEA Readings no. 14. London: Institute of Economic Affairs, 1974d.

Friedman, M. *Unemployment versus Inflation? An Evaluation of the Phillips Curve.* IEA Occasional Paper no. 44. London: Institute of Economic Affairs, 1975.

Friedman, M. "Comment on 'Long Run Effects of Fiscal and Monetary Policy on Aggregate Demand,' by J. Tobin and W. Buiter." In *Monetarism,* ed. J. L. Stein, pp. 310–17, Amsterdam: North-Holland, 1976.

Friedman, M. *From Galbraith to Economic Freedom.* Preface by Arthur Seldon. IEA Occasional Paper no. 49. London: Institute of Economic Affairs, January 1977a.

Friedman, M. "Nobel Lecture: Inflation and Unemployment." *Journal of Political Economy* 85 (June 1977b): 451–72. Also published as Occasional Paper no. 51, Institute of Economic Affairs (London, May 1977).

Friedman, M. "Monetary Policy and the Inflation Rate." Letter to the Editor, *The Times,* London (May 2, 1977c).

Friedman, M. "Milton Friedman, the Chilean Junta and the Matter of Their Association." (An exchange of letters among Nobel Laureates: Friedman with Baltimore and Luria, and with Wald and Pauling.) *The New York Times* (May 22, 1977d).

Friedman, M. "Has the Tide Turned?" *The Listener,* London, pp. 526–8 (April 27, 1978a).

Friedman, M. "Relying on the Free Market." Letter to the Editor, *The Times,* London (August 15, 1978b).

Friedman, M. "Correspondence with Milton Friedman: A Debate on Britain's Policy." *Director*, London (December 1979).

Friedman, M. "Monetarism: A Reply to the Critics." *The Times*, London (March 3, 1980).

Friedman, M. "Detailed Comments on the Hendry/Ericsson [HE] Paper." Mimeo, uncatalogued, Milton Friedman Papers, Hoover Institution, Stanford University, September 1, 1987.

Friedman, M. "Do Old Fallacies Never Die?" *Journal of Economic Literature* 30 (December 1992): 2129–32.

Friedman, M., Despres, E., Hart, A. G., Samuelson, P. A., and Wallace, D. H. "The Problem of Economic Instability." *American Economic Review* 40 (September 1950): 505–38.

Friedman, M., and Kuznets, S. *Income from Independent Professional Practice.* New York: National Bureau of Economic Research, 1945.

Friedman, M., and Meiselman, D. "The Relative Stability of Monetary Velocity and the Investment Multiplier in the United States, 1897–1958." In *Stabilization Policies*, pp. 165–268. A Series of Studies Prepared for the Commission on Money and Credit. Englewood Cliffs, NJ: Prentice-Hall, 1963.

Friedman, M., and Savage, L. J. "The Utility Analysis of Choices Involving Risk." *Journal of Political Economy* 56 (August 1948): 270–304.

Friedman, M., and Schwartz, A. J. "The Stock of Money in the United States, 1875–1955." Mimeo, Box 47, Milton Friedman Papers, Hoover Institution, Stanford University, 1957.

Friedman, M., and Schwartz, A. J. "Money and Business Cycles." *Review of Economics and Statistics* 45, part 2, supplement (February 1963a): 32–64. Reprinted in *The Optimum Quantity of Money*, M. Friedman, pp. 189–235. Chicago: Aldine, 1969.

Friedman, M., and Schwartz, A. J. *A Monetary History of the United States, 1867–1960.* Princeton: Princeton University Press for the National Bureau of Economic Research, 1963b.

Friedman, M., and Schwartz, A. J. *The Great Contraction.* Princeton: Princeton University Press, 1965.

Friedman, M., and Schwartz, A. J. *Monetary Statistics of the United States: Estimates, Sources, and Methods.* New York: Columbia University Press for the National Bureau of Economic Research, 1970.

Friedman, M., and Schwartz, A. J. *Monetary Trends in the United States and the United Kingdom: Their Relation to Income, Prices, and Interest Rates, 1867–1975.* Chicago: University of Chicago Press, 1982.

Friedman, M., and Schwartz, A. J. "Alternative Approaches to Analyzing Economic Data." *American Economic Review* 81 (March 1991): 39–49.

Gilbert, C. L. "Professor Hendry's Econometric Methodology." *Oxford Bulletin of Economics and Statistics* 48 (August 1986): 283–307.

Goodhart, C. A. E. "*Monetary Trends in the United States and the United Kingdom:* A British Review." *Journal of Economic Literature* 20 (December 1982): 1540–51.

Goodhart, C. A. E. *Monetary Theory and Practice*. London: Macmillan, 1984.

Gordon, R. J., ed. *Milton Friedman's Monetary Framework: A Debate With His Critics*. Chicago: University of Chicago Press, 1974.

Gordon, R. J., and Wilcox, J. A. "Monetarist Interpretations of the Great Depression: An Evaluation and Critique." In *The Great Depression Revisited*, ed. K. Brunner, pp. 49–107. Boston: Martinus Nijhoff, 1981.

Granger, C. W. J., and Weiss, A. A. "Time Series Analysis of Error-Correcting Models." In *Studies in Econometrics, Times Series and Multivariate Statistics*, eds. S. Karlin, T. Amemiya, L. A. Goodman, pp. 255–78. New York: Academic Press, 1983.

Gurley, J. "Liquidity and Financial Institutions in the Postwar Period." Study Paper No. 14, Study of *Employment, Growth, and Price Levels*, pp. 3–57. 86th Cong., 1st sess., Joint Economic Committee, January 25, 1960.

Haavelmo, T. "The Statistical Implications of a System of Simultaneous Equations." *Econometrica* 11 (January 1943): 1–12.

Haavelmo, T. "The Probability Approach to Econometrics." *Econometrica* 12, supplement (July 1944).

Haberler, G. *Prosperity and Depression*. Cambridge: Harvard University Press, 1937.

Hahn, F. H. "Equilibrium With Transactions Costs." *Econometrica* 39 (May 1971): 417–40.

Hall, R. E. "*Monetary Trends in the United States and the United Kingdom*: A Review from the Perspective of New Developments in Monetary Economics." *Journal of Economic Literature* 20 (December 1982): 1552–56.

Hamilton, J. D. "Monetary Factors in the Great Depression," *Journal of Monetary Economics* 19 (March 1987): 145–69.

Hammond, J. D. "Monetarist and Antimonetarist Causality." In *Research in the History of Economic Thought and Methodology*, ed. W. J. Samuels, vol. 4, pp. 109–26. Greenwich, CT: JAI Press, 1986.

Hammond, J. D. "Realism in Friedman's *Essays in Positive Economics*." In *Perspectives on the History of Economic Thought*, ed. D. E. Moggridge, vol. 4, pp. 194–208. Aldershot, England: Edward Elgar, 1990.

Hammond, J. D. "Early Drafts of Friedman's Methodology Essay." Paper presented to the History of Economics Society, June 1991.

Hammond, J. D. "The Problem of Context for Friedman's Methodology." In *Research in the History of Economic Thought and Methodology*, ed. W. J. Samuels, vol. 10, pp. 129–47. Greenwich, CT: JAI Press, 1992a.

Hammond, J. D. "An Interview with Milton Friedman on Methodology." In *Research in the History of Economic Thought and Methodology*, ed. W. J. Samuels, vol. 10, pp. 91–118. Greenwich, CT: JAI Press, 1992b.

Hausman, D. M. "Are There Causal Relations Among Dependent Variables?" *Philosophy of Science* 50 (1983): 58–81. Reprinted in *Essays on Philosophy and Economic Methodology*, D. M. Hausman, pp. 109–28. Cambridge: Cambridge University Press, 1992.

Hausman, D. M. "Supply and Demand Explanations and their *Ceteris Paribus* Clauses." *Review of Political Economy* 2 (1990): 168–87. Reprinted in *Essays on Philosophy and Economic Methodology,* D. M. Hausman, pp. 147–62. Cambridge: Cambridge University Press, 1992.

Hausman, D. M. *Essays on Philosophy and Economic Methodology.* Cambridge: Cambridge University Press, 1992.

Hawtrey, R. G. *A Century of the Bank Rate.* London: Longmans, Green and Co., 1938.

Hendry, D. F. "Econometric Modelling: The 'Consumption Function' in Retrospect." *Scottish Journal of Political Economy* 30 (November 1983): 193–220.

Hendry, D. F. "Monetary Economic Myth and Econometric Reality." *Oxford Review of Economic Policy* 1 (Spring 1985): 72–83.

Hendry, D. F. "Econometric Methodology: A Personal Perspective." In *Advances in Econometrics,* ed. T. F. Bewley, pp. 29–48. Cambridge: Cambridge University Press, 1987.

Hendry, D. F., and Ericsson, N. R. "Assertion Without Empirical Basis: An Econometric Appraisal of 'Monetary Trends in . . . the United Kingdom' by Milton Friedman and Anna Schwartz." In Bank of England Panel of Academic Consultants, *Monetary Trends in the United Kingdom,* pp. 45–101, Panel Paper No. 22, October 1983 (with additional references).

Hendry, D. F., and Ericsson, N. R. "An Econometric Analysis of U. K. Money Demand in Monetary Trends in the United States and United Kingdom." *American Economic Review* 81 (March 1991): 8–38.

Hester, D., and Tobin, J., eds. *Financial Markets and Economic Activity.* Cowles Foundation Monograph 21. New York: Wiley, 1967.

Hickman, W. B. *Corporate Bond Quality and Investor Experience.* Princeton: Princeton University Press, 1958.

Hildreth, C. *The Cowles Commission in Chicago.* Berlin: Springer-Verlag, 1986.

Hirsch, A., and de Marchi, N. *Milton Friedman: Economics in Theory and Practice.* Ann Arbor: University of Michigan Press, 1990.

Homan, P. T. *Contemporary Economic Thought.* New York: Harper and Brothers, 1928.

Hoover, K. D. "Two Types of Monetarism." *Journal of Economic Literature* 22 (March 1984): 58–76.

Hoover, K. D. *The New Classical Macroeconomics.* Oxford: Blackwell, 1988.

Horwich, G. "Effective Reserves, Credit, and Causality in the Banking System of the Thirties." In *Banking and Monetary Studies,* ed. D. Carson, pp. 80–100. Homewood, IL: Irwin, 1963.

Huhne, C. "Monetarism's Guru 'Distorts his Evidence.'" *The Guardian,* Manchester, England (December 15, 1983a).

Huhne, C. "Why Milton's Monetarism is Bunk." *The Guardian,* Manchester, England (December 15, 1983b).

Humphrey, T. M. "Role of Non-Chicago Economists in the Evolution of the Quantity Theory in America, 1930–1950." *Southern Economic Journal* 38 (July 1971): 12–18.

Jevons, W. S. *Investigations in Currency and Finance.* London: Macmillan, 1884.

Johnson, H. G. "A Quantity Theorist's Monetary History of the United States." *Economic Journal* 75 (June 1965): 388–96.

Johnson, H. G. "The Keynesian Revolution and Monetarist Counter-Revolution." *American Economic Review* 61 (May 1971): 1–14.

Kaldor, N. *The Scourge of Monetarism.* 2nd. ed. Oxford: Oxford University Press, 1985.

Kareken, J., and Solow, R. M. "Lags in Monetary Policy." In *Stabilization Policies*, pp. 1–96. Commission on Money and Credit. Englewood Cliffs, NJ: Prentice-Hall, 1963.

Keynes, J. M. *Tract on Monetary Reform.* London: Macmillan, 1923.

Keynes, J. M. *The General Theory of Employment, Interest, and Money.* London: Macmillan, 1936.

Keynes, J. M. "The General Theory of Employment." *Quarterly Journal of Economics* 51 (February 1937): 209–23.

Keynes, J. M. "Professor Tinbergen's Method." *Economic Journal* 49 (September 1939): 558–68.

King, R. G., and Plosser, C. I. "Real Business Cycles and the Test of the Adelmans." *Journal of Monetary Economics* 33 (April 1994): 405–38.

Klein, J. J. "German Money and Prices, 1932–44." In *Studies in the Quantity Theory of Money*, ed. M. Friedman, pp. 121–59. Chicago: University of Chicago Press, 1956.

Klein, L. R. *Economic Fluctuations in the United States, 1921–1941.* New York: Wiley, 1950.

Knight, F. H. "Homan's *Contemporary Economic Thought.*" *Quarterly Journal of Economics* 43 (November 1928): 132–41.

Knight, F. H. "Discussion of 'The Theory of Economic Dynamics as Related to Industrial Instability.'" *American Economic Review* 20 (March 1930): 35–7.

Koopmans, T. C. "Measurement Without Theory." *Review of Economics and Statistics* 29 (August 1947): 161–72.

Kuznets, S. "Summary of Discussion and Postscript." *Journal of Economic History* 17 (December 1957): 545–53.

Laidler, D. E. W. "Mayer on Monetarism: Comments from a British Point of View." In *The Structure of Monetarism*, ed. T. Mayer, pp. 133–44, New York: Norton, 1978.

Laidler, D. E. W. "Hawtrey, Harvard, and the Origins of the Chicago Tradition." *Journal of Political Economy* 101 (December 1993): 1068–1103.

Lail, G. M. "The Failure of Frisch's Vision: Frustrated Attempts to Integrate Statistical and Analytical Approaches in Econometrics, 1930–1960." Ph.D. dissertation, Duke University, 1993.

Latané, H. A. "Cash Balances and the Interest Rate – A Pragmatic Approach." *Review of Economics and Statistics* 36 (November 1954): 456–60.

Latané, H. A. "Income Velocity and Interest Rates – A Pragmatic Approach." *Review of Economics and Statistics* 42 (November 1960): 445–49.

Leamer, E. "Let's Take the Con Out of Econometrics." *American Economic Review* 73 (March 1978): 31–43.

Lerner, E. M. "Inflation in the Confederacy, 1861–65." In *Studies in the Quantity Theory of Money,* ed. M. Friedman, pp. 163–75. Chicago: University of Chicago Press, 1956.

Lindert, P. H. "Comments on 'Understanding 1929–1933.'" In *The Great Depression Revisited,* ed. K. Brunner, pp. 125–33. Boston: Martinus Nijhoff, 1981.

Lucas, R. E., Jr. "Review of Milton Friedman and Anna J. Schwartz's *A Monetary History of the United States, 1867–1960.*" *Journal of Monetary Economics* 34 (August 1994): 5–16.

Marschak, J. "Comment on Burns." In *Conference on Business Cycles,* pp. 14–24. New York: National Bureau of Economic Research, 1951.

Marshall, A. *Principles of Economics.* 8th ed. London: Macmillan, 1920.

Mayer, T. "The Inflexibility of Monetary Policy." *Review of Economics and Statistics* 40 (November 1958): 358–74.

Mayer, T. "The Lag in the Effect of Monetary Policy: Some Criticisms." *Western Economic Journal* 5 (September 1967): 324–42.

Mayer, T. "Consumption in the Great Depression." *Journal of Political Economy* 86 (February 1978a): 139–45.

Mayer, T. *The Structure of Monetarism.* New York: Norton, 1978b.

Mayer, T. "*Monetary Trends in the United States and the United Kingdom*: A Review Article." *Journal of Economic Literature* 20 (December 1982): 1528–39.

Mayer, T. *Monetarism and Macroeconomic Policy.* Aldershot, England: Edward Elgar, 1990.

Mayer, T. *Truth versus Precision in Economics.* Aldershot, England: Edward Elgar, 1993.

Mayer, T. *Doing Economic Research: Essays on the Applied Methodology of Economics.* Aldershot, England: Edward Elgar, 1995.

Meltzer, A. H. "Monetary Theory and Monetary History." *Schweizerische Zeitschrift Volkwirkschaft Und Statis* 4 (Spring 1965): 404–22.

Metzler, L. "Wealth, Saving, and the Rate of Interest." *Journal of Political Economy* 59 (April 1951): 93–116.

Meyer, J. R., and Conrad, A. H. "Economic Theory, Statistical Inference, and Economic History." *Journal of Economic History* 17 (December 1957): 524–44.

Mills, F. C. *The Behavior of Prices.* New York: National Bureau of Economic Research, 1927.

Mills, F. C. "The Theory of Economic Dynamics as Related to Industrial Instability." *American Economic Review* 20 (March 1930): 30–35.

Mills, F. C. "On the Changing Structure of Economic Life." In *Economic Essays in Honor of Wesley Claire Mitchell,* pp. 355–91. New York: Columbia University Press, 1935.

Mills, F. C. "Comments on Bye's *Critique* and the Reviews." In *Critiques of Research in the Social Sciences: II An Appraisal of Frederick C. Mills' "The Behavior of Prices",* R. T. Bye, pp. 91–164. New York: Social Science Research Council, 1940.

Mintz, I. *Deterioration in the Quality of Foreign Bonds Issued in the United States, 1920–1930.* New York: National Bureau of Economic Research, 1951.

Miron, J. A. "Empirical Methodology in Macroeconomics: Explaining the Success of Friedman and Schwartz's *A Monetary History of the United States, 1867–1960.*" *Journal of Monetary Economics* 34 (August 1994): 17–25.

Mishkin, F. S. "The Household Balance Sheet and the Great Depression." *Journal of Economic History* 38 (December 1978): 918–37.

Mitchell, W. C. "The Real Issue in the Quantity Theory Controversy." *Journal of Political Economy* 12 (June 1904): 403–8.

Mitchell, W. C. *Business Cycles.* Berkeley: University of California Press, 1913.

Mitchell, W. C. "The Prospects of Economics." In *The Trend of Economics,* ed. R. G. Tugwell, pp. 3–34. Port Washington, NY: Kennikat Press, (1924) 1971.

Mitchell, W. C. "Quantitative Analysis in Economic Theory." *American Economic Review* 15 (March 1925): 1–12.

Mitchell, W. C. *Business Cycles: The Problem and Its Setting.* New York: National Bureau of Economic Research, 1927.

Mitchell, W. C. "Supplementary Statement." In *Critiques of Research in the Social Sciences: II An Appraisal of Frederick C. Mills' "The Behavior of Prices",* R. T. Bye, pp. 299–300. New York: Social Science Research Council, 1940.

Mitchell, W. C. *Business Cycles and Their Causes.* Berkeley: University of California Press, 1941.

Mitchell, W. C. *The National Bureau's First Quarter-Century: Twenty-fifth Annual Report.* New York: National Bureau of Economic Research, 1945.

Mitchell, W. C. *What Happens During Business Cycles: A Progress Report.* New York: National Bureau of Economic Research, 1951.

Mizon, G. E., and Richard, J.-F. "The Encompassing Principle and Its Application to Testing Non-Nested Hypotheses." Paper presented at the European Meeting of the Econometric Society, 1983.

Modigliani, F., and Ando, A., "Impacts of Fiscal Actions on Aggregate Income and the Monetarist Controversy: Theory and Evidence." In *Monetarism,* ed. J. L. Stein, pp. 17–42. Amsterdam: North-Holland, 1976.

Morgan, M. S. *The History of Econometric Ideas.* Cambridge: Cambridge University Press, 1990.

Morton, J. E. *Urban Mortgage Lending: Comparative Markets and Experience.* Princeton: Princeton University Press, 1956.

Neftci, S. N. "Is There a Cyclical Time Unit?" In *The National Bureau Method, International Capital Mobility and Other Essays,* eds. K. Brunner and A. H. Meltzer. Carnegie–Rochester Conference Series on Public Policy, vol. 24, pp. 11–48. Amsterdam: North-Holland, 1986.

Nourse, E. G. "Forward." In *Critiques of Research in the Social Sciences: II An Appraisal of Frederick C. Mills' "The Behavior of Prices",* R. T. Bye, pp. vii–xv. New York: Social Science Research Council, 1940.

Okun, A. M. "Comment." *Review of Economics and Statistics,* supplement. (February 1963): 72–7.

Patinkin, D. "Price Flexibility and Full Employment." *American Economic Review* 38 (September 1948): 543–64.

Patinkin, D. *Money, Interest, and Prices.* 2nd ed. New York: Harper and Row, 1965.

Patinkin, D. "The Chicago Tradition, the Quantity Theory, and Friedman." *Journal of Money, Credit, and Banking* 1 (February 1969): 46–70.

Patinkin, D. "Friedman on the Quantity Theory and Keynesian Economics." In *Milton Friedman's Monetary Framework*, ed. R. J. Gordon, pp. 111–31. Chicago: University of Chicago Press, 1974.

Patinkin, D. *Essays On and In the Chicago Tradition.* Durham: Duke University Press, 1981.

Pigou, A. C. "Review of *Business Cycles*, by W. C. Mitchell." *The Economic Journal* 24 (March 1914): 78–81.

Pigou, A. C. "The Classical Stationary State." *Economic Journal* 53 (December 1943): 342–51.

Pigou, A. C. "Economic Progress in a Stable Environment." *Economica* 14 (new ser.; August 1947): 180–90.

Prescott, E. C. "Theory Ahead of Business Cycle Measurement." In *Real Business Cycles, Real Exchange Rates and Actual Policies*, eds. K. Brunner and A. H. Meltzer. Carnegie–Rochester Conference Series on Public Policy, vol. 25, pp. 11–44. Amsterdam: North-Holland, 1986.

Rasche, R. "A Comparative Static Analysis of Monetarist Propositions." *Federal Reserve Bank of St. Louis Review* 55 (December 1973): 15–23.

Robbins, L. *The Great Depression.* London: Macmillan, 1934.

Robinson, J. *The Economics of Imperfect Competition.* London: Macmillan, 1933.

Romer, C. D. "The Nation in Depression." *Journal of Economic Perspectives* 7 (Spring 1993): 19–40.

Russell, B. "On the Notion of Cause." In *Mysticism and Logic and Other Essays*, B. Russell, pp. 180–208. London: George Allen and Unwin, 1917.

Samuelson, P. A. "Reflections on Recent Federal Reserve Policy." *Journal of Money, Credit, and Banking* 2 (February 1970): 33–44.

Sargent T. J., and Sims, C. A. "Business Cycle Modeling Without Pretending to Have Too Much *A Priori* Economic Theory." In *New Methods in Business Cycle Research: Proceedings from a Conference*, pp. 45–109. Minneapolis: Federal Reserve Bank of Minneapolis, 1977.

Schumpeter, J. A. "Mitchell's Business Cycles." *Quarterly Journal of Economics* 45 (November 1930): 150–72.

Schwartz, A. J. "Understanding 1929–1933." In *The Great Depression Revisited*, ed. K. Brunner, pp. 5–48. Boston: Martinus Nijhoff, 1981.

Schwartz, A. J., and Oliver, E. "Currency Held by the Public, the Banks, and the Treasury, Monthly, December 1917–December 1944." NBER Technical Paper 4. New York: National Bureau of Economic Research, 1947.

Selden, R. T. "Monetary Velocity in the United States." In *Studies in the Quantity Theory of Money*, ed. M. Friedman, pp. 179–257. Chicago: University of Chicago Press, 1956.

Simkins, S. P. "Do Real Business Cycle Models Really Exhibit Business Cycle Behavior?" *Journal of Monetary Economics* 33 (April 1994): 381–404.

Simons, H., and others. "Banking and Currency Reform" (with supplement and appendix). Mimeo, University of Chicago, November 1933.

Sims, C. A. "Exogeneity and Causal Ordering in Macroeconomic Models." In *New Methods in Business Cycle Research: Proceedings from a Conference*, pp. 23–43. Minneapolis: Federal Reserve Bank of Minneapolis, 1977.

Smith, B. D. "Mischief and Monetary History: Friedman and Schwartz Thirty Years Later." *Journal of Monetary Economics* 34 (August 1994): 27–45.

Somers, H. M. "What Generally Happens During Business Cycles – and Why." *Journal of Economic History* 12 (Summer 1952): 270–82.

Sprinkel, B. W. "Monetary Growth as a Cyclical Predictor." *Journal of Finance* 14 (September 1959): 333–46.

Stein, J. L., ed., *Monetarism*. Amsterdam: North-Holland, 1976a.

Stein, J. L. "Inside the Monetarist Black Box." In *Monetarism*, ed. J. L. Stein, pp. 183–232. Amsterdam: North-Holland, 1976b.

Stigler, G. J. "Monopolistic Competition in Retrospect." In *Five Lectures on Economic Problems*, G. J. Stigler, pp. 12–24. Freeport, NY: Books For Libraries Press, 1949.

Tavlas, G. S. "The Light in the Secret Shrine: Chicago, Harvard, and the Doctrinal Foundations of Monetary Economics." Paper presented to the History of Economics Society, June 1995.

Temin, P. *Did Monetary Forces Cause the Great Depression?* New York: Norton, 1976.

Temin, P. *Lessons from the Great Depression*. Cambridge: MIT Press, 1989.

Thomas, W. J., and Znaniecki, F. *The Polish Peasant in Europe and America*. Chicago: University of Chicago Press, 1918.

Tinbergen, J. *An Econometric Approach to Business Cycle Problems*. Paris: Hermann and Cie, 1937.

Tinbergen, J. *Statistical Testing of Business-Cycle Theories.* Vol. I: *A Method and Its Application to Investment Activity;* Vol. II: *Business Cycles in the United States of America*. Geneva: League of Nations, 1939.

Tinbergen, J. *The Dynamics of Business Cycles: A Study of Economic Fluctuations*. Chicago: University of Chicago Press, 1950.

Tobin, J. "The Interest-Elasticity of Transactions Demand for Cash." *Review of Economics and Statistics* 38 (August 1956): 241–7.

Tobin, J. "The Monetary Interpretation of History." *American Economic Review* 55 (June 1965): 464–85.

Tobin, J. "Money and Income: Post Hoc Ergo Propter Hoc?" *Quarterly Journal of Economics* 84 (May 1970a): 301–17.

Tobin, J. "Rejoinder." *Quarterly Journal of Economics* 84 (May 1970b): 328–29.

Tobin, J. "Friedman's Theoretical Framework." In *Milton Friedman's Monetary Framework*, ed. R. J. Gordon, pp. 77–89. Chicago: University of Chicago Press, 1974.

Tobin, J. "Is Friedman a Monetarist?" In *Monetarism*, ed. J. L. Stein, pp. 332–6. Amsterdam: North-Holland, 1976.

Tobin, J., and Buiter, W. "Long-run Effects of Fiscal and Monetary Policy on Aggregate Demand." In *Monetarism*, ed. J. L. Stein, pp. 273–309. Amsterdam: North-Holland, 1976.

Triffin, R. *Monopolistic Competition and General Equilibrium Theory*. Cambridge: Harvard University Press, 1941.

Veblen, T. *The Theory of Business Enterprise*. New York: Charles Scribner's Sons, 1904.

Veblen, T. "The Place of Science in Modern Civilization." In *The Place of Science in Modern Civilization*, T. Veblen, pp. 1–31. New York: Russell and Russell, (1906) 1961.

Veblen, T. "The Evolution of the Scientific Point of View." In *The Place of Science in Modern Civilization*, T. Veblen, pp. 32–55. New York: Russell and Russell, (1908) 1961.

Viner, J. "Mills' Behavior of Prices." *Quarterly Journal of Economics* 43 (February 1929): 337–52.

Viner, J. *Balanced Deflation, Inflation, or More Depression*. Minneapolis: University of Minnesota Press, 1933.

Vining, R. "Koopmans on the Choice of Variables to be Studied and of Methods of Measurement." *Review of Economics and Statistics* 31 (May 1949): 77–86.

Wald, G., and Pauling, L. "The Laureate." Letter to the Editor, *The New York Times* (October 24, 1976).

Warburton, C. "The Volume of Money and the Price Level Between the World Wars." *Journal of Political Economy* 53 (June 1945): 150–63.

Warburton, C. "Quantity and Frequency of Use of Money in the United States, 1919–45." *Journal of Political Economy* 54 (October 1946): 436–50.

Warburton, C. "Bank Reserves and Business Fluctuations." *Journal of the American Statistical Association* 43 (December 1948): 547–58.

Warburton, C. "The Theory of Turning Points in Business Fluctuations." *Quarterly Journal of Economics* 64 (November 1950): 525–49.

"Wet Blankets at the Bank." *The Guardian*, Manchester, England (January 4, 1984).

Whaples, R. "A Quantitative History of the Journal of Economic History and the Cliometric Revolution." *Journal of Economic History* 51 (June 1991): 289–301.

White, E. N. "The Stock Market Boom and Crash of 1929 Revisited." *Journal of Economic Perspectives* 4 (Spring 1990): 67–83.

## Correspondence

Clark, J. M. to Friedman, M., March 31, 1960 (act. 1961), Box 23, Milton Friedman Papers, Hoover Institution, Stanford University.

Culbertson, J. M. to Friedman, M., April 17, 1961, Box 24, Milton Friedman Papers, Hoover Institution, Stanford University.

Dow, J. C. R. to Friedman, M., September 9, 1983, uncatalogued, Milton Friedman Papers, Hoover Institution, Stanford University.

Friedman, M. to Schwartz, A. J., March 3, 1948, Box 90, Milton Friedman Papers, Hoover Institution, Stanford University.

Friedman, M. to Burns, A. F., May 3, 1949, Box 94, Milton Friedman Papers, Hoover Institution, Stanford University.

Friedman, M. to Schwartz, A. J., March 1, 1955, Box 90, Milton Friedman Papers, Hoover Institution, Stanford University.

Friedman, M. to Schwartz, A. J., April 5, 1957, Box 95, Milton Friedman Papers, Hoover Institution, Stanford University.

Friedman, M. to Wehle, M., July 6, 1957, Box 91, Milton Friedman Papers, Hoover Institution, Stanford University.

Friedman, M. to Schwartz, A. J., April 16, 1960, Box 91, Milton Friedman Papers, Hoover Institution, Stanford University.

Friedman, M. to Moore, G. H., January 9, 1962, Box 89, Milton Friedman Papers, Hoover Institution, Stanford University.

Friedman, M. to Moore, G. H., February 13, 1962, Box 89, Milton Friedman Papers, Hoover Institution, Stanford University.

Friedman, M. to Moore, G. H., February 11, 1963, Box 89, Milton Friedman Papers, Hoover Institution, Stanford University.

Friedman, M. to Goodhart, C. A. E., May 10, 1982, uncatalogued, Milton Friedman Papers, Hoover Institution, Stanford University.

Friedman, M. to Hammond, J. D., June 13, 1985, uncatalogued, Milton Friedman Papers, Hoover Institution, Stanford University.

Friedman, M. to Taylor, J. B., September 1, 1987, uncatalogued, Milton Friedman Papers, Hoover Institution, Stanford University.

Friedman, M. to McCallum, B. T., January 10, 1989, uncatalogued, Milton Friedman Papers, Hoover Institution, Stanford University.

Hendry, D. F. to Friedman, M., July 13, 1984, uncatalogued, Milton Friedman Papers, Hoover Institution, Stanford University.

Moore, G. H. to Friedman, M., December 9, 1948, Box 89, Milton Friedman Papers, Hoover Institution, Stanford University.

Moore, G. H. to Friedman, M., January 5, 1962, Box 89, Milton Friedman Papers, Hoover Institution, Stanford University.

Moore, G. H. to Friedman, M., January 25, 1962, Box 89, Milton Friedman Papers, Hoover Institution, Stanford University.

Schwartz, A. J. to Friedman, M., March 27, 1957, Box 95, Milton Friedman Papers, Hoover Institution, Stanford University.

Schwartz, A. J. to Friedman, M., May 7, 1957, Box 91, Milton Friedman Papers, Hoover Institution, Stanford University.

Wehle, M. to Friedman, M., April 13, 1957, Box 91, Milton Friedman Papers, Hoover Institution, Stanford University.

# Index

235